Disabled Children and the Law

Disabled Children and the Law
Research and Good Practice

Janet Read and Luke Clements

Jessica Kingsley Publishers
London and Philadelphia

First published in the United Kingdom in 2001 by
Jessica Kingsley Publishers Ltd
116 Pentonville Road
London N1 9JB, England
and
325 Chestnut Street
Philadelphia, PA 19106, USA

www.jkp.com

Second Impression 2002

Library of Congress Cataloging in Publication Data
A CIP catalog record for this book is available from the Library of Congress

British Library Cataloguing in Publication Data
A CIP catalogue record for this book is available from the British Library

ISBN 1 85302 793 6

Printed and Bound in Great Britain by
Athenaeum Press, Gateshead, Tyne and Wear

For Matthew and his family

Contents

ACKNOWLEDGEMENTS   8

Part I

Chapter 1 Introduction   11

Chapter 2 Human rights, ethics and values   14

Chapter 3 Research and good practice: an overview   23

Chapter 4 The law and frequently encountered legal obstacles   53

Chapter 5 The early years   81

Chapter 6 The school years   112

Chapter 7 Becoming an adult   138

Chapter 8 Children who live away from home   175

Part II: Resource materials

Appendix 1 References   209

Appendix 2 Local authority complaints materials   223

Appendix 3 Social services materials   230

Appendix 4 Education materials   244

Appendix 5 NHS complaints materials   255

Appendix 6 Disability Discrimination Act 1995 materials   258

Appendix 7 Disabled facilities grants materials   263

Appendix 8 Precedent letters   266

Appendix 9 Useful addresses   275

SUBJECT INDEX   288

INDEX OF LEGISLATION AND GUIDANCE   298

AUTHOR INDEX   301

Acknowledgements

A number of people have made helpful suggestions. The Authors would like to thank: Clare Blackburn, John Harris and Christine Harrison of the University of Warwick, John Lawson of the University of Salford, Steve Martin and Bethan Cowan of the Welsh Funding Councils and Francine Bates of Contact-a-Family.

We welcome critical feedback, Suggestions and information. These should be sent to Luke Clements at: clemntslj@cf.ac.uk

PART I

Research, the Law
and Good Practice

CHAPTER I

Introduction

What is this book about?

There are three basic principles underlying this book:

1. Disabled children and their families have a right to a quality of life comparable to that enjoyed by others who do not live with disability.

2. Research, good practice and the law represent a continuum and an understanding of each is essential to ensure that the rights of disabled children and their families are protected and promoted.

3. The route to the law is through research and good practice; the law is not separate.

Accordingly throughout the book, the three elements (research, good practice and the law) are considered in the following order:

*   what research has to tell us about the needs of disabled children and those close to them

*   what research has to tell us about valued services to meet those needs

*   how the law can be used as a tool to make valued and appropriate services available to meet need.

In other words, in relation to different topics, we start with the issues that research tells us are significant for the children and those close to them; we move on to strategies that may make a difference and then consider how the law might help.

Who is the book for?

Disabled children and young people and those close to them often lack essential information about matters that substantially affect their lives. We hope that this book helps tackle this problem. It is written with disabled young people and their families in mind and we hope that they may have direct access to it and find that it contains material which is useful to them. Others may find that the various handbooks and websites which we recommend are much more to their liking than a research-based text. In addition, we hope that the book will be of value to organisations, lawyers, advisors and advocates assisting them or representing their interests. In this way, the children and their families may benefit indirectly from the information that we have provided.

The book is also aimed at practitioners and managers providing and planning services for disabled children and their families and at students training for the relevant professions. In recent years, there has been a growing expectation that the best available research evidence should inform practice and service development. It can prove very difficult, however, for even the most conscientious of practitioners to keep abreast of current research. Similarly, there is evidence that practitioners and managers find at least some aspects of the law related to disabled children complex and demanding (Read and Clements 1999). This book is intended to give service providers access both to a substantial range of research and to related legislation.

How the book is organised

There is no easy way to lay out a book of this nature. A law book would deal with each statute in succession and a practice book might deal with the duties of each public authority separately (i.e. social services, education, the NHS and so on). Since we challenge the inappropriate compartmentalisation of issues that arise in the lives of disabled children we have not favoured either arrangement. We have opted (after trying many alternatives) for a layout based primarily on the stages in a child's development.

The book is organised in two parts: Part I is the main body of the text on research, good practice and the law. Part II contains more detailed legal source materials, precedent letters and useful addresses.

In Part I, following this introduction, there is a chapter on disabled children, human rights and the law. Chapters 3 and 4 provide an overview of research, policy, practice and the law in relation to all disabled children and their families. These chapters form an essential background and are intended to be read in conjunction with others on specific topics. Chapters 5–7 follow the children's life course and deal with issues which routinely become important for them and their families at particular times. Finally, Chapter 8 focuses on children who live away from their families.

Taking this approach to the three elements – research, good practice and the law – has undoubtedly created considerable problems of organisation. In relation to any topic, we have had to draw on a range of research and legislation, appreciating however that most people will not read this book from cover to cover. We have, therefore, tried to find a way of giving readers the best access possible to material that they may need without either being too repetitive or risking a serious omission. Some issues, for example, the need for an effective means of communication for each disabled child, could have been explored in almost every section. Choices had to be made, however, and some matters are dealt with in a particular chapter, not because they belong there exclusively, but often because on balance that seems the most appropriate place for them to be. We have tried to help the reader by providing quite extensive cross-referencing, a detailed index and a list of contents at the beginning of each chapter.

Chapters 5 to 8 are each divided into two sections: the first consists of a review of research and policy in relation to need and services; the second of a legal commentary on those findings.

Finally, to save endless repetition of 'he or she', we have mainly used the male gender indiscriminately to denote both genders.

Note:

Whilst this book is concerned throughout with the safety and well-being of disabled children, it does not deal specifically with procedures in relation to child protection. Similarly, it does not offer information and advice on income maintenance benefits. Reference is made, however, to texts and guides on these topics.

CHAPTER 2

Human Rights, Ethics and Values

Introduction

In this chapter, we outline briefly some of the ethics and values that underpin our approach. These principles and related theoretical work appear in one form or another throughout this book but the aim of this chapter is to make them explicit.

Quality of life and human rights

Our approach is founded on a very simple assumption. We believe that it should not be regarded as an exotic idea for disabled children and those close to them to aspire to a quality of life comparable to that enjoyed by others who do not live with disability. In our view, it should be seen as unacceptable at the beginning of the twenty-first century for the lives and experiences of disabled children and their families to be bereft of those features which many others take for granted; features which make an essential contribution to an ordinary and reasonable quality of life. This is not, of course, the same as saying that all children, disabled or not, need or want exactly the same personal, social and material experiences in exactly the same form. What we are suggesting is that we should aim for basic equality of opportunity and recognise that children and their families will take very different routes and need markedly different supports if there is to be any chance of achieving it.

We should therefore never start from the assumption that an experience which is taken for granted by many non-disabled children and their families should be ruled out on the grounds of a child being disabled. By contrast, if we start by assuming that disabled children and their families should have access to experiences which others routinely expect, the issue then becomes one of finding the route to achieve it and the services that will enable it to happen. To assume that disabled children and their families have the same basic social and human rights as other people is fundamental.

This idea is not new. Increasingly, researchers and disability activists have highlighted situations and experiences which are often fundamental to the lives of disabled children and their families, but which would be regarded as intolerable for those who are non-disabled (e.g. Hirst and Baldwin 1994; Morris 1995). They have pointed to differential standards that apply to the two groups and to the size of the gap between them. In the past few years we have seen increasing challenges to the notion that it is acceptable for such a gap to exist between the expectations and experiences of disabled and non-disabled children and young people.

Our experience as both researchers and practitioners has taught us that while children and their families may have to compromise as they focus their attention on managing the day-to-day rigours of life, many retain a sense of injustice or disquiet about this gap. We cannot be the only people who have been asked by disabled children how we think that others of their age would like it if they had to put up with things that are integral to disabled children's lives. Parents also frequently draw an implied or explicit comparison between their own children's lives and those of others. In doing so, they sometimes use the language of fairness and unfairness. When faced with a battle to get something which they feel would improve their disabled child's quality of life, they often challenge what they regard as restrictions and low standards and in doing so pose questions such as 'Why *shouldn't* she have what other children have?' (Read 2000).

Some of the questions asked by disabled children and young people and their parents should not be assumed to be simply rhetorical. When we attempt seriously to answer the questions that begin 'How would *they* like it if…?' or 'Why *shouldn't* she have the same…?', the unacceptable quality of the opportunities afforded to many disabled children and their families is brought home to us. If, for example, we were to come to the conclusion that it would be unbearable and damaging for a non-disabled child to be without a means of communication or a consistent way of expressing preference or dissent, we immediately have to ask why it is routinely regarded as acceptable for many disabled children to be in that position. Furthermore, if the answer is a resounding 'No' to a question about whether some aspect of the quality of life experienced by disabled children would be good enough for non-disabled children, we need then to interrogate why it should be contemplated. The onus must be on having to explain and to justify it.

One group of practitioners known to the authors used a rough and ready but effective yardstick in relation to these issues. The team undertook a review of services offered to disabled children with complex support needs with the aim of extending their opportunities and enhancing their quality of life. The staff dubbed the project 'Good Enough for Me: Good Enough for You' as a reminder of one guiding principle: that if the children's quality of life did not meet the standards and expectations that staff might have for their own and that of their families, they should immediately question what could be done.

We are aware that some disabled children and young people and their families may feel sceptical about an assertion that there is nothing exotic about the idea that they should have comparable aspirations to others. They may wonder, understandably in our view, if those who suggest it have any idea of what they are up against most of the time. Similarly, hard-pressed practitioners and managers in services with few resources may equally understandably argue that such notions are fine in an ideal world but, sadly, the world is far from ideal. It is precisely because things are so taxing for many disabled children and their families and because good services are so thin on the ground, that it is crucial to be emphatic about the principle. While it may not yet be possible always to achieve the goal of a comparable quality of life and opportunity, the consequences of lowering our sights may be that we work to inferior standards and achieve less. In addition, it needs to be acknowledged that in circumstances where people are offered little, there is a danger that an often quite limited service which makes only a marginal difference to their lives may be presented as more significant than it actually is. We do not wish to suggest that small or incremental gains are always unimportant and we certainly do not want to diminish the efforts of families and conscientious practitioners to create as much room for manoeuvre as they can with whatever limited resources they have at their disposal. We recognise too, that like all individuals and families, disabled children and those close to them make compromises. Nevertheless, it would be dangerous to lose sight of the useful yardstick of how the child's and family's quality of life compares with that of others in the general population.

Parents also frequently point out, however, that they feel it is unwise to spend all their time concentrating on what they regard as the injustices in theirs and their children's lives. Many regard it as essential to emphasise positive strategies and to carve out those defensible spaces in their lives that foster and enhance the well-being of all family members (Beresford 1994; Read 2000). This does not mean, of course, that they are unaware of the gap or unaffected by it. Throughout this book, we shall be detailing the hardships that children and families face, the positive and creative aspects of their lives and services and strategies which can make a difference. One aspect of making a difference is reducing the gap.

Understanding disability

The approach outlined so far is predicated on an assumption that it is possible to make a difference so that the lives of disabled children and their families are improved. This in turn rests on a further set of assumptions about the nature of the difficulties which disabled children and adults and their families face. Later in the book there is more detailed reference to work that has been undertaken in the past two decades on defining and theorising disability. Much of this work has been developed by disabled academics and activists and lays emphasis on the social oppression of children and adults who live with impairment (for example, Morris 1991; Oliver 1996). At this point, however, we want to take time briefly to summarise our understanding of disability and the things that affect the lives of disabled children and adults in both positive and negative ways.

There can be no doubt that some of the most restrictive and difficult features in the lives of disabled children and their families are not a necessary or inevitable consequence of having impairments. Some of the most devastating and eroding factors are socially or politically constructed and can be changed by social and political means. Consequently, in this book we place a great deal of emphasis on the part that can be played by child, family and community support services to enhance opportunity and reduce restriction. These tend to focus on reducing material and social barriers in order to create a supportive and enabling environment in which a child may flourish. We also recognise however that, like other children, those who are disabled can benefit from sensitive and high quality interventions which aim to enhance their individual cognitive and physical development. While some might argue that there has often been too much focus on changing the child and too little on reducing the negative impact of social barriers, we assume that individual and social change are not necessarily mutually exclusive. It is important to state, however, that if we do not appreciate the immense impact of social factors on disabled children and the disabling nature of the structural problems that they face, we fundamentally misunderstand their situation and do them and their families an enormous disservice.

Whose perspectives?

One of the most significant influences in aiding understanding of disability has been the oral and written contribution of disabled children and adults and those close to them. Throughout this book we rely heavily on research and other accounts shaped by these perspectives.

It is also important to recognise that while families may be significant social groupings for most people, in all households individuals have different needs and perspectives, some of which may be difficult to reconcile all of the time. Consequently, it is important to hear the accounts or to gain access to the perspectives of all children and adults intimately involved in the issues that we discuss. While one version of events may take precedence at a particular time, it is crucial that individuals who have a significant stake in a situation are not silenced. It is only too easy for one version or one account to become privileged over another. Because the opinions of disabled children have so often been neglected, considerable emphasis needs to be placed on measures which offset this. Such an assumption carries with it, however, no implication that their fathers, mothers, brothers and sisters need no voice, nor that their opinions are unimportant. Like other parents, those with disabled children assume a major degree of responsibility for their health, development and well-being. Many develop high levels of knowledge and expertise in relation to both their own children and the provision that would meet their needs. They also find very effective coping strategies and ways of living their lives in given circumstances. It is clearly essential that their voices are heard.

In addition to variations within households, there is also a wide gamut of perspectives, opinion and need across the total population of disabled children and adults and their families. While there may be some commonality of experience and views, there is also great diversity. Individuals and groups develop their own distinctive perspectives on disability, the needs derived from it and the interventions that would bring about improvement. These diverse perspectives and the language used to characterise them change and develop in the light of experience. It would be surprising were this not the case. However, while some people expect and accept a range of views, diverse perspectives can sometimes cause conflict. A passionately held belief, self-evident to one individual or group, can seem like dogma to someone else. What is regarded as the voice of authority and leadership by some will be experienced as authoritarianism by others. Individuals derive their attitudes and values from a variety of sources but some are undoubtedly shaped by particularly dominant social and personal experiences in their lives.

The significance of social groupings and divisions

The diversity of social and personal experience will in part be a reflection of the range of social groupings or divisions to which individual children and their families belong. Issues related to socio-economic status, gender, ethnic origin, age and sexuality have a profound influence in all people's lives. Social circumstances and inequality across the entire life course have a major impact on their health and well-being (Ahmad 2000; Shaw *et al.* 1999). Unsurprisingly, therefore, these factors also powerfully shape the experience of disability. Throughout this book, we draw attention to the differential experience of children and their families from a range of social groupings and to some of the ways in which their life chances and access to services are significantly affected. Without adopting an over-deterministic position, it is our view that for many families issues related, for example, to social exclusion and material hardship are so great that they structure their lifestyles and coping strategies in major ways.

Relationships between service users and providers

The impact of these social factors on the needs of disabled children and their families is a key issue for all practitioners involved in service provision. While different professional groups and providers work to varying codes of practice, there has been a growing official recognition in recent years of the necessity to provide more responsive and sensitive services for disabled children and those close to them (for example, Ball 1998; DoH 2000c). Within the social care field in particular, this focus has included an increased emphasis on developing services and professional practice aimed specifically at countering discrimination and social exclusion (Thompson 1993). Since the early 1990s, the notion of the user of public and voluntary sector services as a consumer or customer with comparable rights to those of any other consumers has become common currency.

While we would not wish to undermine any attempts to ensure that disabled children and their families are treated with respect and offered services which are responsive to their needs, it is essential to be clear about the difference between prevailing rhetoric, no matter how well intentioned, and what is often delivered. From the service users' point of view, no amount of user-centred terminology will disguise an assessment that is narrowly resource or provision driven. Similarly, the repetition of mantras about partnership with children and parents cannot conceal the complexities of unequal power relations that frequently exist between service users and professionals. It may be that some families become particularly cynical about an approach which appears to promise much but can only deliver a lot less in the way of tangible benefits.

This presents dilemmas for many conscientious practitioners who know only too well the limitations on resources within their services. These realities are also appreciated by many families. When we characterise them primarily as service users, it is easy to forget that they are also readers of their local newspapers, council tax payers and so on. While the whole orientation of this book is to help raise the level of expectations that disabled children and their families may have, we recognise that few people assume that service providers' resources are unlimited.

Notwithstanding these restrictions, parents and children are likely to appreciate practitioners whose values mean:

- they treat them with courtesy and sensitivity and take their point of view seriously

- they approach them in as straightforward and honest a way as possible

- they do what they say they will do when they say they will do it

- they start with a practical approach and only focus on more personal matters when invited or when a relationship is established

- they are well informed or prepared to find out about matters essential to the well-being of the child and family

- they demonstrate that they have an accurate appreciation of the taxing and busy nature of their lives

- they demonstrate that they appreciate the positive aspects of their experience

- they do not hold them responsible, even by implication, for factors beyond their control.

Such an approach and the values which underpin it form only a baseline, but one which can be adhered to by any informed and competent practitioner. In the chapters which follow, we shall frequently be referring to other standards and responses which families ought to be able to expect. While parents may have a realistic view of restricted public sector resources and the constraints under which practitioners work, we assume that their primary responsibility is to represent their own child in the best way that they can. It is therefore entirely reasonable for any parent to make the most of any lawful opportunity to ensure that their child's needs are met in the best way possible.

Even when practitioners, parents and children share common aims and values in relation to the quality of life that should be available to disabled children, the process of working towards this is by its very nature challenging. Pumpian (1996), exploring the goal of *self-determination across the lifespan*, suggests that there are three deceptively simple questions which disabled people should have the right to be asked:

1.   Where do you want to spend your time living, working, learning and socialising?

2.   What activities are important to you in those settings?

3.   Who are important people to interact with in these environments and activities?

Pumpian points out, however, that the complexity of the questions is revealed once we try to work out what concepts such as self-determination and choice mean in practice:

At first, answering these questions seems simple until we deal with real people in complex situations. Then these questions cause us to question and clarify our values. Our values will be challenged and conflict will be unavoidable. When is a dream, or a choice, a bad dream or just not ours? When is a goal unrealistic or just beyond our ability or willingness to be creative, inconvenienced, engaged, or effective? When is an activity too risky and irresponsible, and when is it a risk worth taking and a necessary part of a person's growth and development?

Pumpian (1996, p.xv)

The struggle to make sense of these issues and others like them, will be familiar territory to many disabled young people, parents and practitioners.

The law and its application

Throughout this text, the review of research and good practice precedes the legal analysis. This approach echoes the basic premise of the study, namely that the route to the law is through good practice. Law is not freestanding; it is not separate, indeed – like good practice and research findings – it is not always clear. If, therefore, the law and good practice appear to conflict, then one should generally be guided by good practice. The law has been drafted with the aim of reinforcing good practice and promoting certain ideals; in general if the law is believed to be dictating a course which conflicts with the best interests of the child, then almost certainly the law has been misunderstood. Gandhi (who was by training a barrister) expressed this concept as 'if we take care of the facts of a case, the law will take care of itself'.[1]

There is therefore no hierarchy of professionals (or indeed non-professionals); lawyers are not superior to practitioners and academics do not necessarily know more than disabled children or their parents. The law is not chiselled in tablets of stone; indeed, if anything, the law is the chisel, not the tablet. It is an active and adaptable tool, not a passive object. While principles and procedures may be written down in law books, the 'law' itself is alive and is what happens in daily life. It is what regulates actions and guides decision making. It is adaptable providing basic principles are respected, the most basic of all being respect for individual rights and respect for people's 'differentness' – their right to be different and to hold different views.

Laws concerning these matters are generally labelled human rights or civil liberty documents, and into this category one might put the international human rights covenants and conventions, as well as our domestic laws which are modelled on certain of these treaties, such as the Human Rights Act 1998, the Children Act 1989 (Parts I and III) and the anti-race and sex discrimination legislation. In addition we have laws for which (arguably)[2] there are no equivalent international covenants, for instance the Disability Discrimination Act 1995. The application of these rights-based statutes is further considered on p.54.

The price of freedom is, however, eternal vigilance. This constant awareness can only be maintained by procedures, routines and practices which seek to protect and promote individual rights and freedoms. Laws concerning these matters are frequently labelled 'due process' provisions in the sense that they must be adhered to strictly. They do not lay down rights, but impose restrictions and administrative obligations upon the state. Into this category one might put the Children Act 1989 (Part VI), the Mental Health Act 1983 and most of the detailed procedural regulations under the Children Act and Education Acts. The law gives public officials very little discretion in relation to the discharge of these obligations. 'Eternal vigilance' is their raison d'être: where vulnerable people are reliant upon the good behaviour and diligence of people discharging public functions, experience has shown that meticulous compliance with certain administrative procedures is one mechanism which helps reduce the risk of abuse and neglect.

When we consider the question of the law, research and good practice we assume that all those concerned with the rights of disabled children are engaged in a common struggle; a struggle to promote equality of opportunity and to combat prejudice. While lawyers, academics and practitioners often use very different language to express these issues (sometimes characterised as gobbledygook, jargon and cliché), adherence to these core principles unites their various endeavours. Not infrequently the most apt articulation of a basic tenet will be found in a research report or in a good practice guide rather than the law (or vice versa); whatever its provenance, it is appropriate that this expression of principle be used when seeking to determine what should happen in any particular situation (be the decision maker a parent, judge or social worker). One principle is however so fundamental that it has achieved a universal expression, namely 'all human beings are born free and equal in dignity and rights'.[3]

Notes

1   M. K. Gandhi, *An Autobiography* (Penguin 1982), p.132.
2   UN General Assembly Declaration on the Rights of Disabled Persons, G.A. res. 3447 (XXX), 30 U.N. GAOR Supp. (No. 34) at 88, U.N. Doc. A/10034 (1975).
3   Art. 1, The Universal Declaration of Human Rights, adopted by the UN General Assembly 10 December 1948.

CHAPTER 3

Research and Good Practice

An Overview

Introduction

Russell (1991) suggests that when we attempt to understand the experience of disabled children and their families it is helpful to see disability as a major and potentially damaging life event which is amenable to intervention and compatible with a good quality of family life. One advantage of such a balanced view is that it neither minimises the problems faced by parents and their sons and daughters nor adopts a stance in relation to disablement that is inevitably negative. Instead, it proposes an approach which identifies both the factors which generate difficulty and the nature of support services and other arrangements which can alleviate the strain and open up positive opportunities.

While it is important never to lose sight of the individuality of disabled children and their families, research and other literature have a great deal to tell us about social trends that may affect them, their most common experiences and needs, the problems they encounter and services and other supports which are generally found to be positive and helpful. Within the literature and policy documents a number of themes consistently come to the fore which are relevant to children of all age groups and their families. They may, however, have different significance at particular times in their lives. Some of these themes and findings refer to matters that have a very direct effect on their ways of living. Others deal with issues which have an equally significant but sometimes more indirect impact.

In this chapter, we review those overarching themes before turning in later chapters to more specific experiences commonly linked with different periods in the life course. We suggest that the following themes should be seen as a backdrop when any of those particular experiences are considered:

1.   Key debates and social trends

- understanding disability, exclusion and lack of opportunity
- disabled children's perspectives
- the changing population of disabled children
- poverty and material hardship.

2.   Disabled children and their families: common needs and problems

- caring in the home: mothers, fathers and siblings
- needs to be met at home
- material, financial and practical problems
- families' experience of services
- critical transition periods
- personal consequences for parents, disabled children and their siblings
- the need for information.

3.   Valued service provision

- a needs-led approach to assessment and integrated family service provision
- co-ordination of services
- key working and advocacy
- interventions to enhance children's development
- assistance with financial and practical problems of daily living
- home care, support workers and short-term breaks.

The majority of this chapter will focus on the situations of children who live at home with either or both of their parents. This is the experience of the vast majority, 91.2 per cent (Gordon et al. 2000). Because it is clear, however, that disabled children have a far greater likelihood than non-disabled children of living away from home for substantial periods, a later chapter is devoted entirely to the experience of being away from their families of origin.

Key debates and social trends

Understanding disability, exclusion and lack of opportunity

Debates on appropriate ways of theorising disability more generally have affected understandings of the experience of childhood disability. As we have suggested in Chapter 2, it has increasingly been acknowledged that some of the most restricting and damaging features in the lives of disabled children and adults and those close to them are not an inevitable or necessary consequence of having physical impairment or learning disability (Baldwin and Carlisle 1994; Barnes and Mercer 1996; Morris 1991; Oliver 1996). A greater focus on the oppressive and exclusionary nature of social and contextual factors has led to the development of what is often termed the 'social model of disability'. Some writers and activists who adopt this approach have sought fundamentally to redefine disability solely in terms of those extrinsic factors which are seen to oppress and restrict people living with impairment (Oliver 1996). Others who are sympathetic to the notion that social, political and ideological forces can be overwhelmingly damaging in the lives of disabled people have expressed reservations about some work on the social model which has appeared to give limited attention to the potentially restricting nature of impairment (Crow 1996; Read 1998, 2000; Williams 1996). Despite some differences in analysis and emphasis, there has nevertheless been a growing consensus about the fact that some of the greatest restrictions and limitations experienced by disabled children and adults are undoubtedly created by the way that society is organised to exclude them, by other people's damaging attitudes, by limited and unequal opportunities and by inadequate service provision. There has been a growing emphasis on the need to challenge these features in the lives of the disabled children and adults concerned and to create provision which offsets their effects.

These shifts in understanding show through clearly in the literature, research and official policy documents on disabled children and young people and their families (for example, Baldwin and Carlisle 1994; Ball 1998; Beresford *et al.* 1996; DoH 2000a; DoH, DfEE and Home Office 2000; Social Services Inspectorate 1998). Increasingly, there has been a challenge to what is seen as the over-medicalisation of children and their experiences and it has been argued that services have often been constrained by too narrow a medical and educational focus (McConachie 1997).

In recent years, there has been considerable debate on the different standards that have often been applied in making judgements about what is regarded as acceptable for disabled compared with non-disabled children. In almost all aspects of their lives, experiences that would be regarded as too narrow, unsettling, exclusionary or damaging for a non-disabled child have often not even required justification for their disabled peers. The repeated questioning of such assumptions and arguing for disabled children and their rights to be governed by the same standards as those applied to their non-disabled peers can be seen as a major breakthrough in policy, research and other literature in the last decade of the twentieth century (DoH 2000a; Hirst and Baldwin 1994; Morris 1995, 1998a, 1998b, 1998c). Related to this general trend has been a greater focus on policies and practices which create opportunities for the inclusion of children with diverse needs and characteristics in mainstream services and facilities (Booth 1999; Booth *et al.* 1992; Reisser and Mason 1992; Social Services Inspectorate 1994). Substantial work on inclusion in education began to emerge in the early 1980s, but initiatives in this and other fields have accelerated in more recent times.

Recent years have also seen a growing awareness in research and other literature of the way in which disability, gender, ethnic origin, age, sexuality and social status should be seen as major mediating factors which differentially structure the experience of individuals and groups (Ahmad 2000; Butt and Mirza 1996; Twigg and Atkin 1994).

While the whole population of disabled children and their families shares some common experiences, it is of course made up of individuals and groups with very diverse backgrounds and characteristics. Factors related to gender, ethnic origin, social and economic status and sexuality are shown to be very significant in shaping almost every aspect of people's lives. This has frequently been given less attention than it merits and it has been salutary for service providers and policy makers to realise the degree to which social and ethnic background and characteristics affect children's and their families' access to services which meet their needs. Research has consistently shown that poor people and those from minority ethnic groups, for example, can be very disadvantaged in this respect. Families often have to work very hard to find out their entitlements, and even when they have done so there is no guarantee that what is available will fit what the children and adults require. Sometimes, those under the greatest pressure because of a combination of stressful life events, social exclusion and very limited resources are least likely to be able to find their way through the maze and come out at the other end with something that really meets their needs (Ahmad and Atkin 1996; Baxter *et al.* 1990; Begum, Hill and Stevens 1994; Butt and Mirza 1996; Chamba *et al.* 1999; Dyson 1992, 1998; Shah 1992, 1997; Sloper and Turner 1992). Consequently, increased attention has been given to practice and service organisation designed to challenge and redress such discriminatory experiences (Baxter *et al.* 1990; Begum 1992; Dalrymple and Burke 1995; Shah 1992, 1997; Thompson 1993).

Another theme which has emerged consistently over recent years is related to the growing disquiet about the ways in which disabled children have been represented in some professional literature, in the media and some charity advertising.

There have been increasing challenges to the tendency to misrepresent disabled children as tragedies or burdens and a greater consensus about the need to be vigilant in protecting the disabled child's right to dignity and respect in all situations (Beresford 1994; Goodey 1991; Hevey 1992; Read 2000; Ward 1997).

Disabled children's perspectives

In the past few years awareness has grown about the limited degree to which the opinions and perspectives of disabled children themselves have been sought in both research and practice. Some researchers have argued that disabled children have been consigned to a passive role rather than being seen as active subjects who should be fully included in those processes which have a bearing on their lives (Priestley 1998). There is increasing recognition that it can never be assumed that disabled children 'have nothing to say', even though they may be living with profound impairment and have significant barriers to communication (Russell 1998). In addition, since the early 1990s, there has been a challenge to the notion that it is sufficient for anyone seeking to further the interests of children to rely solely on the views of adults who are close to them. Consequently, we have seen a growth in work which seeks to obtain disabled children's accounts and opinions directly and gives status to their perspectives. This has included attempts to involve them as active participants in research, development and service evaluation (Beresford 1997; Kennedy 1992; Lewis 1995; Marchant and Page 1992; Minkes, Robinson and Weston 1994; Russell 1998; Ward 1997). Because disabled children's voices have routinely been ignored for a very long time, it may prove necessary for a while at least to give counterweight to the established order of things by placing the need to consult with them high on the agenda.

There is clearly no reason, however, why more sustained attempts to seek the perspectives of disabled children need be seen to devalue the opinions or contributions of parents and significant others in their households and families. Listening seriously to children does not carry with it any assumption that their mothers, fathers and siblings need no voice, nor that the children's perspectives are inevitably privileged over others. While acknowledging that the needs and perspectives of children and parents should not be viewed as indistinguishable, research also recognises that, particularly in the case of young children living at home, theirs and their parents' needs and well-being are often inextricably linked (Beresford 1994). Consequently, in most circumstances parents of disabled children, like any others, should be asked for consent and kept fully informed when their children's opinions are being sought (Ball 1998; Russell 1998).

The changing population of disabled children

Parker (1998), drawing on the reanalysis of the OPCS data of 1985–89, indicates that there were an estimated 327,000 disabled children under the age of 16 years living in the UK. The majority of these (91.2 per cent) lived at home with their parents. Other children were being cared for by a relative (0.6 per cent), 2.5 per cent were looked after by foster carers and 4.4 per cent were at boarding school on a termly or weekly basis. A smaller number (1.5 per cent) lived in communal establishments on a permanent basis.

It is also important to recognise that over the past twenty years developments in medical technology have brought about a shift in the population of disabled children (McConachie 1997). Greater numbers of low birthweight babies and those with severe and complex disorders are surviving and are being cared for at home. Some individual children may each have a substantial range of impairments. The reanalysis of the OPCS data indicates that disabled children between the ages of 5 and 15 living in private households had an average of 2.6 disabilities. Within the cluster of those defined as severely disabled, however, this average rose to 8.6 and is higher still (9.4) in the under-5 age group (Parker 1998).

The issue of multiple impairment has significant implications for the lives of the children and their families as well as services attempting to meet their needs. The lives of a growing number of children with complex impairments are sustained by means of technological procedures and equipment usually managed by their mothers at home. These include, for example, tube feeding, assisted ventilation and resuscitation procedures (Social Services Inspectorate 1998). The children may frequently require a high level of sensitive, well-organised health care and social support on an ongoing basis. There may sometimes be problems over the organisation of medical care, disputes or uncertainty about the respective responsibilities of different service providers in relation to these complex needs, as well as issues related to the adequacy of staff training (Ball 1998; Social Services Inspectorate 1998; Townsley and Robinson 2000).

Poverty and material hardship

Later in this chapter we shall consider how factors related to the presence of a disabled child in a household predispose a family to a greater degree of financial hardship than others like them in the general population. There is growing concern about the ways in which the increased general trends in childhood poverty, the restructuring of the labour market, higher levels of unemployment and greater incidence of lone parenthood may impact particularly harshly on households of disabled children, adding to their pre-existing economic disadvantage (Baldwin and Carlisle 1994; Blackburn 1991; McConachie 1997). In many cases, their position may be rendered even more fragile by these broader social trends.

Disabled children and their families: Common needs and problems

If we are to provide services that are sensitive and effective, it is essential to appreciate what research tells us about the common needs of disabled children and young people, the care and assistance they require, who usually provides support and what are the problems routinely encountered by everyone involved. By doing this, we have a greater chance of understanding what is needed, where it should be targeted and how we may provide an integrated system of family support that takes into account the needs, activities and resources of all members of households.

Caring in the home: Mothers, fathers and siblings

The majority of disabled children are brought up at home in their families of origin and the parents, particularly the mothers, have the main responsibility for their care. The patterns of care for disabled children reflect childcare arrangements in families more generally with women tending to assume primary responsibility (Abbott and Sapsford 1992; Atkin 1992; Beresford 1995; Read 1991, 2000). In two-parent households, however, fathers frequently play a significant and active role in relation to both the disabled and other children. They are often identified by mothers as their most important source of practical and emotional support (Atkin 1992; Beresford 1995; Read 2000).

Mothers undertake a greater volume of the work overall and this cannot be fully explained simply by the fact that in two-parent households fathers are more likely than mothers to undertake paid employment outside the home. Even when fathers are unemployed or at home for other reasons, the caring workload and responsibility usually remain weighted towards mothers (Atkin 1992).

Fathers and mothers also tend to undertake different types of caring tasks. The ongoing, day-to-day care, particularly intimate personal care, most often falls to mothers who, in addition, frequently undertake physical and practical tasks. Fathers tend to take on some of those practical and physical jobs which do not include personal care and assistance. They may also undertake tasks related to the children's leisure activities from time to time or on a regular basis (Atkin 1992).

Mothers tend to take ultimate responsibility for orchestrating things that need to be done in relation to both the disabled and other children and for attending to issues related to emotional as well as physical well-being. They often assume the role of jugglers and mediators who balance out the interests of different individuals within the household (Glendinning 1983; Graham 1985; Morgan 1996; Read 2000).

The key role played by mothers of disabled children as mediators between the child and the formal health and welfare system is well documented (Beresford 1995; Glendinning 1983, 1986; Read 1991, 2000; Sloper and Turner 1992; Strong 1979). In two-parent households, fathers of the children may have difficulty in attending appointments (Beresford 1995), but may become involved in non-routine matters that have been identified as significant (Strong 1979; Read 2000).

It is important to emphasise that there are large numbers of women who as lone parents carry the full responsibility for the care and upbringing of their disabled children. The majority of lone-parent households are headed by women (OPCS 1991) and, compared with the general population, a greater proportion of households with disabled children have a lone parent (Beresford 1995). These findings are important because of the limitations on household income that often accompany lone parenthood and because of the support which many women in two-parent households acknowledge they receive from a partner (Beresford 1995). Whether the lone parent is a man or, as in most cases, a woman, managing everything single-handed may prove enormously taxing.

The caring tasks to be accomplished may change over time but many mothers find themselves having a very intimate and protracted involvement with their sons and daughters. As time progresses, the experience of the mother of the disabled child can diverge considerably from that of her peers who have non-disabled children. In the present circumstances, whatever mothers and their disabled sons and daughters might otherwise wish, the options for each to live independently of the other are drastically reduced compared with the experience of non-disabled young people and their families (Hirst and Baldwin 1994; Read 2000). Externally provided support services to meet the children's needs are simply not made available for the majority and this means that it often falls to mothers to continue to provide care and assistance to their sons and daughters on an ongoing and long-term basis. This state of affairs may persist simply because mothers and their sons and daughters have been offered no other positive and viable alternative. The mothers' opportunities to have a career or to undertake any paid work outside the home are consequently very restricted indeed and their position in this respect has worsened during the past decade (Baldwin and Glendinning 1983; Beresford 1995). The situation not only has personal implications for both the women and their sons and daughters as individuals, but also has a negative effect on the total household income.

Fathers' labour market participation is affected in different ways from that of mothers, but it may still have repercussions for the household income and for the career and job prospects of the individual men concerned. Fathers do not tend to give up their jobs but many report that their work is adversely affected by having to take time off to attend to matters related to their disabled child (Atkin 1992).

While the pivotal role of parents, particularly mothers, has been recognised for some time, in recent years there has been an increasing acknowledgement of the fact that many siblings offer quite substantial amounts of support, care or assistance on a regular basis to their disabled brothers and sisters (Atkinson and Crawforth 1995; Dearden and Becker 1998). Sometimes this can take the form of directly helping a disabled brother or sister or by undertaking tasks which assist the parent providing most of the care. In a sample of 2284 children and young people known to young carers projects in the UK, 24 per cent were defined as offering care or assistance to a disabled brother or sister (Dearden and Becker 1998).

Some young people may feel happy with what they do in this respect. Some may baulk particularly at any suggestion that they be given the label of 'young carer', feeling that it places an unwelcome connotation on their relationship with a disabled brother or sister. They may also worry about the implications of calling their situation to the attention of those in authority. Others may believe, however, that what is asked of them goes beyond what they think of as reasonable, places too great restrictions on their lives or skews their relationship with the disabled child or young person. Some may welcome formal or semi-formal recognition of what they do.

Needs to be met at home

While the upbringing of all children may prove taxing at times, it has to be recognised that the care of a disabled child frequently makes demands that exceed what is usually required of parents of non-disabled children (Baldwin and Carlisle 1994; Baldwin and Glendinning 1982; Beresford 1995; Glendinning 1983; Sloper and Turner 1992). The volume of work to be undertaken directly with the child on both a routine and non-routine basis tends to be greater and the caring tasks more complex. A combination of factors related to circumstances and human and practical resources may make balancing the needs of disabled and non-disabled family members a challenging proposition. Trying to be even handed in meeting the sometimes incompatible needs of different children in the household and making sure that nobody misses out is something that undoubtedly preoccupies many parents and may be a cause of stress (Glendinning 1983; Read 2000).

Beresford's (1995) national survey of 1100 families with a disabled child confirmed the findings of many other studies on the high levels of personal care and assistance being offered by mothers to their severely disabled sons and daughters of all ages. Help is frequently needed with bathing, washing, eating, toileting, mobility and communication. Special dietary needs have to be met, medication administered, physiotherapy and other programmes undertaken. Some children need to be watched over or require a great deal of attention and stimulation if frustration is to be kept at bay. In addition, social, communication and behavioural problems are identified as significant in the lives of substantial numbers. It has to be remembered, as other studies have shown, that this work is not confined to the daytime. Many disabled children need attention during the night for a range of reasons and this can result in disrupted sleep, not only for the main caregiver but also for other members of the household (Atkinson and Crawforth 1995; Haylock *et al.* 1993; Sloper and Turner 1992).

The literature describes graphically the ongoing and long-term nature of the caring commitments. While some children's needs for care and assistance are undoubtedly reduced as they mature, for large numbers this is not the case. For example, in Beresford's research (1995) four out of five of the young people in the 12 to 14 age group still needed help with self-care. One in two needed substantial assistance with washing, dressing, toileting and mobility. Two-thirds needed to be supervised and kept occupied. The point has frequently been made that as a child gains in height and weight, the physical demands on many mothers and other carers also become greater.

In addition, Beresford's (1995) survey indicated that behavioural, social and communication problems tended to increase in prevalence and severity as children grew older. The negative impact that they were seen to have on a range of necessary or desirable daily tasks and activities also became more marked. Challenging behaviour in an older and bigger child can be much more difficult to accomodate and manage than in one who is younger and smaller.

Getting out and about and undertaking activities which others take for granted can require a great deal of planning, organisation and energy for families with disabled children of all ages. Notwithstanding issues related to the some children's mobility or behaviour, going shopping or taking a day trip out can be made difficult by a combination of transport problems, an inaccessible built environment, a restricted budget, the need to transport equipment and parental fatigue (Beresford 1995). It is also by no means unusual for parents and children to have to face negative or insensitive reactions by other members of the public (Glendinning 1983; Read 2000).

Parents of disabled children may find that the measures which other parents use to offset the demands of child rearing are less available to them. Babysitting, 'child swaps' and other informal systems of moral and practical support that prove crucial for many parents do not come their way so easily (Read 1991; Russell 1991). Such arrangements are often based on reciprocity and upon participants having agreed needs and circumstances in common. The child who is viewed as markedly different and who sometimes has unusual needs to be met may not fit within the informal rules governing such arrangements. In addition, many people may feel uncomfortable with disabled children and uncertain as to whether they can offer them care. As families with disabled children are not unlikely to find themselves living on a limited budget, parents may not have the choice of buying in childcare or other practical sources of help and diversion for both adults and their children. Consequently, the social lives of all members of the households of disabled children can become more restricted and there is an ever-present danger of their feeling a sense of isolation or exclusion.

Material, financial and practical problems

It has long been establised that the presence of a disabled child has a significant financial impact on the household (Baldwin 1985). This results from two main factors: the costs of disabled living are high and therefore expenditure increases; simultaneously, as we have already indicated, the child's need for care reduces the opportunities that parents, particularly mothers, have for earning income outside the home. Even when families are aware of their full benefit entitlements, research has demonstrated that in relation to children of a range of ages and with a variety of impairing conditions there is a substantial shortfall between the maximum benefit entitlement and the minimum essential costs associated with disability (Dobson and Middleton 1998). For example, in Dobson and Middleton's work (1998), the shortfall was estimated on average to be around 20 per cent for primary school age children who are unable to walk and as much as 50 per cent for children of five years and under regardless of impairment.[1] They conclude that even when children in the sample are in receipt of maximum entitlement (and many are not), benefit levels would need to be increased substantially to offset the minimum essential costs of disabled living.

As a result of these factors, living standards in households with a disabled child are lower than those of comparable families in the general population and it has to be recognised that some are living in conditions of extreme material hardship. There has been increasing official recognition of the fact that households with disabled children are at risk of living in poverty or on its margins (Ball 1998). Again the fragile financial position in this respect of lone parent households cannot be stressed too strongly. In addition, recent research has also drawn attention to the particularly vulnerable population of more than 7500 families in the UK who have more than one disabled child (Lawton 1998; Tozer 1999). In these families there is an increased rate of unemployment among parents, a greater incidence of lone parenthood and a greater likelihood of being dependent on income support.

Restricted financial resources are also partly responsible for another major material problem in the lives of families with disabled children. Such families often find themselves living in housing conditions that are very restrictive and unsuitable for both child and carers (Beresford 1995; Oldman and Beresford 1998; Sloper and Turner 1992). Some of the most severe housing problems are to be found among low-income families and those from minority ethnic communities. Some are living in accommodation that is hazardous and of very poor quality. Even when families have a place to live that might be judged reasonable when general criteria are applied, it often does not have the space, layout and adaptations suitable for the needs of a disabled child, the carers and other family members. Disabled children are frequently precluded from participating in ordinary activities associated with childhood simply by the existence of physical barriers within their home environment (Oldman and Beresford 1998). In the face of serious shortfalls in public financial assistance and the absence of suitable public housing, families frequently overstretch themselves financially by moving house or undertaking adaptations at their own expense (Oldman and Beresford 1998).

Ownership of both special equipment and standard consumer durables can also prove to be a problem. Research tells us that low income families are disadvantaged in their access to disability aids and equipment (Gordon *et al.* 2000). It has also been argued repeatedly that the ownership of ordinary consumer durables and systems such as cars, refrigerators, telephones, freezers, washing machines and central heating is essential for the families in that it can help them to absorb the additional demands of bringing up and meeting the needs of a disabled child (Baldwin and Carlisle 1994; Beresford *et al.* 1995). There is evidence that the rate of ownership of these important items is lower among families of disabled children than the general population, with lone parent households being particularly disadvantaged (Baldwin and Carlisle 1994; Beresford *et al.* 1995). For example, transport is a very significant resource for most families with disabled children. There are serious and well-documented difficulties associated with use of public transport, making car ownership extremely important (Beresford *et al.* 1996). This can prove to be a major problem for already overstretched households. Suitable cars that are big enough to accomodate growing children and their essential equipment tend to be more expensive. In addition, once a car has been purchased, wear and tear (and consequently running costs) are likely to be higher than for other families. A national survey indicated that only half of the parents with disabled children had access to a car compared with two-thirds of those in the general population (Beresford 1995). There is some variation in research findings on this issue, however, as a recent study of 300 disabled children and their households suggests a slightly higher rate of car ownership and, consequently, higher associated costs (Dobson and Middleton 1998).

Research indicates, then, that some of these households which have irrefutably high levels of need for practical and financial support and both ordinary and specialist equipment frequently cannot access even those things which many in the general population regard as basic to an ordinary standard of living.

Giving consideration to the material and financial problems encountered by families is important in its own right. In addition, however, it is important to be aware that there is substantial research evidence of a clear association between high levels of parental stress and concerns about money, housing, transport and other vital material assets (Beresford *et al.* 1995). It is crucial not to underestimate the eroding nature of this level of stress on those parents who experience it over substantial periods as their children grow towards adulthood. It is also important to be aware of the fact that those who do not have a little extra money to buy in something that makes life easier or more enjoyable for children or adults, or who cannot afford decent transport or housing adaptations, frequently have only their own resilience, energy and muscle power to fall back on yet again.

Families' experiences of services

In addition to the direct caring work at home and the practical and material problems that have been identified, becoming the parent of a disabled child also necessitates involvement with a multiplicity of different agencies and professionals (Glendinning 1986; Sloper and Turner 1992; Yerbury 1997). This in itself constitutes tiring, time-consuming and often frustrating work.

Across almost two decades, a wide range of literature and official reports records considerable levels of unmet need and substantial parental dissatisfaction with many services. Further, it has been shown that parents have to be extremely active and persistent in order to gain access to what they regard as appropriate information and provision. There is a strong sense of their having to find out about, negotiate and fight for quite basic things. Provision which parents regard as suited to their own and their children's needs is often simply not available or is provided inconsistently. Services are also delivered by an increasing range of specialists working within organisational systems of baffling complexity. There are problems associated with co-ordination and joint planning between key agencies and disciplines at all levels and an ever-present danger that disabled children and their parents fall through the gaps or become marginalised (Appleton *et al.* 1997; Audit Commission 1994; Ball 1998; Baxter *et al.* 1990; Beresford 1995; Butt and Mirza 1996; Glendinning 1986; Hall 1997; Haylock *et al.* 1993; McConachie 1997; Social Services Inspectorate 1994, 1998; Sloper and Turner 1992).

Many parents experience enormous difficulty in finding their way through the terrain and they report conflict and frustration with professionals. Good services can undoubtedly be powerful mediators of stress, but the difficulties which have already been described can actually make parents feel worse, particularly if their views on needs differ from the professionals (Beresford 1995; Dyson 1987; Goodey 1991; Gough, Li and Wroblewska 1993; Hubert 1991). Parents report that they have to over-emphasise their own and their children's problems and deficits in order to get a response from a service (Ball 1998). Even when they know what could be available parents, in particular mothers, need to be very active indeed if they are to access the services they want. Those families under the greatest pressure because of a combination of stressful life events and very limited resources are least likely to be able to take on these formidable tasks (Sloper and Turner 1992). A number of studies have highlighted children and families from black and minority ethnic communities, lone parents and those on low incomes as being vulnerable to having unmet needs for support (Baxter *et al.* 1990; Beresford 1994; Chamba *et al.* 1999; Robinson and Stalker 1993; Shah 1992, 1997). In some services, the under-representation of poorer children and their families and those from black and minority ethnic communities is a cause for concern (Robinson and Stalker 1993; Butt and Mirza 1996).

Family support services also tend to be provision led. It has been reported that many children and their families receive multiple and duplicate assessments, often without the purpose being clear (Ball 1998; McConachie 1997; Social Services Inspectorate 1998). Most children and families appear to be assessed for existing provision only and comprehensive assessments of their needs for family support tied in with consistent follow-up action still seem quite rare (Ball 1998; Social Services Inspectorate 1998). In the light of these findings, it is not surprising that parents report they regard dealing with service providers as one of the most stressful aspects of bringing up a disabled child (Beresford 1995).

Critical transitional periods

Another general theme which can be pieced together from research and other literature is that there are a number of key transitional periods in the lives of disabled children and their families which merit particular attention because they have the potential to increase the vulnerability of the children and adults concerned (Baldwin and Carlisle 1994). It is useful to view these as experiences which are likely to be hazardous and stressful for all concerned if need is not addressed appropriately.

The notion of a transitional period refers to a critical stage where something important changes and a significant adjustment of individuals, circumstances and arrangements is required. This might, for example, be related to the child's age or development, to family circumstances, to external arrangements and services or a combination of some or all of them. Discovering disability, entering the education system, starting to live independently, changing from children's to adult services provide four examples of critical transition points experienced by disabled children and young people and those close to them. Typically at one of these times, the territory is unfamiliar and a great deal of new knowledge, understanding and information has to be accessed, absorbed and applied if positive progress is to be made. Because significant outcomes hang on this, however, the stakes can feel very high indeed for all concerned. It is not difficult to see why a combination of such circumstances may induce stress. It is also likely that such times could present opportunities for useful and positive intervention by service providers.

The personal consequences for parents, disabled children and their siblings

When all of the experiences and circumstances that we have reviewed are taken together, it is not surprising that there can be substantial personal consequences for all the adults and children concerned. While positive attitudes and experiences are apparent, the evidence suggests that there is a danger that those involved are coping with too great demands without adequate supports or resources to offset them.

In such circumstances, there can be an impact on the physical and psychological health of those who have the greatest responsibility for providing informal care (Russell 1991). Parents of disabled children, particularly mothers, have been found to experience higher levels of stress than those in the general population. Again, lone parents are found to be particularly vulnerable and there is also some evidence that there are links between stress levels and the severity of disablement in the child and the existence or lack of support from a partner (Baldwin and Carlisle 1994). Feeling tired or in many cases exhausted for a great deal of the time is a problem that many parents live with long term.

The factors that generate stress or promote personal well-being are complex, however, suggesting the need to be cautious about generalisation (Russell 1991). Some work in recent years has sought to uncover the ways in which parents manage stressful circumstances by actively developing their own personal and characteristic coping strategies in order to create an equilibrium in their lives (Beresford 1994). However positive these are, it has to be recognised that such are the pressures on families that any balance they create can be rather fragile and easily upset by one of the unexpected events which are prone to occur in their lives (Beresford 1994, 1995). Also, because of limited resources and support services, many families' choices about strategies for managing their lives may be made within rather narrow confines. With a greater availability of resources, they could still put their own personal stamp on situations, but their scope and choice would be greater.

A great deal has been written about the impact of having a disabled child upon marital or similar adult relationships. The situation is by no means clear with some ambiguity in research findings. Overall, however, while some men and women report their adult relationships strengthened by the experience of having a disabled child, mothers of disabled children generally have an increased chance of becoming lone parents and therefore of having a particularly onerous degree of responsibility for the upbringing and care of their sons or daughters in restricted financial circumstances (Baldwin and Carlisle 1994).

In considering the personal consequences for disabled and non-disabled children of the circumstances we have reviewed so far, a key issue has to be that substantial numbers are living on low incomes and therefore face many of the same restrictions commonly experienced by all children living at or near the poverty line. It is clear from the more general poverty studies how a lack of material resources insidiously affects almost all aspects of their lives and significantly erodes their choices, opportunities and well-being (Blackburn 1991; Graham 1993). These restrictions and exclusionary experiences may be magnified still further by both the extra demands and limitations placed on disabled children and their families. Many other families with disabled children who are not living on the lowest incomes nevertheless also face significant human and material resource problems.

We have already referred to work that has highlighted the way in which a number of factors conspire to generate a gap between aspirations regarded as ordinary for disabled compared with non-disabled children and young people (for example, Hirst and Baldwin 1994). A number of studies also report that many parents are concerned about the limitations placed on both their disabled and non-disabled children by a combination of circumstances. For example, Dobson and Middleton (1998) found that those in their study were acutely aware of their disabled children's isolation and restricted opportunities. They regarded them as children first and foremost and therefore sought experiences which they saw as being integral to any child's birthright and development. These were quite often difficult to come by and only arranged at some cost.

Other studies report that parents worry about not giving their non-disabled children enough time or attention and their opportunities and activities being restricted by the necessity to organise many features of family life around the disabled child. These concerns are sometimes offset by an acknowledgement of outcomes that are seen to be positive such as siblings having as a greater degree of maturity, understanding and a caring outlook (Glendinning 1983; Read 2000).

There has also been some research which seeks directly the views of siblings of disabled children (Atkinson and Crawforth 1995; Dearden and Becker 1998). As with parents, children record mixed reactions. Those in Atkinson and Crawforth's study express positive attitudes towards their disabled brother or sister, but also talk of being upset because of limitations placed on their lives. Unsurprisingly, a disproportionate amount of parental attention directed towards the needs of a disabled sibling, disrupted sleep and restrictions on family outings and leisure pursuits result in some children being jealous or angry. Of the research sample 70 per cent also reported being teased or bullied at school because of their brother's or sister's disability.

Parents may find that extraordinary effort is often required on their part if their disabled and non-disabled children are not to miss out significantly on experiences and standards of living regarded as ordinary by their peers. This may prove an additional demand in a routine that is already exceptionally taxing.

The need for information

Across the whole of childhood and the transition to adulthood, clear information needs to be available to the adults and children concerned, in an accessible and usable form. This can be about the child's condition, the responsibilities of various agencies, entitlements to benefits, practical support and other services. It has been consistently reported that parents and children have difficulty finding information that is essential to their well-being (Ball 1998; Beresford 1995; Chamba et al. 1999; Sloper and Turner 1992; Social Services Inspectorate 1998). Sadly, many families do not seem to have access even to the basics.

Parents' and children's need for information as well as their ability to absorb it varies across time and circumstances. Familes are more likely to make use of material that is geared to events and circumstances which are a priority to them at a particular point. For example, when they are entering a new phase in their lives, a critical transition period, for example, their need for specific information may be particularly acute. Aside from any concerns that budget holders may have about generating increased demand on limited resources, it has proved difficult for agencies to develop information systems which are sophisticated and user friendly enough to cope with both the complexity of the information to be delivered and the diversity of circumstances of those needing to receive it. The plethora of voluntary agencies offering specialist information to parents of disabled children can be seen as both an indication and a recognition of unmet need. In addition to the general shortfall, it is clear that the availability of culturally appropriate information, as well as interpreting and translation facilities for those whose mother tongue is not English, presents problems (Baxter et al. 1990; Chamba et al. 1999; Shah 1997).

It has sometimes been argued that were effective local registers of disabled children in existence, they could be used not only as a database for planning purposes but also as a means to target information appropriately to those who need it (Association of Metropolitan Authorities 1994). As there have been considerable difficulties in many local authorities with establishing registers at all, the day when they could be employed as accurate and effective service-user information systems may be some way off.

The seriousness of the problem in relation to the unmet need for information has found recognition in recent policy development. *Quality Protects*, the governmental programme which aims to transform the management and delivery of social services for children, has emphasised the need to provide information to disabled children and their parents about services to help them (DoH 2000).

Valued service provision

We turn now to some of the services which have been identified as valuable to disabled children and their families. It is worth noting that one objective of the *Quality Protects* programme is to increase the use of services so that disabled children and their families can live as ordinary a life as possible (DoH 2000).

It is seen increasingly as unacceptable to adopt an approach towards intervention that simply lives in hope that it may achieve what it sets out to do. As Beresford *et al.* (1996) point out, to date there has been very little research on the effectiveness of family support and community care services for disabled children and their households and few attempts to review them consistently. Among other things, it has proved difficult to identify the effectiveness of particular services which are not isolated, but embedded within packages of support provided for diverse groups of children and households. Recent work by Bamford *et al.* (1999) has proposed a framework which centres on quality of life outcomes. Their approach seeks to identify factors that are associated with a good quality of life and to monitor whether they occur and are maintained following the application of routine social care practice.

It is important to acknowledge, however, that there is a great deal of research which has consistently identified needs indicating the direction services could take if they are to offer positive support to disabled children and their families. There is also evidence of tried and tested approaches which can produce increased levels of parental satisfaction, enhance the rewarding aspects of bringing up the children concerned while providing a richer experience of growing up. Families identify the presence of appropriate services as a factor that makes a huge difference to their lives and they often single out for mention a practitioner or provision that they rated highly (Haylock *et al.* 1993).

As we have already established, the majority of disabled children are brought up by their families of origin at home. While it is true that most families simply get on with things, this does not mean that they should be expected to do so without support, for there is no doubt that many parents and children encounter substantial difficulties. For a very long time there has been evidence that they frequently have to fight quite hard to keep their heads above water and that the balance they maintain can be fragile and easily upset by unforeseen events and crises. Those caring for a disabled child at home often lack vital services and both formal and informal supports (Baldwin and Carlisle 1994; Baxter *et al.* 1990; Beresford 1994, 1995; Haylock *et al.* 1993; Philp and Duckworth 1982; Statham and Read 1998).

A needs-led approach to assessment and integrated family service provision

In recent years, there has been increasing recognition that disabled children and their families have diverse needs which cannot be met by uniform services and that a greater degree of flexibility is required (Appleton *et al.* 1997; Baldwin and Carlisle 1994; Ball 1998; Beresford 1994; Hall 1997; Russell 1988; Social Services Inspectorate 1998). It has been argued that it is necessary to adopt an assessment and care management framework which has hitherto been more familiar in adult social care provision (Appleton *et al.* 1997). Good practice would therefore demand that together with the children and adults concerned practitioners consider the needs which have to be met in their daily lives, plan an individualised package of provision that addresses those needs, monitor and review how it is working at agreed intervals and modify it as needs and circumstances change.

Such an approach is reflected in the recent Guidance *Framework for Assessing Children in Need* (DoH, DfEE and Home Office 2000). The Guidance has a companion volume of Practice Guidance (DoH 2000a) which contains detailed material on the way in which the *Framework* should be applied to disabled children and their families. The practitioner is required to look at any child in the context of the whole family and local community. The *Framework* consists of three domains and within each there are a number of dimensions to be explored.

1.   Domain A: Child's Developmental Needs

- health
- education
- emotional and behavioural development
- identity
- family and social relationships
- social presentation
- self-care skills.

2.   Domain B: Parenting Capacity

- basic care
- ensuring safety
- stimulation
- guidance and boundaries
- stability.

3.   Domain C: Family and Environmental Factors

- family history and functioning
- housing
- employment
- income
- family's social integration
- community resources
- involving disabled children in the assessment process.

The Practice Guidance takes the view that practitioners need to start by assuming that disabled children have the same basic needs as all children, but because they are living with impairments some may require additional support, assistance and intervention. Considerable emphasis is placed upon social factors which restrict and disable. The Guidance demands that the needs, capacities and opinions of all family members, including the disabled child, are taken into account. Those undertaking assessments are required to consider the direct impact of the child's impairment, the barriers which impede access to experiences which are regarded important in the lives of all children and their families, and ways of overcoming such barriers.

There is already an established literature on valued approaches to working with families and particularly on ways of working in partnership with parents (Appleton and Minchom 1991; Cunningham 1983; Mittler and McConachie 1983). It has been argued that the most effective services aim, where possible, to support directly or indirectly parents' own personal styles and strategies for managing their lives (Appleton *et al.* 1997; Beresford 1994). This is not, of course, the same as assuming that every parent knows exactly what they would like or what might be best for their child at any point. They may never have had access to information on the full range of options and how they might be made to work for individual children and their families. If they have not had the chance for discussion either with other families or with sensitive and informed professionals, they may simply opt for approaches and supports that they happen to know about, restricting themselves or their children unnecessarily. Given the opportunity, they may be only too happy to identify a range of desirable quality of life outcomes, despite the fact that these had hitherto been seen as beyond the reach of the children and adults in their households. Preferences also differ and it is increasingly recognised that, like other families, those with a young disabled child have their own distinctive approaches to child-rearing, lifestyle and coping strategies. Services which take the family's preferences and ways of living at least as a starting point, however, are more likely to meet with success (Beresford 1994; Mukherjee, Beresford and Sloper 1999).

There has been consistent emphasis on the need to negotiate carefully with parents and for professionals to regard them as partners contributing their own skill, knowledge and expertise (Appleton *et al.* 1997; Russell 1991; Stallard and Lenton 1992). Like other people, parents of disabled children tend to prefer to be taken seriously and treated with respect! It should also come as no surprise that empathy, warmth and good interpersonal skills rank high on the list of characteristics they value in the practitioners with whom they are involved (Sloper and Turner 1992; Russell 1991). Parents report being able to form positive working relationships with professionals whom they believe genuinely to value and accept their child (Ballard *et al.* 1997). It may be important, however, to sound a cautionary note about approaching notions such as partnership uncritically. These may often amount to little more than rhetoric, particularly when the essential power balance in professional–user relationships shifts very little. Service users may come to feel understandably cynical about ideas of partnership that do not appear to go beyond words.

As we have established, listening to parents does not and should not preclude listening to children. While it may be true that some parents find it unusual that a practitioner wishes to seek the disabled child's opinions, we have also seen that parents have positive regard for practitioners whom they believe value and appreciate their disabled children. Provided that the practitioner has some of the required skills, consults appropriately about the the most effective means of communication and is sensitive to the feelings of the child, it is likely that many parents will welcome their child's being involved and consulted. There is a range of tried and tested approaches to consulting with disabled children that can be employed by the practitioner who is able to be to be flexible enough to engage in the process (Beecher 1998).

We have seen earlier in this chapter that many disabled children have substantial and often complex needs for care and assistance; needs which are frequently met by their parents, usually their mothers, in their own homes. For a considerable time, the need to develop integrated systems of family support has been recognised (Russell 1991) Research and official reports highlight the importance of services being needs led, flexible and focused on the family as a whole rather than solely on the disabled child (Appleton *et al.* 1997; DoH 2000a; DoH, DfEE and Home Office 2000; Sloper and Turner 1992; Social Services Inspectorate 1998). It has been consistently argued that, particularly in the case of younger children, their own needs and those of the rest of the household are inextricably bound together. While some services that are directed specifically at the disabled child may be seen to be helpful, it is sometimes equally beneficial to introduce provision which in one way or another simply creates the opportunity, time and space for members of the whole family to live a more ordinary life. Families' needs and circumstances vary to such an extent that if provision is to be effective tailor-made packages are essential. While paying attention to the household as a unit, it is also important to consider parents, the disabled children and their siblings as individuals with distinctive needs and rights. In addition, services which are seen as helpful and appropriate for their children, tend to be regarded by parents as indirectly beneficial to themselves (Beresford 1994). The majority of parents are simply unlikely to use services which they feel inappropriate for their child, even if others believe that making use of them might help the adults concerned.

Because we know from research that many families with disabled children are lacking even basic information about their entitlements or about services which they may regard as helpful, any practitioner responsible for assessment will need to ensure that the discussion has sufficient scope to enable the family to think through the range of needs and interventions that might be supportive to them. The practitioner who is using the *Framework for Assessment* may need to find a way of gathering information that is comfortable for the family. There are many methods of doing this. For example, with the family's consent, a practitioner might ask them to talk in detail about what happens from morning till night (and in some cases through the night) over two or three days during a week and weekend. By doing this, the practitioner may begin to understand the pattern of their lives and caring commitments in addition to the barriers they face in trying to do things that others often take for granted. The practitioner can also gain a sense of the family's perceptions of things that are really important and which therefore need reinforcing or supporting, as well as the major problems they would like to see solved. In view of research findings on unmet needs, it might also be helpful for practitioners and service users to bear the following brief checklist in mind:

- Has the service users' elegibility for both general income maintenance and disability related benefits been checked? Do they qualify for financial help from the Family Fund? Do they qualify for financial help related to hospital and other NHS costs such as prescription, optical and dental charges?

- Do they need housing adaptations, or assistance to apply to move to suitable public housing?

- Do they need aids and other equipment?

- Would parents and children benefit now or in the future from any of the range of short-term breaks, either outside or inside the home: for example, someone providing assistance, support or care directly with the disabled child, a sitting-in service, a family link scheme, etc?

- Would the parents value help from homecare or domiciliary services to meet the disabled child's needs for care, assistance and supervision on an ongoing basis?

- Would parents value help with general household duties to relieve stress and, for example, create more time to spend with children or meet the demands of direct caring?

- Does the disabled child have a reliable means of comunication or is one being developed? Who understands the child best and how can their knowledge be used?

- Would other children in the family benefit from a service in their own right?

- Does the parent who has main responsibility for care wish to return to work now or in the future and what arrangements would facilitate this?

Even if a practitioner does not approach the task of assessment for services in this way, there is no reason why service users themselves should not adopt such a focus if they find it useful.

Co-ordination of services

The importance of co-ordination and co-operation between the services and personnel involved has long been recognised. Research and official reports show just how difficult this has proved to achieve (Appleton *et al.* 1997; Audit Commission 1994; Ball 1998; Hall 1997; Social Services Inspectorate 1994, 1998; Yerbury 1997). The lack of co-ordination between agencies, along with related disputes over their respective responsibilities, undoubtedly exacerbates the considerable difficulties that we have already established families experience in their dealings with services. Frequently identified problems include:

- health, education and social services departments are not coterminous

- a lack of agreement between agencies on priorities and few mechanisms to achieve them

- a lack of agreement about what is to be achieved and a timescale for doing it
- inadequate management information systems
- a lack of clarity about responsibility for disabled children in health authorities
- the omission of health authorities and trusts from planning groups.

The need for development of appropriate organisational, financial and managerial mechanisms to overcome these problems and to ensure joint planning, joint commissioning and co-ordinated service delivery to meet need effectively has been powerfully argued (Appleton *et al.* 1997; Audit Commission 1994; Ball 1998; Social Services Inspectorate 1994, 1998). In addition to major strategic and organisational arrangements, there need to be agreements between key agencies about who takes a lead role at particular points and how practitioners and managers with whom families have contact in one service will ensure that they know their entitlements from other services and how these can realistically be accessed. This link needs to be made in a proactive way that will have some outcome for the family rather than a token form of notification. It is not enough for these matters to be left to the initiative of individual practitioners as this makes the situation too fragile and unreliable for the children and families concerned. Clear agency and inter-agency agreements are not only in the interests of the families but also provide a sound context in which the individual practitioner can operate. The process is undoubtedly easier and more effective in places where there are established procedures for inter-agency co-operation. A key recommendation of a major report by the Association of Metropolitan Authorities (1994) was that social services, health and education authorities should make local cross-agency agreements and in turn take the lead role in brokering services required in the disabled child's early life. In many areas, however, it is clear that comparable organisational arrangements have not been put into operation (Audit Commission 1994; Ball 1998).

Key working and advocacy

When we bear in mind the difficulties that parents and children have in obtaining comprehensive and reliable information, as well as accessing complex and fragmented services, it is hardly surprising that research has repeatedly emphasised one of the most effective and valued provisions as the allocation of a particular worker to parents and their child (Appleton *et al.* 1997; Baxter *et al.* 1990; Chamba *et al.* 1999; Glendinning 1986; Haylock *et al.* 1997; Mukherjee *et al.* 1999; Shah 1997; Stallard and Lenton 1992). The recommended tasks for such practitioners vary from the provision of information and guidance through to much more active facilitation, advocacy or care management. These individuals are not only well placed to fill the information deficit so often described, but also to act as a guide through the maze, to take some of the strain of negotiation from parents and to help them access services they need and want. They may also be effective in tackling the problem that those most in need are often least well placed to gain support. Finally, they may when appropriate offer personal and emotional support through experiences that are upsetting, difficult or wearing.

A recent study defined a key worker as a named person whom parents can approach for advice about any problem related to their disabled child. Key workers may be practitioners from a number of different agencies who have responsibility to collaborate with professionals from their own and other settings (Mukherjee *et al.* 1999). The findings suggest that it is crucial for those practitioners identified as key workers to have a clear understanding of the task, to assume fully the role as defined and to have protected time to carry it out. Families reported particular features that made key working a beneficial and distinctive form of support:

- proactive contact by the key worker
- an open relationship
- a holistic, family-centred approach
- working across agency boundaries
- working with the family's strengths and ways of coping
- working and advocating for the family rather than the agency.

When we take this into account, it is probably not surprising that the existence of specialist workers or teams is also associated with higher levels of service user satisfaction (Ball 1998). It is not only that such practitioners and managers develop essential expertise in relation to the children and their families, but they also provide a clear point of contact and an avenue to other appropriate services for both service users and colleagues from other agencies.

Just as families appreciate workers who focus on their interests and advocate on their behalf, on occasion, so too do individuals within those households. It may be positive and appropriate in some circumstances for the disabled child to have his or her own separate advocate, particularly as they get older (Russell 1998). Many non-disabled children find that in the normal run of things they have the chance to establish relationships and points of reference outside their immediate household. Fewer situations may occur naturally for the disabled child to do something similar unless positive steps are taken to create the opportunity for this to happen. Again, it is important to stress that this should not be taken as a criticism of the child's parents. If the arrangement is discussed and put into practice with sensitivity, it may be seen as providing both child and parents with something that many other children take for granted. In addition, as we have already reported, some young carers' projects continue to provide support, advocacy and diversion for non-disabled brothers and sisters (Dearden and Becker 1998).

Interventions to enhance children's development

There is consistent evidence that many parents value and feel supported by provision aimed at aiding the child's development either through work undertaken by professionals directly with the child or in collaboration with parents. Examples include opportunity groups and nursery classes, daycare, early intervention or teaching programmes such as Portage, home teaching services and conductive education, as well as speech and language therapy and physiotherapy (Cameron 1997; Hall 1997; Haylock *et al.* 1993; Read 1996). The provision of specialist equipment may also be seen as a way of enhancing a child's development. Apart from the valued aims in terms of the child's development, some schemes may help to give parents confidence in themselves and their child. As we have already suggested, contact with a centre or professional providing a specialist service frequently gives parents and children access to valuable information, support and other benefits that are not directly linked to the primary purpose of the agency. It has been argued by some that because services which aim to enhance children's development are so valued by parents, it may be important to provide them even though appropriate methods of evaluating all aspects of their outcomes are not yet available (Hall 1997; McConachie *et al.* 1997).

While some services developed specifically for disabled children are undoubtedly valued by some families, there continues to be a debate about the degree to which some of the specialised or separate interventions are desirable or necessary. Some have warned against an emphasis on special teaching and therapy, particularly if it is founded on uncritical normalisation. It has been argued that some specialist interventions may create an over-structured and contrived upbringing (Gregory 1991) or serve to undermine disabled children's sense of intrinsic worth by pressing them to aim for goals which are established as desirable with reference only to non-disabled children (Middleton 1999; Read 1998). Some families may see it as most enhancing for a child to be included in mainstream activities and facilities and regard it as a priority to to have those practical and professional supports which make this possible.

In recent years there has been a growing awareness of the importance of trying to enable every child to have an effective means of communication. There has been concern about the numbers of disabled children who have never been given the opportunity to learn ways of letting others know about significant things that have happened to them or of expressing sometimes even the most basic preferences and choices (Beresford 1997; Kennedy 1992; Marchant and Page 1992; Russell 1998). There is now greater recognition of the value of systems of communication that can be used in addition to speech or as an alternative. Sometimes these are elaborated into a formal system such as Makaton, British Sign Language or Bliss. Sometimes approaches are tailor-made to particular children, their needs and abilities. The use of multiple systems and a variety of media can be extremely helpful for some children and there is now a range of literature and accounts of innovatory projects to aid those parents and practitioners wishing to ensure that they are best informed (Beecher 1998; Burkhart 1993; Russell 1998). Whatever the system, it is clear that enhanced opportunities for effective communication aid children's cognitive and social development and give them the chance to act upon their world rather than simply being acted upon by others. Because improved opportunities to communicate offer such significant possibilities for disabled children and young people, it is crucial that the means to achieve this are understood, taken seriously and employed by everyone in key service settings where they spend time. We shall give further consideration to the issue of communication in the chapter which deals with the school-age years.

Assistance with financial and practical problems of daily living

Families benefit from practical assistance and financial support to relieve them of the additional personal and monetary costs brought about by the extra needs which result from having a disabled child in the household. Their needs in relation to a range of aids, equipment, transport and minor and major adaptations to the home should be established as part of a social or community care assessment. The annual *Disability Rights Handbook* (Disability Alliance 2000) includes an excellent guide to benefit entitlement and the applications families may make to the Family Fund for cash grants to offset the costs of certain items related to the care and upbringing of a disabled child.

Short-term breaks, homecare and support workers

Schemes which offer parents and children a range of short-term breaks, formerly known as 'respite care', are also seen as valuable by many who use them. It has been pointed out, however, that it should not be construed as the primary or only service to be offered to children and their families, nor as a universal panacea (Ball 1998; Russell 1996). The government has identified the increase of short-term breaks and domiciliary services for disabled children and their families as an objective of the *Quality Protects* programme.

The more traditional or established models of short-term break provision consist of residential units and family link schemes. Some hospices also offer provision to children with life-limiting or life-threatening conditions (Robinson and Jackson 1999). Domiciliary services consisting of workers going to the family home to support the child are gaining favour but are a much more recent development.

It is estimated that only 5 per cent of all disabled children are using any type of short-term break service, though the figure rises to 17 per cent among those who are most severely disabled (Robinson 1996). There is concern about the under-representation of black and lone-parent households among users of these services despite high levels of need (Ball 1998).

There may be many reasons why families do not use short-term break provision and a lack of take-up should not be assumed to mean either that families do not want or need a break of some kind or that they do not need any other services. First, research on low take-up of short-term breaks indicates that substantial numbers of families do not have information about available schemes (Robinson 1996). It also needs to be recognised that even when families have information provision is in quite short supply generally and they may not be able to obtain what they need at a point when it is most helpful to them. There is a general shortage of family link placements and children and young people who have challenging behaviour, profound and complex impairments or who require lifting are less likely to be placed in them. Disabled children from poor families and those from minority ethnic groups are also under-represented in family-based schemes (Robinson 1996; Stalker 1991). Some studies have shown that black families and those on low incomes tend to be users of institutional care in the form of health service units or residential homes (Robinson 1996).

There are important questions to be asked about the degree to which short-term break provision has been sensitive to the social and cultural needs of potential users and whether the lack of information available to users has created a significant barrier to take-up (Robinson 1996). In addition, it is crucial to acknowledge that what is acceptable and useful varies from household to household, from child to child and from time to time. It is perfectly legitimate for most parents to exercise their judgement that some things are suitable for their children and others not. While the importance of having diversity of provision has been repeatedly emphasised (Aldgate, Bradley and Hawley 1996; Robinson 1996; Russell 1996), the range of services which would allow families to choose something that really fits their needs and circumstances is simply not on offer in many areas. Some parents find the link with another family providing short-term, family-based breaks immensely supportive. Some families feel that a residential unit is most appropriate. Other parents do not find it acceptable to place their disabled child away from home (Beresford 1994; Russell 1996) and would prefer a regular sitting-in service, domiciliary support or a homecare worker to spend time with the disabled child at home or to take them out. In some circumstances it may be advantageous to regard someone from outside the family as a child's or young person's personal assistant or enabler. They may undertake those tasks which the children cannot accomplish themselves in order to increase autonomy and enable access to new experiences. While the case has long since been made for the provision of such personal assistants for disabled adults (Morris 1993), it is regarded as a relatively new idea in services for disabled children. Some families may also appreciate a support worker who will on occasion concentrate on the needs of the non-disabled children in the family.

Whatever the arrangement, however, it is increasingly clear that parents as well as good professional practice demand that breaks outside the home as well as schemes involving support workers, personal assistants and homecare provision should be seen as a positive experience for both the disabled child and the rest of the family (Robinson 1996). Successful provision can offer a child an enjoyable and wider experience with people other than family members and sometimes, with support, the opportunity to do things which non-disabled children more often take for granted, giving a break to those who usually take most responsibility for care. Parents may also have the opportunity to spend time on other things which are important to them and can so easily be pushed aside or made difficult by the rigours of everyday caring.

Concluding remarks

In this chapter we have drawn together some key themes from the research on the experiences and needs of disabled children and their families when they are living together at home for most of the time. We have also considered some of the approaches to service provision which are either tried, tested and valued, or which attempt to address deficits which research has repeatedly identified. We have also acknowledged the importance of researching and monitoring the outcomes of interventions that are intended to improve the quality of life of children and their families (Bamford *et al.* 1999).

In the next chapter we move on to consider the legal commentary on these overarching issues and explore how the law can be seen as a tool to enable good policy and practice in relation to disabled children and those close to them. We consider what disabled children and their families can expect of the law and whether it can help both service users and providers to create the opportunities which research indicates are essential for their well-being.

Note

1   It is not unlikely that the latter shortfall will have been reduced to some degree due to the change in the benefit regulations affecting preschool children since the publication of Dobson and Middleton's findings.

CHAPTER 4

The Law and Frequently Encountered Legal Obstacles

Introduction

While all disabled children are unique, unfortunately the legal problems they and their parents face are not. Experience has shown that certain difficulties or issues of concern recur time and time again. Some problems arise at particular moments in the child's development, whereas others (such as poor communication between different agencies) can be ever present.

The purpose of this chapter is to provide an overview of the legal framework relevant to all disabled children and their families. In addition, we consider the legal principles that are relevant to the recurring themes and problems which have been identified as important in the previous chapter. We shall therefore review the following:

1.	What is meant by 'the law'.

2.	The specific obligations and powers of local authorities for the provision of:

    - social services departments
    - education
    - housing
    - the obligations and powers of the NHS

3.	The duties of statutory agencies to co-operate with each other.

4.	The problems that arise at transitional periods in the disabled child's development.

5.	The disabled child's perspective.

6.   The perspective of the parents and siblings.

7.   Confidentiality and access to information.

8.   The procedures for making representations and complaints.

What is meant by 'the law'

Rights based law

As we have noted above (see pp.21–22) certain laws are of importance because of their basic human rights content. The clearest examples are of course the international covenants and conventions which have emerged from the United Nations and the Council of Europe. The UN treaties include, most importantly for our purposes, the UN Convention on the Rights of the Child (1989).[1] Although the UK has ratified this Convention it is (like most other UN treaties) not directly enforceable by aggrieved individuals. Its principal purpose is to act as an internationally agreed standard as to the basic rights of children. In addition, however, every four years the UK has to lodge a report with the UN explaining how the government is ensuring that the rights in the Convention are being implemented.[2]

British courts will not generally have regard to UN Conventions of this type, since they are not part of our domestic law, but merely international treaties. Judges will only have regard to them if UK law is ambiguous or unclear. In such cases, when deciding how to interpret a provision, the courts endeavour to give it a construction that does not conflict with any treaty the government may have signed.[3]

Unlike most UN covenants, the European Convention on Human Rights (ECHR) was drafted with the intention that it would be enforced by aggrieved individuals and to this end the Council of Europe made provision for a court (the European Court of Human Rights) to oversee its enforcement. The ECHR has now been incorporated into our domestic law by the Human Rights Act 1998. Conventions which have enforcement procedures tend to concentrate upon 'negative' rights. Such rights are those which can generally be fulfilled by the relevant state refraining from acting a particular way. Thus the ECHR requires the state to refrain from killing people (Art. 2), torturing them (Art. 3), enslaving them (art. 4), unlawfully imprisoning them (Art. 5), and so on. The ECHR does not, however, protect many of the positive rights found in other 'free-standing' treaties. Examples of such positive rights include the right to 'adequate food, clothing and housing and to the continuous improvement of living conditions';[4] the right 'to rest, and leisure and to engage in play';[5] and the right of disabled persons to 'vocational training, rehabilitation and resettlement'[6].

The ECHR was drafted over 50 years ago and during the intervening period many of its apparently 'negative' provisions have, upon analysis by the Court, been shown to contain 'positive' characteristics. Thus, although Art. 3 merely asserts that 'no one shall be subjected to torture or to inhuman or degrading treatment or punishment', the Court has held that this obliges states to:

- have laws and procedures which protect individuals from abuse[7]

- ensure that it does not single out a group of persons for grossly different treatment on the basis of race or other grounds[8]

- conduct independent investigations when ill-treatment in a public institution appears to have occurred.[9]

Likewise the requirement in Art. 8 of 'respect' for individuals' private and family life and home has been interpreted as requiring positive measures by the state. It must, for instance, ensure that people who are harassed[10] or abused[11] are protected by prosecuting their assailants and that in certain cases people be provided with access to their social services files.[12]

Now that the ECHR has been incorporated into domestic law, there is every likelihood that our courts will continue to develop the case law by providing greater protection for disabled people. By way of example, our courts may hold that the right under Art. 10 (freedom of expression) brings with it a positive obligation on the state to help people with speech difficulties to communicate; that the right to private life under Art. 8 not only includes a right to a sexual life,[13] but also for people with profound physical impairments the provision of sexual aids and assistance; that the rights under Art. 3 (degrading treatment) require the state to legislate to protect vulnerable adults and the rights under Art. 2 (life) are violated by the presently unregulated system by which doctors make 'do not resuscitate' decisions.

The Human Rights Act 1998 is not the only statute which contains broad civil liberty provisions. In the context of disabled children, the Children Act itself is of particular relevance. Part I of the Act lists certain guiding principles, that apply when a decision materially affecting a child is to be made:

1. The 'best interests principle': namely that the paramount consideration is always the child's best interests (for which the Act provides at s.1(4) a checklist of factors to be borne in mind).

2. The delay principle: namely that in general delay in making decisions is detrimental to the child's interests.

3. The 'no order' principle: namely that if faced with a choice of making a court order affecting the interests of a child, or making no

order, then no order should be made, unless it can be shown that the making of an order is better for the child.

We see in other domestic legislation statements of general human rights principles, for instance, in the Race Relations Act 1976, s.71,[14] which obliges public authorities to promote (among other things) equality of opportunity and good relations between persons of different racial groups. Likewise the Disability Discrimination Act 1995 obliges (in certain situations) employers, service providers and the owners of premises to take steps to ensure that they do not discriminate against disabled people.

Statutes
e.g. Children Act 1989 Disability Discrimination Act 1995 Education Act 1996 Human Rights Act 1998
Regulations, Orders, etc.
e.g. Review of Children's Cases Regulations 1991 Education (Special Educational Needs) Regulations 1994 Representation Procedure (Children) Regulations 1991
Guidance: Policy Guidance (what social services must do)
e.g. Volume 6 Children Act Guidance 'Children with Disabilities,' policy guidance (1991) Framework for the Assessment of Children and their Families, policy guidance (2000)
Guidance: Codes of Practice
e.g. Code of Practice on the Identification and Assessment of Special Educational Needs 1994
Guidance: Practice Guidance **(suggests what should be done – in general)**
e.g. Assessing Children in Need and Their Families, practice guidance (2000) Carers (Recognition and Services) Act 1995, practice guidance (1996) Private Sector Renewal: A Strategic Approach 17/96 (DETR guidance on – among other things – disabled facilities grants.

Figure 4.1 The law and guidance: its relative importance

The hierarchy of the law: Statutes, regulations and guidance

The body of law of primary relevance to disabled children in their relationship with public authorities is legislation approved by parliament.[15] At its simplest one can express such law as a simple hierarchy (Figure 4.1). At the top of the scale, we have primary statutes, such as the Children Act 1989, the Education Act 1996 and the NHS Act 1977. In general statutes create the basic structure of the public body's obligations but, like a skeleton, they need to be fleshed out with detail, which is done by subordinate legislation such as regulations, orders and rules.

By way of example, s.26 Children Act 1989 seeks to ensure that children who are being looked after by a local authority have their needs regularly monitored. The basic principle is established by s.26, which then states that 'the Secretary of State may make regulations requiring the case of each child who is being looked after by a local authority to be reviewed in accordance with the provisions of the regulations'. In due course the 'Review of Children's Cases Regulations 1991' were issued, which provide a detailed scheme to ensure regular reviews occur.

Subordinate legislation of this type has to be approved by Parliament (although the actual process is generally routine) and accordingly it has almost equal legal force to primary statutes.

Lawyers do not generally regard government 'guidance' (such as guidance issued by the Department of Health or the Department for Education and Employment) as having the force of law. However, such guidance is something to which a public officer must have regard when reaching a decision (for instance, when deciding whether or not a service should be provided to a disabled child). Thus if it can be shown that in taking a decision relevant guidance was ignored or not followed, then the court may be prepared to cancel the decision and order the authority to consider the matter again, having regard to the relevant guidance. Thus it is frequently asserted by lawyers that government guidance does not have to be followed 'slavishly', but is something that a decision maker must bear in mind when reaching a decision.

This analysis of general guidance has one slight refinement in relation to what is known as social services 'policy guidance'. In general, Department of Health guidance to social services departments is labelled 'practice guidance' (and issued by the Social Services Inspectorate). This guidance advises authorities on how they should go about implementing a legislative obligation. Such guidance is essentially 'practical' and need not be followed to the letter where, for sound reasons, good practice dictates another approach. Examples of practice guidance include, for instance, the Department of Health's guidance on *Assessing Children in Need and their Families* and the practice guidance issued under the Carers (Recognition and Services) Act 1995.[16] Guidance issued to non-social services departments (such as education and housing) generally has the same status as practice guidance; for instance, the guidance issued to housing departments concerning disabled facility grants, namely 'Private Sector Renewal: a Strategic Approach DETR 17/96' (see p.262).

Policy guidance, however, must be followed in all but the most exceptional situations: it is guidance which tells authorities what they must do in order to implement a statutory provision. Policy guidance is issued under s.7(1) Local Authority Social Services Act 1970 and its binding nature derives from the wording of the section. In *R v Islington LBC ex p Rixon* [1996][17] the court explained the effect of such guidance in the following terms:

> Parliament in enacting s.7(1) did not intend local authorities to whom ministerial guidance was given to be free, having considered it, to take it or leave it.

and

> Parliament by s.7(1) has required local authorities to follow the path charted by the Secretary of State's guidance, with liberty to deviate from it where the local authority judges on admissible grounds that there *is* good reason to do so, but without freedom to take a substantially different course.

Examples of 'policy guidance' of relevance to disabled children include the guidance volumes issued under the Children Act 1989, for instance, Vol. 6, *Children with Disabilities*[18] and the *Framework for the Assessment of Children in Need and their Families.*[19]

Central government may also issue guidance in the form of a 'code of practice'; such guidance has more weight than ordinary practice guidance. Authorities are required to have regard to such guidance and the ombudsman and judges pay it especial regard when making decisions. The most relevant code of practice in relation to disabled children concerns the 'Code of Practice on the Identification and Assessment of Special Educational Needs' (discussed on p.127).

The general obligations and powers of the statutory agencies

A number of statutory agencies have specific responsibilities for disabled children and their families. Most notably these include social services and education departments and the NHS, as well as housing and the benefits agency.

Although, as we have seen, legislation spells out with varying degrees of precision the powers and duties of these agencies, they must also (for reasons of administrative efficiency if no other) adopt local policies to facilitate the implementation of these obligations in their particular geographic area. However, in framing these local policies, agencies cannot decide to ignore, or not to follow, the statutory responsibility in question. Unhappily, however, many disabled children and their families experience severe problems because local professionals and policy makers fail properly to appreciate the relevant legal opportunities and duties that exist. Practising lawyers frequently come across cases where a family has been told that a service is simply not available. Typically this might be expressed thus:

- 'We don't do carers assessments in this local authority.'

- 'Our authority no longer provides respite care.'

- 'Although Matthew needs a day centre place, due to cutbacks we cannot provide this.'

- 'Our department doesn't believe that residential placements are appropriate for disabled children.'

All these statements are unlawful. Statutory agencies, like everyone else, must obey the law; they cannot pick and choose what laws they will comply with and ignore the rest. This is known in legal parlance as 'fettering' their discretion or duty. If the law says that local authorities must carry out a Carers Act assessment when certain criteria have been satisfied (as it does)[20] then the local authority has no choice over the matter. If an authority has a power to provide a particular service, then it cannot decide for reasons of dogma or resource constraints that it will never provide that service. If an authority has a duty to provide a service and has decided that a disabled child needs it, then it must provide that service, regardless of whether it has budgetary problems.[21]

Although this much is clear, statutory agencies do make such comments and often because they have adopted a practice which has not been challenged by service users. This practice is then so often repeated that it becomes part of the culture of that agency. There are good reasons why service users do not challenge policy and practice which runs counter to their interests. They are often bereft of information and support, extremely busy and not infrequently exhausted. A combination of such factors can make people unassertive. When, however, someone has the temerity to seek the forbidden service, the request is met with same incomprehension that greeted the young child's comments in the 'Emperor's New Clothes'. In such situations the service is usually only obtainable by making an early complaint and taking the request to the level at which the agency's general policy is capable of review (we review the procedures for making a complaint on pp.76–78).

The specific obligations of local authorities

We have already noted that, strictly speaking, the duty to discharge a statutory obligation is not placed upon an individual department, but on the authority as a whole. Thus if Surrey County Council's social services department acted unlawfully, one would not sue the department but the council itself. We consider (on p.68) why this distinction is an important one, although in general parlance one can speak of departmental legal responsibilities. Thus in this section we consider these various obligations under the heading of the departments which customarily are primarily responsible for ensuring that they are discharged.

The specific obligations of social services departments

The responsibilities of the various agencies (health, education, housing, etc.) vary over time such that disabled children and their parents have to negotiate many transitions. Throughout, however, it is the social services department that is charged with ensuring that these transitions run smoothly. Social services are, in effect, the 'safety net' service. They should always be available (even if they are not actually providing a service) and ready to step in if, for whatever reason, one of the other agencies fails to deliver.

The most obvious (and arguably most fundamental) social services obligation to disabled children and their families is the duty to provide a social worker service. In addition, however, social services departments have a duty:

- to prepare strategic plans in order to meet the needs of disabled children
- to maintain registers of disabled children
- to assess individual disabled children and their carers and, where appropriate, to provide a range of services to meet their needs
- to provide information about services that may be available.

A social work service

A major innovation of the National Assistance Act 1948 was its recognition of the importance of a social work service which would provide 'advice and support as may be needed for people in their own homes or elsewhere'.[22] The Act identified the need that disabled people had for social workers to perform as 'brokers' by dealing with all the various agencies who might be able (or obliged) to provide services. The 'social work service' duty owed to disabled children and their families is now contained in the Children Act 1989 at s.17 and in Part 1 of its Second Schedule.[23] This places a duty on local authorities to provide (among other things) advice, guidance and counselling services.[24] 'Advice' clearly includes the provision of welfare benefits and general social security advice. In addition to the general support and assistance provided by social workers, there are now many specific obligations; including the duty to plan and to carry out assessments (considered below, p.62) and the duty to inform (p.65).

As we have noted, research has shown that access to a named social worker is a service highly valued by families. All too often, however, disabled children have no named social worker responsible for ensuring that their care needs are monitored and satisfied by the provision of properly co-ordinated services.

Although a failure to assign a social worker may be due to staff shortages within the local authority, any prolonged failure should be challenged. A precedent letter to this effect is shown in Appendix 8, p.265 and 268. If this fails to result in a satisfactory response, then it will generally be appropriate to instigate the review procedures (p.222).

Advocates

Advocates are persons who help disabled people and their families communicate their wishes and feelings in various contexts. While the law does not accord them as having any particular standing[25] – and while the local authorities have no legal duty to provide them – there is much Children Act and Community Care guidance which presupposes their existence; for instance, the practice guidance *Assessing Children in Need and their Families* (2000)[26] states (at para. 3.18) that 'some families would like friends, advocates or relatives to support them during assessments and this should be facilitated'.

While there are many varieties of advocate, the most commonly referred to are 'crisis advocates' and 'citizen advocates'. Social services departments should be able to direct disabled children and their parents to such advocates when requested. In general advocacy services receive funding from a variety of sources, including from the local authority.

The crisis advocacy relationship with the disabled person or his/her family is generally short term and limited to assistance in resolving a specific issue. The guidance on health and social services complaints procedures advises that complainants should have access to crisis advocates in appropriate situations.

Citizen advocacy involves the advocate developing a longer term relationship with the disabled person.[27] It is a form of advocacy where 'an ordinary citizen develops a relationship with another person who risks social exclusion or other unfair treatment because of a handicap. As the relationship develops, the advocate chooses ways to understand, respond to, and represent the other person's interests as if they were the advocate's own'.[28]

The duty to plan and keep registers

The Children Act requires local authorities to plan their services with the object of safeguarding and promoting the interests of disabled children in their area.[29] Authorities must produce 'Children's Services Plans',[30] which spell out their priorities and procedures for joint working with the statutory and voluntary agencies who have responsibilities towards 'children in need'. We consider the definition of this phrase in detail on p., but under s.17 Children Act 1989 all disabled children are deemed to be 'children in need'. As part of this 'planning and monitoring' process they are obliged to keep a register of children with disabilities.[31] The register is considered in detail on p.104.

The social services assessment and service provision obligations

In addition to providing advice, counselling, guidance and other personal support services for disabled children and their families, social services authorities have specific 'assessment' and service provision obligations in relation to individuals. The legal basis for these obligations is not always simple, and as we consider on p.21 above, practitioners should always concentrate upon good practice issues where the law appears to be contradictory or uncertain.

While the Children Act 1989 effected a radical reform of local authorities' duties and responsibilities in relation to all children, it unfortunately complicated matters in relation to disabled children by creating new rights and duties which apply alongside and overlap with the pre-existing legislation. As a consequence, disabled children and those close to them have rights to child and family support services under both the Children Act and Community Care regimes. Legally this means:

- they have a right to be assessed under both the Children Act 1989[32] and the NHS and Community Care Act 1990[33]
- they have a right to receive services under s.17 Children Act 1989 and s.2 Chronically Sick and Disabled Persons Act 1970.

While it is no simple matter to explain the interrelationship between these various statutes, in practice the problems are less daunting, and can be summarised as follows.

Assessments

Under the Children Act s.17, local authorities have obligations to assess and provide services for 'children in need'; and as we have noted above, all disabled children come within this definition. The obligations under the Act are, however, limited to providing services for children and young people (i.e. people under 18, although in certain situations up to the age of 21, see p.198).

Under a separate set of statutes (known as the Community Care legislation) disabled people have a right to services from social services departments. The obligations under some of these Acts only arise in respect of adults (i.e. people over 18) but some of the duties are owed to disabled people of any age. The most important of these Acts is the Chronically Sick and Disabled Persons Act 1970. Under s.2 of this Act, disabled people of any age (child or adult) have a right to services.

In order to decide whether or not to provide services to a disabled child, social services departments must carry out what is known as an assessment. There is nothing magical or obscure about an assessment; it is, no more, no less, an information gathering exercise whose aim is to ascertain the needs of the disabled child and his/her family. Once an assessment has taken place, the next stage is to decide what services (if any) should be provided in order to meet the identified 'needs'. (Assessments are considered in detail on pp.229–232 below.)

A legal complication in relation to the assessment of a disabled child's needs is that in order to obtain services under the Children Act an assessment must be carried out under that Act, whereas in order to obtain services under Chronically Sick and Disabled Persons Act 1970 an assessment must be carried out under the NHS and Community Care Act 1990, s.47. Of course in practice this is not a problem. All that need occur is that the social services department carry out one assessment which combines both obligations.[34] It then decides what services are required.

As we note below, the services that can be provided under the Chronically Sick and Disabled Persons Act 1970 are specific (i.e. home help, a day centre placement, home adaptations, etc.), whereas those provided under the Children Act are very wide ranging indeed, being virtually anything which could 'safeguard and promote' the welfare of the disabled child. In practice it is generally irrelevant as to whether a particular service is made available under the Children Act or the Chronically Sick and Disabled Persons Act 1970; as long as it is provided, the child and parents may consider the issue academic – and so it is, in the vast majority of situations. In a few cases however, it is necessary to know 'pursuant to which statute does the service obligation arise'. Most commonly this question crops up when the local authority is failing to provide the service, or is seeking to withdraw or curtail it. The reason for this is that the obligation under the 1970 Act is considered to be more binding on the local authority than the obligation under the Children Act.[35] As a general rule of thumb, if the service could be provided to the disabled child under the 1970 or 1989 Act, it will in fact be provided under the 1970 Act. Thus the only services provided to disabled children by social services under the Children Act 1989 are those services which cannot be provided under the 1970 Act.[36]

Residential accommodation

Where the assessment reveals that the disabled child requires the provision, by social services, of residential accommodation, this accommodation will almost invariably be provided under Part III of the Children Act.[37]

The provision of residential accommodation by social services department is considered in detail in Chapter 8. It should be noted, however, that in appropriate cases the accommodation that may be provided to the child and his/her parents under the Children Act may comprise little more than an ordinary tenancy; this arrangement is considered on p.170.

Non-residential services

As noted above, where the assessment concludes that it is necessary to provide services of the type listed in the Chronically Sick and Disabled Persons Act 1970 (i.e. practical help in the home, a day centre placement, aids and adaptations, etc.) then these must be made available. Services under the Chronically Sick and Disabled Persons Act 1970 are considered in detail on p.234.

Where the assessment concludes that other non-residential services are required (i.e. services not available under the 1970 Act, for instance, advice, coun- selling, respite care vouchers, direct cash payments, laundry, etc.) then these services will be made available, almost invariably, under the Children Act 1989. Non-accommodation services under the Children Act 1989 are considered in detail on p.232.

Social services duties towards carers

As a result of two Acts, the Carers (Recognition and Services) Act 1995 and the Carers and Disabled Children Act 2000, social services departments have specific responsibilities for parents and other people who provide unpaid care for disabled children. Although the 2000 Act has received Royal Assent, it is not expected to come into force until April or possibly October 2001. The social services obligation under these Acts is detailed on pp.237–40, but can be summarised as follows.

The 1995 Act does not provide services to carers, but instead requires social services to assess the ability of certain carers to care and continue to provide care. The Act (as with the 2000 Act) applies only to unpaid carers who are providing (or intending to provide) regular and substantial care.

If a carers' assessment reveals, for instance, that the carer is suffering a stress or other related health risk due to the extent of their caring responsibilities, then it may be that changes have to be made to the disabled child's care plan to reduce the reliance on the carer for help and increase the provision of outside assistance.

The 1995 Act applies to young carers (i.e. carers under the age of 18) and the implications of this are outlined on pp.238–9.

The 2000 Act increases the rights of carers, primarily by entitling them to receive services in their own right. The Act does not spell out with any precision what these services may be, merely stating that they must be services which help the 'carer care for the person cared for'. The Act in addition makes provision for vouchers to be paid to carers to enable them to have a break from their caring responsibilities (i.e. the vouchers being redeemable for respite care or short-term breaks). Social services are permitted to charge carers for any services they receive under this Act.

The social services' duty to 'inform'

Para. 1 of Schedule 2 Children Act 1989 requires social services departments (SSDs) to identify the extent to which there are children in need in their area and to publicise the availability of services. This duty is considered in Vol. 6 of *The Children Act Guidance: Children with Disabilities*, which makes the following observations:

> 3.6 ...SSDs should build on their existing links with community groups, voluntary organisations and ethnic minority groups to involve them in planning services and as a sounding board when formulating policies. The publicity required must include information about services provided both by the SSD and, to the extent they consider it appropriate, about such provision by others (e.g. voluntary organisations). Publicity should be clearly presented and accessible to all groups in the community, taking account of linguistic and cultural factors and the needs of people with communication difficulties. SSDs should take reasonable steps to ensure that all those who might benefit from such services receive the relevant information.

The power of social services departments to charge for services

Local authorities are entitled to charge for the services they provide under the Children Act 1989, although it is doubtful whether there is a power to charge for services provided to a disabled child under the Chronically Sick and Disabled Persons Act 1970.

The rules relating to the assessment of charges for residential and non-residential services are considered in detail on pp.240–1. In essence however the local authority may impose such charges as they consider reasonable, but if the parents are in receipt of income support, working family tax credit or disabled person's tax credit, no charge may be made. The parents' income is only relevant where the disabled child is under 16. The amount of a charge in relation to a service provided to a young person aged 16–17 is assessed on that young person's income alone.

The specific obligations of education authorities

While education is of course a 'lifelong commitment', in practice the specific obligations of education authorities generally arise at specific phases of a disabled child's development. The duty to provide general and special educational needs education is first engaged in the child's early and school age years and is accordingly considered on pp.107,124–33. The obligation in relation to further and higher education generally arises during the young person's transition into adulthood and therefore is considered on p.155.

The specific obligations of housing authorities

Without the provision of appropriate accommodation, other efforts to promote the quality of life of the disabled child may be of no avail. As the practice guidance notes, 'when houses are well adapted for a particular child, the family's life can be transformed'.[38] Housing authorities have duties to process disabled facilities grants for adaptations (reviewed on p.262), and their obligation to accommodate homeless people is considered on p.169. In addition social services authorities have powers to provide accommodation for disabled children under the Children Act (this function is considered on p.170).

NHS obligations to disabled children

The obligations on the NHS towards disabled children are substantial. At birth an NHS trust's acute paediatric service may be involved, and thence services via the NHS community trust such as health visitors, speech and language therapists and physiotherapists. These general duties, including the obligation of family GPs, are outlined in Chapter 5. The obligation of the NHS to provide continuing care, short breaks or respite care, and longer term residential care are considered on p.100, and 167, respectively.

The duties of statutory agencies to co-operate with each other

Both the Children Act and the community care legislation[39] underpin social services departments' key co-ordination role in ensuring that services are made available to meet the care needs of disabled children. S.27 of the Children Act provides:

> (1) Where it appears to a local authority that any authority mentioned in subsection (3) could, by taking any specified action, help in the exercise of any of their functions under this Part, they may request the help of that other authority, specifying the action in question.
>
> (2) An authority whose help is so requested shall comply with the request if it is compatible with their own statutory or other duties and obligations and does not unduly prejudice the discharge of any of their functions.
>
> (3) The authorities are: –
>
> (a) any local authority;
>
> (b) any local education authority;
>
> (c) any local housing authority;
>
> (d) any health authority, special health authority, or NHS trust; and
>
> (e) any person authorised by the secretary of state for the purposes of this section.

It will be seen that a social services request for assistance not only obliges the other authority to consider the request and to respond constructively, but also to comply with it unless it would unduly prejudice the discharge of its functions. Thus the mere fact that providing assistance would prejudice their functions, is insufficient. S.27 cannot, however, be used by social services as a mechanism for shifting its responsibilities to another authority.[40]

The good practice implications of the duty to co-operate are amplified in the Children Act guidance[41] in the following terms:

> Care management arrangements also take account of the multiple service providers which will be required to meet the majority of special needs. The approach aims to encourage the identification of the full range of services which may be needed. The SSD will have overall responsibility for the co-ordination of the services required. However, the day to day management and provision of these services may rest elsewhere. Packages of support can be put together using the statutory and the voluntary and independent sectors thereby making use of whatever pattern of provision has been developed within the context of a particular SSD.

Frequently it is difficult if not impossible to say with precision which particular statutory agency is responsible for providing a particular service, or (put another way) which agency is at fault in any given situation. The experience of practising lawyers is that all too often agencies end up blaming each other and suggesting that it is to the other that complaint should be made. There a large number of statutory provisions which require agencies to co-operate. These include:

- s.27 Children Act 1989, as detailed above

- s.22 NHS Act 1977 and s.26 Health Act 1999 oblige local authorities, health authorities, NHS trusts and primary care trusts to co-operate with each other to secure and advance the health and welfare of the people of England and Wales

- s.47(3) NHS and Community Care Act 1990, which obliges social services authorities to refer to health or housing authorities any health or housing needs which may become apparent while carrying out a community care assessment

- s.213(1) Housing Act 1996 places a duty on a housing authorities to respond to any request for assistance from a social services authority

- ss.5 and 6 Disabled Persons (Services, Consultation and Representation) Act 1986 which require education authorities to consult social services authorities to establish whether a child over the age of 14 who has been 'statemented' under Part IV Education Act 1996 is likely to require support from the social services department when s/he leaves school.

Where delay is caused by an inter-agency dispute, it is generally appropriate for a complaint to be made against each authority primarily on the basis that they have failed to 'work together' in violation of their specific statutory obligations (see p.76 where the complaints process is considered). The ombudsman has repeatedly criticised authorities for allowing disabled children and their families to suffer while they squabbled over their respective obligations. A recent complaint concerned the failure of a health authority and social services department to co-operate. The local governement ombudsman considered that the health authority's involvement had been 'reluctant, if not unhelpful' and in consequence the service user became caught in the cross fire. She nevertheless held that since the social services department had accepted that a need existed, it should have 'grasped the nettle' and secured the provision, before entering into protracted negotiations with the NHS on liability for the care costs.[42]

In many cases, the failure of 'joint working' is an internal, rather than an inter-agency, failure. Social services departments and education departments are always part of the same authority, and in many cases so too is the housing department (i.e. in unitary authorities, metropolitan and London boroughs). Frequently, disabled children or their parents are told by the education department that a particular need is a social services responsibility and that the family should therefore make a formal approach to that department. This is manifestly unprofessional practice, since there should be internal liaison by which the education department officer automatically refers the need to the social services department. As we have pointed out earlier, at law there is no such thing as an 'education department' or a 'social services department'; there are only local authorities. There would be nothing wrong for instance in an authority combining its social services and education departments as a number of authorities have amalgamated their housing and social services departments. Thus a request made to a 'local authority' for help will trigger obligations in all departments of that authority. Indeed certain local authority obligations are triggered not by a request for help, but by the 'appearance of need'.[43]

Transitional periods in a disabled child's development

As we have emphasised above, negotiating transitions is one of the key problems faced by disabled children and their families. New requirements brought about, for example, by a child growing older or by changes in other circumstances mean that the service user has to move from a familiar agency and find out about and access new services. These transitions are not only from one agency to another (typically from the health service then to social services, then to education, then to the benefits agency and then to housing) but may also be within departments or particular sectors, typically from a social services child care team to an adult team, from the hospital health team to the GP, from local education authority to further or higher education funding. In addition, because there is a high turnover among some healthcare, social services and education staff, there are the inevitable transitions from one worker to another. This being so, commitments made by an individual worker are only of use if that worker remains or puts the commitment in writing as part of a formal agreement or plan.

Legislative recognition of these difficulties exists in relation to a child's transition into adulthood and this stage is considered in detail in Chapter 7. If a transition between departments or workers is not properly managed and results in difficulties, it will be clear evidence of a joint working failure, and where appropriate this should form the substance of any complaint (see p.222).

The disabled child's perspective

Over the last 50 years, the law has gradually moved from the perspective of 'the state doing things to/for' disabled children and their families, to the state 'enabling and empowering' disabled children and their families to participate as fully as possible in ordinary social life. Today social services and education statutes specifically recognise the importance of involving disabled children in the decision-making process. While such explicit references are absent from statutes dealing with health, housing and social security, that does not mean these agencies have no equivalent duty. All agencies have a general obligation to take account of the wishes and feelings of a disabled child and a failure in this regard will frequently constitute maladministration[44] and/or a breach of a professional code of practice.

Social services

The formal guidance under the Children Act 1989 requires social services departments to 'develop clear assessment procedures for children in need... which take account of the child's and family's needs and preferences, racial and ethnic origins, their culture, religion and any special needs relating to the circumstances of individual families'.[45] The guidance continues (at para. 6.6):

> Children and young people should be given the chance to exercise choice and their views should be taken seriously if they are unhappy about the arrangements made for them. Plans should be explained, discussed and if necessary, reassessed in the light of the child's views... With young children, the social worker should make efforts to communicate with the child to discover his real feelings. All children need to be given information and appropriate explanations so that they are in a position to develop views and make choices.

And, at para. 6.7:

> If the child has complex needs or communication difficulties arrangements must be made to establish his views. Decisions may be made incorrectly about children with disabilities because of ignorance about the true implications of the disability and the child's potential for growth and development ... Even children with severe learning disabilities or very limited expressive language can communicate preferences if they are asked in the right way by people who understand their needs and have the relevant skills to listen to them. No assumptions should be made about 'categories' of children with disabilities who cannot share in decision-making or give consent to or refuse examination, assessment or treatment.

The importance of involving children in the assessment process is emphasised in the policy guidance, *Framework for the Assessment of Children in Need and their Families*,[46] which at para. 3.41 stresses:

> Direct work with children is an essential part of assessment, as well as recognising their rights to be involved and consulted about matters which affect their

lives. This applies to all children, including disabled children. Communicating with some disabled children requires more preparation, sometimes more time and on occasions specialist expertise, and consultation with those closest to the child. For example, for children with communication difficulties it may be necessary to use alternatives to speech such as signs, symbols, facial expression, eye pointing, objects of reference or drawing.[47]

In similar vein, the guidance accompanying the NHS and Community Care Act 1990 requires that the disabled person 'and normally, with his or her agreement, any carers should be involved throughout the assessment and care management process. They should feel that the process is aimed at meeting their wishes. Where a user is unable to participate actively it is even more important that he or she should be helped to understand what is involved and the intended outcome'.[48]

A failure properly to involve a disabled child in his or her assessment (even if there are profound communication problems) may well result in a court holding the procedure unlawful.[49]

Education

The *Code of Practice on the Identification and Assessment of Special Educational Needs*[50] stresses the importance of 'involving the child' in any assessment or planned intervention in his or her life, stating that as a matter of principle 'children have a right to be heard. They should be encouraged to participate in decision-making about provision to meet their special educational needs'. The guidance continues (at para. 2.36):

> Schools should, therefore, make every effort to identify the ascertainable views and wishes of the child or young person about his or her current and future education. Positive pupil involvement is unlikely to happen spontaneously. Careful attention, guidance and encouragement will be required to help pupils respond relevantly and fully. Young people are more likely to respond positively to intervention programmes if they fully understand the rationale for their involvement and if they are given some personal responsibility for their own progress.

NHS services

The statutory duties placed upon health bodies are expressed in broad and general terms, such that there is no specific requirement that health professionals involve disabled children when choices need to be made about their health care needs and the services that may be available to them.

We emphasise throughout this text the crucial importance of maximising the disabled child's ability to communicate, and (on p.101–2) argue that since this amounts to a fundamental human right it places a substantial obligation on the NHS to ensure that the child's wishes and feelings are taken into account.

The issue of user involvement is also a matter of relevance to the common law and professional ethics. Where the child is mentally competent[51] the doctor is unable to do anything that is invasive or intrusive in the absence of the child's specific consent unless sanctioned by the court or permitted by the Mental Health Act 1983. The Children Act guidance makes this point clear, stating '[the ability of disabled children] to give consent or refusal to any action including examination, assessment or treatment is only limited by the general conditions regarding sufficient understanding which apply to other children under the Children Act.[52]

The perspective of parents and siblings

The difficulties experienced in meeting the needs of disabled children frequently have a profound and negative impact on the lives of other household members. It is therefore essential that account is taken of this impact, not only as an aid to ensuring the disabled child's needs are satisfied, but also to enable his or her parents and siblings to have as full and normal life as possible.

Social services, education and the health service all have responsibilities in relation to parents of disabled children. 'Partnership with parents' is a central theme of the Children Act which has implications for the way social service staff are expected to work. The formal guidance asserts that partnership includes an appreciation that 'the family has a unique and special knowledge of a child and can therefore contribute significantly to that child's health and development – albeit often in partnership with a range of service providers'.[53] The guidance continues, at para. 6.4:

> Equally partnership and consultation with parents and children on the basis of careful joint planning and agreement is the guiding principle for the provision of services whether within the family home or where children are provided with accommodation under voluntary arrangements. Such arrangements are intended to assist the parent and enhance, not undermine, the parent's authority and control.

The practice guidance *Assessing Children in Need and their Families*[54] notes that 'services should seek to build on parents' strengths, and since parents cope in very different ways an approach sensitive to individual difference is necessary' and that the 'siblings of disabled children have often been invisible to professional eyes'.

In addition to the social services' obligation to work in partnership with parents are the duties owed to them as carers by virtue of the Carers (Recognition and Services) Act 1995, and the Carers and Disabled Children Act 2000. These

Acts, which are considered in detail (on pp.237–40), oblige social services departments (among other things) to carry out an assessment of the ability of 'substantial and regular' carers with a view to ascertaining what additional services may be required by the household.

The *Code of Practice on the Identification and Assessment of Special Educational Needs*[55] acknowledges that 'the relationship between parents of children with special educational needs and the school which their child is attending has a crucial bearing on the child's educational progress and the effectiveness of any school-based action'. The guidance continues by emphasising the importance of ensuring that assessments take account of the wishes, feelings and knowledge of parents at all stages:

> Children's progress will be diminished if their parents are not seen as partners in the educational process with unique knowledge and information to impart. Professional help can seldom be wholly effective unless it builds upon parents' capacity to be involved and unless parents consider that professionals take account of what they say and treat their views and anxieties as intrinsically important.[56]

Guidance issued under the Carers (Recognition and Services) Act 1995[57] drew the attention of NHS staff, and in particular primary care staff (including GPs and community nurses through their contact with users and carers), to the fact that they were in a good position to notice signs of stress, difficulty or rapidly deteriorating health particularly in carers. It advised such staff that the provisions of the Act would assist them:

> ...to meet the medical and nursing needs of their patients who are carers. When making a referral for a user's assessment they should be able to inform the carer that they may also have a right to request an assessment and will be well-placed to encourage patients whom they consider will benefit most to take up the opportunity. Social services departments should make sure that primary care staff have relevant information about social services criteria and know who to contact to make referral.

In recent years, there has been a growing awareness of the needs of siblings and the importance of services being responsive to them. The Children Act guidance reminds social services that the 'needs of brothers and sisters should not be overlooked and they should be provided for as part of a package of services for the child with a disability. They may however be children in need in their own right and require separate assessment'.[58]

Research suggests that the siblings of disabled children are frequently young carers 'carrying out significant caring tasks and assuming a level of responsibility for another person, which would usually be taken on by an adult'.[59] Accordingly the Children Act 1989[60] makes provision not only for disabled children, but also for other 'children in need'. Guidance[61] issued by the Social Services Inspectorate refers to (and accepts) research which has demonstrated that:

> Many young people carry out a level of caring responsibilities which prevents them from enjoying normal social opportunities and from achieving full school attendance. Many young carers with significant caring responsibilities should therefore be seen as 'children in need'. Once a young person is accepted as a 'child in need' the social services department is able to make a wide range of services available to that person (and his family) to safeguard and promote his or her welfare.[62]

The Carers (Recognition and Services) Act 1995 also obliges social services authorities to make provision for 'young carers' and this duty is considered on p.238.

Confidentiality and access to information

Confidentiality

Personal information about disabled children and their families held by profesionals and agencies is subject to a legal duty of confidence and should not normally be disclosed without the consent of the subject.[63] This duty of confidence applies to children as well as to adults, provided that if they are under the age of 16 'they have the ability to understand the choices and their consequences'.[64] *The Framework for the Assessment of Children in Need and their Families* policy guidance (2000) provides a brief overview of social services departments' obligations in relation to the law of confidentiality as well as an abbreviated checklist in relation to their duties under the Data Protection Act 1998.[65]

The duty on public bodies to 'maintain confidences' is not, however, an absolute one (for instance, it is displaced if the protection of a child requires it). It also important to appreciate that it exists to protect the interests of the disabled person and not the local authority. Public bodies should always analyse precisely why they are asserting 'confidentiality' and ask themselves whether this does indeed promote the disabled person's best interests. Is confidentiality being claimed to protect themselves rather than the disabled person? In its guidance on protecting vulnerable adults, 'No Secrets',[66] the Department of Health emphasise this point (at para. 5.8), stating 'principles of confidentiality designed to safeguard and promote the interests of service users and patients should not be confused with those designed to protect the management interests of an organisation. These have a legitimate role but must never be allowed to conflict with the interests of service users and parents.

Department of Health practice guidance requires that advocates are given access to relevant information concerning the person for whom they advocate and are enabled to consult with appropriate individuals in order to establish the best interests of that person.[67] The local government ombudsman has also suggested that 'confidentiality' should not be used as a reason for not disclosing relevant information in such cases. In criticising a council for not sharing information with the parents of a 24-year-old man with serious learning difficulties, she commented:

> I accept that this would not be regular practice when the Council is looking after an adult: the privacy of the individual demands that the parents be kept at some distance. But [the user] had such a high level of dependency that the Council should have been willing to reconsider its approach to parental involvement in this case.[68]

Even where the Data Protection Act 1998 makes no provision for documents to be made available to the disabled child or his/her parents, the public body retains a discretion to disclose the information.[69] In other words, even if an individual has no right to insist on seeing a particular document or piece of information, the public body has a discretion to allow that access.

Access to information

In an earlier section, we dealt with social services departments' obligations to provide information about available services in order to help children and their families to access provision. In this section we are concerned with the right of individuals to have access to information held about them by public bodies.

Disabled children and their families have the same rights of access as other children and adults to information held about them by social services, health service or in any other official records.[70] Access to such records is governed by the Data Protection Act 1998. General guidance on the Act has been issued by the Data Protection Commissioner,[71] as well as specific social services guidance by the Department of Health as LASSL (99)16.

The Act applies eight basic principles to the disclosure of information. These essentially require data to be processed fairly, legally and accurately and that the information be retained no longer than necessary. They restrict the transfer of data as well as unnecessary reprocessing of data and require organisations holding such information to take appropriate measures to restrict unauthorised access to it.

The Act gives a right of access by individuals to any personal information held by the authority about them. Where the information concerns other individuals (for instance, a local authority file on an entire family), one member is not in general entitled to see information about another member without that person's consent. The Act permits the disclosure of information notwithstanding that it has been provided by a third party and that party has not consented to the disclosure, although in deciding whether to agree to disclosure regard is to be had to various factors, including the duty of confidence to the third party, the steps taken to obtain his or her consent (and whether s/he is capable of giving such consent), and the reasons for any refusal given by the third party.

The guidance makes clear that where a person under 18 seeks access to their records the authority must decide whether or not s/he has 'sufficient understanding to do so' which means 'does he or she understand the nature of the request'. If the requisite capacity exists, then the request for access should be complied with. If however insufficient understanding exists, the request may be made by a person with parental responsibility who can make the request on the child's behalf. Disclosure to parents in such cases should only occur after the authority has satisfied itself that:

- the child lacks the necessary capacity to make the request in his or her own name and
- the disclosure would not result in serious harm (para. 2.10).

A precedent letter seeking access to such information is contained in Appendix 8. If a dispute arises concerning access to information, then the usual response would be for a complaint to be made. The legislation however provides for a procedure by which disputes can be resolved either by the Data Protection Commissioner or the courts; the choice of remedy is up to the applicant.

Procedures for making representations and complaints

Many disabled children and their parents have nothing but praise for the help they receive from the statutory agencies. Not uncommonly, however, problems do arise. While these may often be resolved informally, statutory procedures exist to ensure that persisting problems are dealt with expeditiously.

Complaints procedures

In most cases the appropriate procedure will be for a local complaint to be made and then dealt with under the local authority or NHS complaints procedures (see pp.222 and 254).

If the complaints process does not resolve the problem, it is possible then to refer the matter to the ombudsman or for a judicial review. Both these procedures are briefly outlined below. Where there is a possibility of a judicial review, expert assistance should be sought at an early stage (as the procedure is complex and subject to strict time limits).[72]

Where the disabled child lacks sufficient mental capacity[73] to articulate a complaint, a parent or other 'friend' may do so on his or her own behalf. This is also the case with complaints to the ombudsman and indeed in court proceedings such as a judicial review.

Local government ombudsman procedures

The Commissioners for Local Administration in England and Wales (the local government ombudsmen) investigate complaints from members of the public who claim to have suffered injustice in consequence of maladministration in connection with action taken by or on behalf of an authority. Maladministration is unacceptable (though not necessarily unlawful) behaviour by a public body. It is concerned with the manner in which decisions by the authority are reached and the manner in which they are or are not implemented and has been held to include such matters as 'bias, neglect, inattention, delay, incompetence, ineptitude, perversity, turpitude, arbitrariness and so on'.[74]

Complaints must in general be made within 12 months from the date on which the person first had notice of the matters alleged in the complaint. In general the local ombudsman cannot investigate a complaint unless it has first been drawn to the attention of the local authority, and that authority has been afforded an opportunity to investigate and reply to the complaint. In general this means that the ombudsman will expect the complainant to have gone through the formal complaints procedure locally.

The local ombudsman's website is at: [www.open.gov.uk/lgo/index.htm] and the contact addresses are in Appendix 9.

Health Service Ombudsman

The Health Service Commissioner (generally called the Health Service Ombudsman) has wide powers to investigate complaints concerning GPs, trusts and health authorities, including clinical practice. As with the local ombudsman, he cannot in general consider a complaint until the relevant NHS complaints procedures have been exhausted.

Complaints should be made within one year of the date when the action complained about occurred. Complaints must concern issues of maladministration. The ombudsman's website is at: [www.health.ombudsman. org.uk/health.html] and his contact address is given in Appendix 9.

Judicial review

Judicial review is a procedure by which the High Court reviews the lawfulness of decisions made by public bodies, such as the departments of state, local authorities and NHS bodies.

Public bodies must act 'reasonably' and what is 'reasonable' depends upon the nature of the decision and the context in which it is to be made. It will invariably require that in reaching a decision all relevant matters be considered; that all irrelevant matters are disregarded; that the body correctly applies the relevant law (including that it has the power to make the decision). In certain situations reasonableness may require that prior to making a decision consultation take place with persons who are likely to be affected. Likewise reasonableness may require that a particular decision-making procedure be followed, if affected parties have a 'legitimate expectation' that this will occur. Even if a public body adheres to all these principles, its ultimate decision will be capable of judicial challenge if it bears no sensible relationship to the material facts on which it was based (if it in essence 'defies logic') or if the decision amounts to an abuse of power.

Judicial review is not available where an equally convenient, expeditious and effective remedy exists. In general therefore an applicant should first utilise the complaints procedures.

If it is contemplated that a legal challenge be taken by way of a judicial review, it is essential that contact be made with a lawyer specialising in this field at a very early stage (as in general proceedings must be issued, at the very latest, within three months of the date when the decision being challenged was taken). Judicial review proceedings are complex and relatively expensive, although legal aid is available to assist with the costs if the applicant has insufficient resources. Frequently the applicant (and accordingly the persons whose 'resources' are assessed) will be the disabled child – albeit that the proceedings will be issued on his or her behalf by the parent or some other 'litigation friend'.

Notes

1   Copies of all UN Treaties can be accessed from the UN website [www.un.org/] although the University of Minnesota has an excellent website for all human rights documents, including non-UN treaties [www.umn.edu/humanrts/treaties.htm].
2   For a summary of the government's (1999) report see: www.homeoffice.gov.uk/hract/part1.htm#Article 24 – Rights of Children
3   Governments are unlikely to enact laws which conflict with undertakings given at the international level; see *R v Secretary of State for the Home Department, ex p. Brind* [1991] 1 AC 696.
4   Art. 11, UN International Covenant on Economic, Social and Cultural Rights 1966.
5   Art. 32 UN Convention on the Rights of the Child 1989.
6   Art. 15 Revised Euopean Social Charter on the Council of Europe 1996.
7   *A v UK* [1998] 27 EHRR 611.
8   *Patel v UK (the East Africans case)* [1973] 3 EHRR 76.
9   *Assevov v Bulgaria* [1999] 28 EHRR 652.

10   *Osman v UK* [1999] 29 EHRR 245.
11   *X & Y v Netherlands* [1985] 8 EHRR 235.
12   *Gaskin v UK* [1989] 12 EHRR 36.
13   *Norris v Ireland* [1985], 13 EHRR 186.
14   As amended by s.2 Race Relations (Amendment) Act 2000.
15   As opposed to the 'common law' which was created on a case by case basis by judges.
16   1996; LAC (96)7.
17   1 CCLR 119, at 123; (1996) *Times* 17 April. For a fuller account of the legal effect of such
     guidance see L. Clements, *Community Care and the Law*, 2nd edn (2000) London: Legal Action
     Group. para. 1.20.
18   *The Children Act 1989 Guidance and Regulations, Vol. 6, Children with Disabilities* (HMSO, London,
     1991); indeed all the volumes of guidance issued under the Children Act 1989 are expressed as
     being 'policy guidance'.
19   (HMSO, London, 2000), see p.41; also available at [www.the-stationery-office.co.uk/doh/
     facn.htm].
20   S.1 Carers (Recognition and Services) Act 1995, see p237. below.
21   See p.235 below.
22   S.29 National Assistance Act 1948 & Appendix 2 LAC (93)10, para. 2(1)(a).
23   This duty is reinforced by s.6(6) Local Authority Social Services Act 1970 which requires the
     local authority to provide 'adequate staff' in order to assist the director of social services.
24   Para. 8(a), Part 1 Schedule 2 Children Act 1989.
25   Ss.1–2 DP(SCR)A 1986, which was to put advocates ('authorised representatives') on a statutory
     footing, has not been implemented by the government because of 'its resource and administrative
     implications'.
26   See also para. 38 in *Care Management and Assessment – Practitioners' Guide* which stresses the
     importance of advocates 'taking a full part in decision making'. (Department of Health, London.)
27   For an excellent account, see A. Dunning, *Citizen Advocacy with Older People: a Code of Good Practice*
     (CPA, London, 1995).
28   See B. Sang and J. O'Brien, *Advocacy: the United Kingdom and American experiences* (King's Fund,
     London, 1984) p.27. King's Fund Project paper No. 51.
29   S.17 and para. 1 of Schedule 2.
30   Children Act 1989 Schedule 2 Part I, para. 1A; copies of these plans should be available free of
     charge from local social services departments.
31   Para. 2 of Schedule 2; see also para. 4.2 Vol. 6 of the Children Act Guidance (Children with
     Disabilities).
32   Para. 3 of Schedule 2 to the Children Act 1989.
33   S.47(3) NHS and Community Care Act 1990.
34   The combined assessment must comply with the good practice guidance issued under both the
     Children Act and Community Care regimes. Since the Children Act guidance is more extensive
     and appropriate it follows that this guidance will largely dictate the assessment process.
35   For a detailed discussion of this question see L. Clements, *Community Care and the Law*, 2nd edn
     (Legal Action Group, London 2000), para. 1.7 et seq. and 5.79.
36   Ibid.
37   Residential accommodation for disabled adults is generally provided by social services under s.21
     National Assistance Act 1948. Prior to its amendment by the Children Act, s.21 services were also
     available to disabled children. Disabled children who have been detained under s.3 Mental
     Health Act 1983 may be entitled to residential accommodation under s.117 of the 1983 Act.
     Consideration of this provision is outside the scope of this text. For an analysis see L. Clements,
     Community Care and the Law, 2nd edn (Legal Action Group, London 2000), para. 4.91.
38   *Assessing Children in Need and their Families: Department of Health Practice Guidance* (HMSO, London,
     2000), para. 3.115.
39   S.47(3) NHS and Community Care Act 1990 obliges the social services department to seek help
     from the NHS or housing department if a health or housing need is identified.
40   *R v Northavon DC ex p Smith* [1994] 3 All ER 313, HL.

41   *The Children Act 1989 Guidance and Regulations, Vol. 2, Children with Disabilities* (HMSO, London, 1991), para. 5.9.

42   Complaint 96/C/3868 against Calderdale MBC.

43   *R v Gloucestershire County Council ex p RADAR* [1995] 1 CCLR 476: see p.229 below.

44   See p.77 where these remedies are considered.

45   *The Children Act 1989 Guidance and Regulations, Vol. 6, Children with Disabilities* (HMSO, London, 1991), para. 5.1. See p.41 and 229 where this duty is considered in greater detail.

46   (Stationery Office, London, 2000), see p.41; also available at [www.the-stationery-office.co.uk/doh/facn.htm].

47   See also the practice guidance from the Department of Health, *Assessing Children in Need and their Families* (HSMO, London, 2000), para. 3.128 et seq. which refers to the fact that there may be surprise among others that the child be involved in the process.

48   Para. 3.16 *Community Care in the Next Decade and Beyond Policy Guidance* (HSMO, London, 1990), para. 3.16.

49   *R v North Yorkshire CC ex p Hargreaves* [1994] 1 CCLR 105.

50   Department for Education and Welsh Office (1994), para. 2.34 et seq.

51   As defined by the House of Lords in *Gillick v West Norfolk & Wisbech Area Health Authority* [1985] 3All ER 402.

52   *The Children Act 1989 Guidance and Regulations, Vol. 6, Children with Disabilities* (HSMO, London, 1991), para. 6.7.

53   *The Children Act 1989 Guidance and Regulations, Vol.6, Children with Disablilities* (HSMO, London, 1991), para. 6.1.

54   Department of Health (2000), para. 3.104 et seq.

55   Op. cit. para. 2.28 et seq.

56   Ibid.

57   Para. 30 LAC (96)7.

58   Ibid., para. 6.4.

59   SSI guidance letter 28 April 1995; CI (95)12.

60   S.17(10).

61   SSI guidance letter 28 April 1995; CI (95)12.

62   S.17(1) Children Act 1989; see p.238 where this duty is considered in greater detail.

63   *Framework for the Assessment of Children in Need and their Families, Policy Guidance* (HSMO, London, 2000), para. 3.47.

64   Ibid., para. 3.48.

65   Ibid at para. 3.46 et seq. and at Appendix E.

66   Local Authority Circular LAC (2000) 7 issued by the Department of Health and in Wales as 'In Safe Hands' National Assembly of Walse Circular 27/2000.

67   *Care Management and Assessment Practitioners Guide* (HMSO, London, 1991), para. 3.28.

68   Local Government Ombudsman Complaint No 97/C/4618 against Cheshire (1999).

69   *R v Mid Glamorgan FHSA ex p Martin* [1994] BMLR.

70   *The Children Act 1989 Guidance and Regulations, Vol. 6, Children with Disabilities* (HMSO, London, 1991), para. 6.7.

71   *The Data Protection Act 1998 – An Introduction* (Data Protection Commissioner Wilmslow, 1998). Data Protection Commissioner's Office, Wycliffe House, Water Lane, Wilmslow, Cheshire SK9 5AF.

72   For detailed consideration of this issue, see L. Clements, *Community Care and the Law*, 2nd edn (Legal Action Group, London, 2000) para. 12.77.

73   The legal definition of 'mental capacity' is considered at p.172 below.

74   For a fuller account see L. Clements, *Community Care and the Law*, 2nd edn (Legal Action Group, London, 2000), para. 12.60 et seq.

CHAPTER 5

The Early Years

Introduction

In this chapter we concentrate on some specific aspects of the experiences and needs of parents and their young disabled children that may be associated with the early years. In doing so, we revisit some of the themes already established in Chapter 3 but we consider their importance as the parents become aware of the child's impairment and begin, together with their children, to establish their own way of living with disability. In this chapter, we concentrate mainly on the preschool years but we are aware that in some families the early stages of living with disability occur later in the child's life. Such is the impact and significance of these early times that they are frequently remembered in sharp relief by those involved, particularly parents (Scope 1996). Not only does this early period have a specific importance of its own, but it can also be seen as a time when the foundations may be laid for attitudes, behaviours and ways of living that become established and enduring. In this chapter we consider:

- discovering disability
- establishing a way of living with disability
- the need for information
- accessing services
- services to aid children's development and behaviour
- daycare, playgroups, nursery education and short-term breaks
- accessing education.

Discovering disability

Research and other sources have consistently indicated that the process of discovering they have a disabled child, whether at birth or later, is experienced as exceptionally stressful by substantial numbers of parents (Audit Commission 1994; Scope 1996; SCOVO 1989a). While some men and women may not experience shock or distress, there are very many reasons why others may feel desperate when they discover that they are the parents of a child they were not expecting. Individual reactions are diverse and complex and it is important that we do not make predictions based on generalised assumptions about what someone will feel or want to do in this situation.

When negative perceptions about disability are so prevalent in the population as a whole, however, it is reasonable to assume that many parents of disabled children initially approach the experience with at least some of the attitudes that they may later come to modify or even wholeheartedly reject. Many parents report that as a result of getting to know their children and finding themselves involved in a loving, care-giving relationship with them, they not only become close to their particular child but also adopt changed views about some aspects of disability generally (Goodey 1991; MacHeath 1992; Murray and Penman 1996; Read 2000; Traustadottir 1991). This is not of course, to suggest that some do not continue to wish that their children were without their impairments. While it is crucial to recognise the distress that many parents experience when their child is identified as being disabled, it is also important to be aware of the impact that discussions about this issue can have on disabled children and young people themselves. If the prevailing attitude is that parents need to be helped to cope with something that is unequivocally tragic, disabled children may feel devalued and undermined.

In addition to their perceptions of disability and their personal reaction to the fact of having a disabled child, some parents may be unsure whether they can cope with what they think will be demanded of them. They may not wish their lives to change in ways that they assume will happen.

Depending on the child's condition, parents may also be desperately concerned about the child's health or even survival. They may be very unfamiliar with the impairments or medical condition and understandably anxious about the immediate and longer term implications. They may find themselves spending a great deal of time with numbers of unfamiliar health service and other professionals and feel that their lives are 'on hold' for a while until they see the outcome of various investigations. For some children and their families, the early stages may be characterised by a health or medical focus.

It is not only the fact of finding themselves parents of a disabled child that is reported by many parents as the cause of the initial distress and disorientation; it is also the response of some professionals and their organisations that is regarded as a major problem. Many studies have discovered high rates of dissatisfaction among parents about the services they receive at the crucial time when they are finding that they have a disabled child. In relation to the diagnosis or identification of a specific condition, concern is expressed about both the nature of the information that they were given and the manner and circumstances in which it was delivered (Green and Murton 1996; Scope 1996; SCOVO 1989a; Sloper and Turner 1993). A number of studies have also highlighted the fact that in many cases, parents are the first to suspect that there is something unexpected or unusual about a child's development, and that their anxiety may be exacerbated by professionals who do not appear to be taking their concerns seriously (Audit Commission 1994; Hall 1997; Quine and Pahl 1986).

Apart from concerns which these findings raise about the standards of practice which families should be able to expect from service providers at this time, it is important to acknowledge the enduring sense of hurt and injustice that remains with many parents who believe they and their child received less than they deserved at so important a turning point in their lives (Scope 1996: Statham and Read 1998).

Beresford et al. (1996) review the research on the process whereby families learn that their children are disabled. They report that professionals sometimes argue that parental dissatisfaction should be seen as part of the inevitable personal reaction to the news that they are being given rather than a reliable indicator of the quality of services. Beresford et al. refute this, pointing to studies which indicate that when services are shaped by research findings on practice that is valued by parents, the process of disclosure is evaluated as being much more positive and effective (e.g. Cunningham, Morgan and McGucker 1984).

In considering the unsatisfactory aspects of the experience, Beresford et al. (1996) draw attention to studies which have found that professionals are sometimes more negative than parents about the impact of a disabled child within a family and also have lower expectations of the child's progress. Professionals can be uncomfortable about giving what they regard as 'bad news' and this can appear to the parents to be an over negative attitude towards the child. Beresford et al. also point to some professionals' lack of communication and counselling skills as factors which make for difficulties. Finally, they highlight the lack of consistent policies within and between services which ensure clear, co-ordinated and guaranteed procedures at this critical point.

There is evidence that the process of identification of disability and the encounters with professionals and organisations that accompany it can be particularly difficult for some parents and children from minority ethnic communities (Baxter et al. 1990; Shah 1995, 1997; Sheik 1986). Services responsive to their needs, including culturally sensitive forms of counselling, may be very thin on the ground. It can be very difficult indeed for those who do not have English as a mother tongue to gain access to essential information and other supports either verbally or in writing. It has also been argued that predominantly white European professionals often hold quite damaging and generalised assumptions about the lifestyles of service users from minority ethnic communities and that this affects the quality and nature of the provision they are offered at this (among other) crucial times. As has already been suggested, some professionals may be unfamiliar with impairing conditions which predominantly affect minority ethnic populations (Dyson 1992, 1998).

The delivery of information at the point when parents are first finding out that they have a disabled child is crucial, as are the manner and circumstances of its delivery. A number of writers and organisations have proposed procedures and practices designed to offset some of the major difficulties and build on positive experiences that parents have identified (Beresford *et al.* 1996; Cunningham 1994; SCOVO 1989b). A number of key points emerge from this and other related work:

1.   Parents' fears and worries should never be dismissed or treated lightly.

2.   Practitioners should share information as soon as possible, even if they are uncertain about a diagnosis or the outcome of an assessment.

3.   Information about a child's condition, its implications and any proposed medical or other interventions needs to be clear and straightforward.

4.   Information needs to be realistic and honest without over-emphasising the negatives.

5.   Parents need enough time and encouragement to take in important information, go over it and ask questions in initial and subsequent meetings.

6.   Parents should be given information that is important or upsetting in private, preferably in the presence of a partner, friend or relative. They should be able to have time together without the presence of the professionals if they wish.

7.   The child should be present or near at hand when parents are given significant information.

8.   One-off information sessions are unsatisfactory; after an initial discussion, a follow-up session or series of sessions should be

arranged so that further information can be shared as it becomes available.

9.   The main information that parents are given verbally should be put in writing for them in a clear form, possibly a Parent Held Record, so that they can refer to it and show it to other people who need to know.

10.   Parents should be given the name of a contact person to whom they can refer for clarification of matters that occur to them between appointments or meetings.

11.   Arrangements for discussion of important matters should reflect the needs of all significant family members: for example, care needs to be taken not to exclude fathers from future involvement.

12.   Professionals who show warmth and seem to understand parents' concerns are valued.

13.   Information about services is regarded by families as important, as well as contact with someone who will help them access information and support at an appropriate point.

14.   Contact with support groups or networks, including those made up of other families with disabled children, may be a positive option for some families.

15.   It should be regarded as a basic minimum standard for written information to be provided in minority languages and for interpreting services to be available for those who need them.

Despite the problems that many parents experience around the time of the identification of the child's impairments, the evidence is that the majority adjust to their new situation and find a way of living that both accommodates the needs of their disabled child and manages all the things that go along with having a son or daughter growing up with disability. As we have suggested, it would be a mistake to assume that families characterise their children as burdens to be shouldered. Many radically alter their stance on disability through getting to know their own disabled child. As we have seen in Chapter 3, however, many establish a positive way of living against the odds and cope with very many stressful situations in isolation.

Establishing a way of living with disability

Some issues and experiences which have a great impact during the early period may continue to have an ongoing significance in the lives of the children and their families. In the early days, however, children and parents may be encountering these things for the first time and in a situation where both the idea and experience of living with disability is new. Given the right support during this period, families may be helped to establish with confidence a preferred way of living that stands them in good stead for the future as well as the present.

We have described in Chapter 3 an approach to needs-led assessment and provision of tailor-made packages of child and family support services. The flexibility built in to such an approach when it is working well may be particularly appropriate for families of young children who are still establishing their own way of living and growing up with disability. Any family with a new child, whether disabled or not, may need to try and test different approaches to care and living arrangements in order to see what works for them. Given the unfamiliarity and complexities of the situation in relation to many disabled children, it is important that parents and other family members have the chance to try things, change their minds and adjust arrangements till they are the best fit for everyone concerned. This has implications for the degree of flexibility that is required of service provision if it is to meet the needs of individual children and their families effectively.

It is not only that families may need to test things out to see what works for them, it is also important to recognise that needs can change quite substantially within a relatively short period in the lives of any young children, their parents and their brothers and sisters. This demands at least some regular review and adjustment in services in order to ensure that they do their job effectively. Similarly, a specific factor can change unexpectedly, for example, a young disabled child's becoming ill and spending time in hospital. As a result, the profile of the practical, financial and personal needs of all family members can alter quite dramatically. If parents and children are not given the opportunity to review the changing needs and preferences of different members of the household, some arrangements may become an established way of life simply by default, whatever those concerned might otherwise wish.

One example is the way in which mothers of disabled children may become locked into being the main provider of care in the home over a protracted period, without ever having the choice of employment outside (Baldwin and Glendinning 1985; Beresford 1995; Read 2000). Some mothers of preschool disabled children may not find it unusual to be at home and may feel strongly, as do many other women, that they wish to give the majority of their time and attention to their son or daughter during their early years. The mother of the disabled child may not anticipate, however, that without the provision of appropriate services, this pattern is likely to persist long after the preschool years are over. With time, the mother of a non-disabled child can reasonably expect that the two of them will have an increasing degree of independence from each other and she may consider taking paid employment outside the home and so on. Not only are the practical arrangements which allow this to happen less easily available for young disabled children and their mothers, but disabled children's needs for care, attention and support may well increase as they get older. Even if this state of affairs does not concern her at the start, as time goes on it may be so well established that she may feel there is little to be done about it.

It is worth remembering that research has shown that one-third of parents, the majority being mothers who are looking after their disabled children full time, would prefer to have the opportunity to go out to work (Beresford 1995). Some mothers would undoubtedly wish to return to paid employment soon after the birth of a child. Research has indicated just how difficult it is for parents with disabled children to manage jobs outside the home (Kagan, Lewis and Heaton 1998).

Isolation and lack of support

Without denying the positive and supportive experiences that some families have, all the available evidence suggests that we should view the early years as a potentially hazardous time for young disabled children and those close to them. One way of characterising the very early years is to view this time itself as the first of a number of key transitional periods in the lives of children and their families. We should not underestimate the consequences of attempting to deal with a situation that is both new and very complex in practical and emotional terms. The taxing level of activity demanded of parents of disabled children may frequently be accompanied at this early stage by understandable anxiety about the child's health, the outcomes of medical interventions as well as other key decisions about, for example, nursery or primary school placement and other services. The impact of the extra costs of disabled living combined with reduced income may bite quite early (Dobson and Middleton 1998).

A wide range of research studies and official reports has repeatedly revealed substantial numbers of families of preschool disabled children who feel isolated, unsupported and ill informed (Audit Commission 1994; Baxter et al. 1990; Haylock et al. 1993; Sloper and Turner 1992; Stallard and Lenton 1992). Studies report parents' experience of being fraught with anxiety as they struggle to cope with a very new situation without adequate information and support. There may not be an appropriate professional available to discuss major questions about planning for the child's future (Stallard and Lenton 1992). Individual families from all social backgrounds can experience these problems but those on low incomes, those from minority ethnic populations and those caring for children severely affected by impairment are particularly vulnerable to high levels of unmet need (Baxter *et al.* 1990; Chamba *et al.* 1999; Sloper and Turner 1992). Baxter *et al.* (1990) describe the circumstances of many black and ethnic minority parents with preschool children with learning disabilities as 'particularly bleak':

> Most of the research carried out among black women carers points to their extreme isolation. The myth of the cohesion of Asian communities belies the loneliness and isolation faced by many carers. Black and ethnic minority people may have a greater need for support than their white peers. Migration may have severed their traditional networks of support. Even where there are relatives in Britain, they may live in other cities. Many black and ethnic carers to whom we spoke felt isolated and desperate. (Baxter *et al.* 1990, p.60)

The need for information

As we have seen in an earlier chapter, families of disabled children of all ages experience difficulties in accessing crucial information. Throughout the early years the provision of information and advice is vital and there are critical times, such as the point of diagnosis and the transition to nursery or primary school, when it is particularly important to ensure that families are well served in this respect (Appleton *et al.* 1997; Baldwin and Carlisle 1994). Unfortunately, the available research points to families with preschool children lacking very basic information about essential services and financial benefits (Appleton *et al.* 1997; Audit Commission 1994; Baxter *et al.* 1990; Haylock *et al.* 1993; Robinson and Stalker 1992; Sloper and Turner 1992; Stallard and Lenton 1992). Studies of families' experiences in this respect frequently paint a picture of parents of young disabled children searching for crucial information for themselves in the face of complex and fragmented organisational systems. They have to be extremely active and persistent to find things out and often happen upon something important by chance. Those whose opportunities are already more restricted because of poverty, stressful events in their lives or minority ethnic status, are likely to experience greater barriers to accessing information (Baxter *et al.* 1990; Sloper and Turner 1993).

In the demanding situation in which families find themselves, it has to be recognised that many still rely on informal sources of information such as other parents whom they happen to meet at a place which is offering a service to their children. In fact, as we have already suggested, one of the bonuses which parents associate with having access to specialist facilities such as opportunity groups and other early intervention schemes is that they find out invaluable information that is unrelated to the primary purpose of the particular service (Haylock *et al.* 1993).

Some families may find that a helpful source of support and information comes through joining a support group or organisation designed to serve the needs of families with disabled children. These take many forms. Some are small, localised groups, some national or international organisations, some bring together families whose children have particular impairments or conditions, some are focused on specific issues such as education. Only a minority of families report that they belong to any such voluntary organisation (Beresford 1995). Consequently, while we may acknowledge the positive help that some undoubtedly obtain through such contact, it is important not to see it as something that suits everyone or is a panacea. In addition, it is helpful to recognise that some people may not wish to join an organisation or become actively involved, but may simply appreciate having contact from time to time in order to gain information as and when appropriate.

Accessing services

As we have seen in Chapter 3, official reports and research findings have frequently concluded that services for disabled children and their families are unco-ordinated and fragmented with the ever-present danger that the service user falls through the gaps or experiences enormous frustration in trying to access essential provision. The research on families' experience of trying to obtain helpful services during the preschool years indicates that many have to struggle to make headway and that outcomes of their efforts are at best uncertain (Appleton *et al.* 1997; Baxter *et al.* 1990; Goodey 1991; Haylock *et al.* 1993; Sloper and Turner 1992; Stallard and Lenton 1992). Frequency of contact with professionals and service organisations gives no guarantee that needs are met (Sloper and Turner 1992) and in some cases the encounters are experienced as frustrating and unhelpful. While this may be the situation for parents and children for many years to come, we need to be aware of the impact on parents and their children who may be facing these barriers for the first time.

The process of accessing services is undoubtedly easier and more effective in places where there are established procedures for inter-agency co-operation. A report by the Association of Metropolitan Authorities (1994) emphasised the importance of making local cross-agency agreements between social services, health and education authorities, with each taking the lead role in turn to broker the services required in the disabled child's early life. Appleton *et al.* (1997) describe a system in which an assessment and care management model was developed for preschool disabled children and their families in a particular authority. Care co-ordinators undertook inter-agency work to develop care plans for the children concerned. In many areas, however, it is clear that comparable organisational arrangements have not been put into operation (Audit Commission 1994; Ball 1998).

In the early days, families undoubtedly need allies on the ground. When we take into account the complexity of services combined with the dearth of usable information available to parents with preschool disabled children, it is hardly surprising that keyworkers, linkworkers or care co-ordinators of some description are so frequently regarded as practitioners who can really make a difference. Bearing in mind how new, taxing and isolating are the circumstances of many families with young disabled children, the keyworker may have a particularly valuable role. A practitioner specifically linked to a particular family may provide a clear point of reference and a first port of call for them. It is not unlikely that the understanding practitioner who acts as a guide through the maze in these difficult times may also become the person to whom the family feels able to turn for more personal discussions. There is clear evidence that people in this key role are valued by the families concerned (Appleton *et al.* 1997; Audit Commission 1994; Chamba *et al.* 1999; Glendinning 1986; Haylock *et al.* 1993; Mukerjee *et al.* 1999; Stallard and Lenton 1992).

We have seen how at the outset health and medical services are the main providers for some families and some studies have revealed that only a small proportion of those with disabled preschool children have contact with social workers (Haylock *et al.* 1997). Despite this, it is important to emphasise that the provision of family support services is the responsibility of local authority social services departments. This indicates how important it is for practitioners working for one agency, say the health service, to see it as their responsibility to put a family in touch with another service which may have a duty to make provision for them.

Services to aid the child's development and behaviour

There is consistent evidence that parents of young disabled children appreciate and feel supported by services which are designed to aid their children's development, whether through work with parents or undertaken directly with the child. These services may be found in the public, voluntary and private sectors and may be mainstream or specialised. Examples include opportunity groups, playgroups and nursery classes, early intervention and teaching programmes such as Portage, home teaching and conductive education, as well as speech and language therapy and physiotherapy (Cameron 1997; Hall 1997; Haylock *et al.* 1993; Read 1996). It has also been argued that programmes which are effective in helping parents to deal with commonly reported difficulties such as challenging behaviour or broken sleep patterns are also valued (Beresford *et al.* 1996; Quine 1993).

While it has been acknowledged that the long-term impact of some programmes on the development of the children concerned remains unproven, it has been argued that the direct and indirect benefits on parents and children, particularly in the short term, warrant their continuing to be provided (Hall 1997; McConachie, Smyth and Bax 1997).

Some concern has been expressed about the fact that some systems designed for disabled children may place undue demands upon already over-burdened families, over-professionalise parenting or render the child's upbringing too stilted and unusual (Appleton and Minchom 1991; Gregory 1991). Some have also questioned whether an undue focus on constantly trying to change or 'improve' children may be undermining to their self-esteem and identity (Middleton 1999). Perhaps the point to be made here is that services of this kind should aim to enhance the positive and individual aspects of the parent–child relationship as well as the child's upbringing more generally, rather that detract from it or place extra pressure on the adults and children concerned. As in other families, many with disabled children eventually find an equilibrium between the things that they would ideally like to do with and for their children and what they can all manage or tolerate at a particular time. Many families also create a successful balance between encouraging, for example, their child's cognitive, motoric and speech and language development to an appropriate level, while being perfectly accepting of their impairments and consequent requirements for aids, adaptations, effective communication systems and other assistance. In other words, as is the case with many other families, parents of young disabled children walk the fine line of encouraging a child to develop while accepting them for whom and what they are.

There is a further issue to be raised. It need not be assumed that all interventions which assist a disabled child's development are those which have the 'special' label attached to them. Mainstream facilities may prove enhancing for both the children and their parents (Newton 1995; Sebba and Sachdev 1997). Parents may nevertheless find that such services do not always exist in their areas and 'special' arrangements may have to be made (and even argued or fought for) to allow their disabled child to participate in mainstream provision.

Daycare, playgroups, nursery education and short-term breaks

Good daycare or nursery provision, whether specialist or mainstream, can serve at least two purposes in the lives of disabled children and their families. As with other preschool children, it can offer the disabled child the chance to learn and socialise in an enjoyable setting outside the home. Access to appropriate and affordable provision will also be one of the main factors which determines whether a mother can choose to work outside the home (Beresford 1995). Apart from the chance to increase the household income, having the opportunity to undertake paid work outside the home is one of the factors known to reduce mothers' stress and enhance their well-being (Sloper *et al.* 1991).

The lack of co-ordination between health, social services and education authorities in relation to preschool provision has been recognised as a problem for some time. While the Children Act requires local authority social services and education departments to carry out joint 'Section 19' reviews of their available services for under-eights every three years, integrated education and daycare services are still something of a rarity (Moss and Penn 1996; Pugh 1992; Statham and Read 1998).

As is the case with much of the provision for disabled children and their families, there is considerable variation from area to area in daycare and other related services, making generalisation difficult. In some areas, the concern to ensure that young disabled children have access to mainstream facilities has been a political and operational priority for children, while in others less has been achieved in this respect. Beresford *et al.* 1996 report that despite some obvious benefits for child and family, childminders are often reluctant to take disabled children and that specialist training which might encourage them to do so is available in very few places. Some social services department day nurseries offer priority places for disabled children, but in many areas such resources are very limited and under pressure. Some voluntary sector organisations offer daycare and in some areas local authorities have purchased places for disabled children in the private sector. Surveys of independent daycare providers have shown that the majority are willing to offer places to children with impairments and 'special needs' (Cameron and Statham 1997). The special needs referral system, operated in most counties of Wales, was reported to be a positive way of ensuring that children with learning disabilities gained access with the right sort of support and to appropriate playgroups (Statham 1996). Funded by the Welsh Office and local social services departments, the scheme provided co-ordinators to find places in local playgroups for children with learning disabilities, to arrange for any special equipment and extra helpers needed as well as supporting parents and staff. Again, although the scheme was widely regarded as successful and non-stigmatising, there often proved to be too few places to meet demand.

In Chapter 3, we stressed the important part that flexible short-term breaks in the home and elsewhere can play in offering a positive form of separation for disabled children, their parents and brothers and sisters. We have also acknowledged that the informal childcare arrangements on which many parents of young children depend are less available for those with a disabled child. Russell (1996) stresses that parents want short-term break arrangements which are age appropriate. Many of those with very young children regard domiciliary based services provided in the child's own home as the age-appropriate option.

We have already discussed the way that mothers can almost by default become their children's full-time carers throughout their lives. If women and their sons and daughters are gradually to have choice about the degree of independence they have from each other in the early days as well as at a future time, practitioners may need to be extremely proactive in searching for and offering safe and enhancing daycare and play opportunities for the child.

Accessing education

While we deal with access to the school system mainly in the next chapter, we recognise that many disabled children will begin an assessment of their special educational needs before the age of two years in order to facilitate their access to nursery education. While some will go to mainstream nursery schools, others will be placed in the nursery departments of special schools. In many cases, the latter arrangement may make their transition to special school at primary age almost inevitable.

The process, usually known as 'statementing', through which a child's educational needs are assessed and provision allocated, can be a stress-inducing situation for preschool children and their parents. The statementing procedure has received widespread criticism and was revised through the introduction of a new code of practice in 1994 (Audit Commission 1992; DfEE 1994; Spastics Society 1992).

It is not difficult to see why this process should be regarded as so hazardous for the service user. Another key transitional point in the child's life has been reached and the decisions made are crucial to present and future well-being. As we have seen, parents may be asked to consider decisions related to educational provision at a much earlier stage than would be the case for a non-disabled preschool child. In addition, the procedures involved are likely to be very new and quite daunting to many parents of young disabled children. They may not know any other parent going through the same process. They may also be unfamiliar with the range of educational provision that can be made available to disabled children and may not have had the opportunity, for example, to think through the pros and cons of mainstream or special schooling, let alone the range of options within those two broad categories. While the law prescribes assessment that is needs led rather than provision led, the likelihood is that in some authorities families are steered predominantly towards the educational facilities already available within the locality. The information which would help parents familiarise themselves with what is a whole new territory and make confident and informed choices in their children's best interests is simply not available to many in a form that they can use. Formal and informal material often comes their way in a fragmented fashion and many feel that it is too much down to luck as to whether they find out what they need to know at a time when it would be useful. Clearly, a child's transition into the education system provides an important point where a care co-ordinator or keyworker can supply a valuable service to the child and the parents (Appleton *et al.* 1997).

LEGAL COMMENTARY

Introduction

Disabled children and their parents testify that if they are to avoid social exclusion and ensure that they receive appropriate services, they need to acquire an enormous range of skills and knowledge. This becomes important as soon as they embark on the process of establishing a way of living with disability. As we have seen, they are frequently left to do this without sufficient support and information.

Once the statutory agencies are aware that a child has a physical and/or intellectual impairment, it is likely that a number of professionals will appear and seek to confirm the diagnosis. As we have seen from research, it is not uncommon for children and their families to undergo serial assessments which result in little that is tangible in the way of ongoing service provision. As soon as a condition or impairment has been identified or diagnosed, service professionals may fade away without any support or significant information being provided for the family. All too often nothing further is done until a crisis develops. In the legal arena, therefore, disabled children and their parents need to acquire:

- a detailed knowledge of the responsibilities of the various statutory authorities and what one has the right to expect from them
- the ability to plan ahead and to anticipate the next obstacle that the legal system will require to be traversed.

As we have outlined above, good practice dictates that help should be readily available throughout the disabled child's life and, most importantly, that this contact is established in a positive way from the outset. In this section we consider the legal obligations that are of particular relevance in the early years, and in doing so highlight the role of the NHS, since it will frequently be the health service which is the first statutory service provider to make contact with a disabled child and his or her parents. At this stage the family may well be unaware of even the most basic of organisational matters such as:

- the role of social workers

- the divisions between the responsibilities of the NHS trust and the primary care teams (or even what an 'NHS trust' is or what 'primary care' means)

- who has responsibility for co-ordinating care arrangements upon discharge from hospital; for instance, who liases with the GP to ensure continuity of health care

- who employs/is responsible for the performance of health visitors, community nurses, GPs, social workers, etc.

- who arranges transport to and from a hospital or clinic if it is some distance from the family home.

While we highlight the important role that the health services should play in the life of a young disabled child, this is not intended to imply that during these years social services are entitled to take a 'back seat'. The local authority's legal responsibilities, which were outlined in the previous chapter, apply as much in the early years as at any other time in the lifecourse of the child.

Before seeking to clarify the legal situation in relation to these specific issues, it is necessary to consider the general obligation of the health service to provide specific health care treatments and services.

The NHS and hospital services

In-patient treatment

While parents of young disabled children will necessarily be anxious to ensure that their child receives the best possible medical and health care, the legal obligations on health authorities to provide specific health care treatments are limited.

The National Health Services Act 1977 (ss.1 and 13) places only a general and indeterminate obligation on health authorities to promote a comprehensive health service in their area. This does not of itself mean that a particular service must be made available for a particular child. Their general discretion is however constrained by three factors:

1. The authority must aim towards the provision of a 'comprehensive service', so if it decides not to make available any services in a particular discipline (or grossly inadequate services) then the court may intervene on behalf of an aggrieved child or parent. For example, in R v North and East Devon Health Authority ex p Coughlan [1999][1] it was held unlawful for a health authority to decide not to provide health services for patients who had a need for substantial, but non-specialist nursing care, on the basis that the local authority could make provision for such persons in nursing homes.[2]

2.   Health authorities must take into account and generally follow guidance issued by the Department of Health, Welsh Assembly or the NHS Executive. At p.57 we briefly review the effect of such guidance. By way of example however, in *R v North Derbyshire Health Authority ex p Fisher*[3] the court ruled that the respondent authority had failed, without good reason, to follow government guidance[4] on the prescription of beta-interferon drugs to people with multiple sclerosis and accordingly held that its actions were unlawful.

3.   The fundamental requirements of the Human Rights Act 1998: s.6 of the Act requires health authorities and trusts (among others) to uphold the rights of individuals under the European Convention on Human Rights. This therefore places upon such organisations a positive duty to protect life (Art.2) as well as to ensure that patients do not suffer degrading treatment (Art.3) and that proper respect is shown for their private and family life (Art.8).

In general however the courts are reluctant to interfere with the decisions of doctors and health authorities as to what treatments should be provided and what treatments are inappropriate. In *R v Cambridge Health Authority ex p B*,[5] for instance, the issue concerned 'the life of a young patient'. The child's father challenged the health authority's decision that, because of its cost and its poor prospects of success, it would not fund any further chemotherapy treatment for his daughter. The Court of Appeal rejected the father's application stating:

> Difficult and agonising judgements have to be made as to how a limited budget is best allocated to the maximum advantage of the maximum number of patients. That is not a judgement which the court can make... It is not something that a health authority...can be fairly criticised for not advancing before the court.

The decision does not mean, however, that courts will not scrutinise very carefully questions which engage fundamental human rights. In the above case the court heard evidence of the lengths to which the health authority had gone to weigh up the likelihood of the treatment being successful and the adverse effects of the treatment, and had consulted with the family. It concluded that the decision was taken on an individual basis and supported by respected professional opinion. In such cases, where the key consideration is expertise that the court does not possess, even with the enactment of the Human Rights Act 1998, the courts will inevitably hesitate to substitute its opinions. The situation will however be otherwise where the issue concerns questions of law or logic.

The Human Rights Act will however impose a positive obligation on all NHS bodies to justify any decision not to provide treatment, where the consequence could be the earlier death of the child (Art.2), or increased suffering (Art.3) or discrimination (Art.14). Thus, by way of example, a decision to restrict funding on kidney dialysis machines could certainly lead to deaths and increased suffering. Accordingly, if challenged, that decision would be carefully scrutinised by the court. Relevant factors in this analysis would be: the cost of such equipment; the extent of the health authority's resources; the other calls upon those resources; and the regard that was taken of government guidance and of individual patients suffering from kidney failure. If however the authority decided that it would not offer dialysis to children with a particular condition, for instance, Down's syndrome, then this would be discriminatory action (contrary to Art.14),[6] which would be extremely difficult for the health authority to justify (unless there were particular medical reasons why a person with Down's syndrome was less likely to benefit from the treatment than a person without that condition).

Hospital discharge planning

The *Hospital Discharge Workbook*[7] spells out what patients and their families are entitled to expect from the NHS when the patient is ready to be discharged. The workbook refers to the Patients' Charter, which places an obligation upon the hospital managers to ensure that before discharge a decision is made about any continuing health or social care needs that the patient may have:

> Your hospital will agree arrangements for meeting these needs with agencies such as community nursing services and local authority social services departments before you are discharged. You and, with your agreements, your carers will be consulted and informed at all stages.

The workbook summarises the care services and assistance that disabled children (amongst others) and their carers are entitled to expect from the hospital authorities:

- to be admitted to hospital only when their needs cannot be appropriately met in the community
- a written and verbal explanation before, or at the time of admission, about what they can expect to happen during their hospital stay
- to be asked only once for all basic personal details, and to be given appropriate opportunities to share further information at all stages of their admission and hospital episode
- to be taken seriously and listened to
- that all relevant medical and social information should be available at the time of admission, or ideally within 48 hours at the outside
- to receive appropriate assessment of health and social care needs

- to receive appropriate investigation, treatment and rehabilitation
- to have an agreed discharge plan and their own copy of it
- to experience no unnecessary delays in discharge, but to be given sufficient time and support to make important decisions
- to experience no big surprises in what happens to them, and that discharge happens according to plan
- that everyone involved in their care will receive any information they need within 24 hours of discharge
- that continuing health and social care needs will be met as planned
- that whenever practicable individuals will be enabled to return to their own homes.

Too often, it is the experience of parents that they are not properly informed about general health care arrangements and in particular about what will happen after their child is discharged. Where clear and consistent information is not provided about such matters, then this should be taken up with both the hospital social worker and the senior ward nurse. If the problem is not rapidly resolved, it may be appropriate that a formal letter be sent expressing concern (even if, by then, discharge has already occurred). All too often disabled children and their families believe that a failure by the statutory agencies will be the last. It is only after repeated failures that a complaint is made, and at that stage there is little in the way of 'prior expressions of formal concern' to refer to as evidence that the failure has been persistent. Suggested precedent letters for this purpose are contained in Appendix 9. If the problems persist or the responses to the letters are inadequate, then formal complaints may be appropriate. The NHS and social services complaints procedures are outlined in Appendixes 2 and 3.

Role of the hospital social worker

While the hospital and the primary care team (GP, community nurse, health visitor, etc.) have much of the responsibility for ensuring that the above obligations are met, the hospital social worker's role is also pivotal. While the social worker may be hospital based, he or she will be an employee of the local authority social services department. In respect of the social worker's role in discharge planning, the Children Act Guidance notes: [8]

Where a child's stay in hospital is prolonged, the hospital social worker may have an important role to play. Chronic illness places enormous strain on a family's emotional and financial reserves. Counselling, practical and financial support (for example, for hospital visits, baby-sitting, etc.) during and immediately after hospitalisation will do much to avoid longer term problems. SSDs will need to work closely with health services including GPs and health visitors to support families when the child returns home.

Primarily, then, the social worker's responsibility is to ensure that the social services department's obligations towards the disabled child and the family are fulfilled. Most importantly, the social worker needs to ensure that the disabled child's care needs, and those of the carers, are properly assessed and services provided to enable them to live as independent a life as possible at home. In addition, however, the hospital social worker will frequently need to act both as an advocate for the family and as a general facilitator, explaining how the system operates and assisting with arrangements such as transport; overnight parents' accommodation; duties to carers.

Transport to and from hospital

If travel arrangements are difficult, the hospital should arrange for the transport of the disabled child to and from hospital (by ambulance or hospital taxi as the case may be). A disabled child and his/her parent are entitled to receive help with the cost of fares and other expenses if they are on a low income:

1. The travel cost to and from hospital for the child and his/her parent (if needed as an escort) will be covered by the hospital scheme if the parent is in receipt of income support or income-based jobseeker's allowances (or in certain situations, disabled persons working tax credit or working families tax credit).

2. If however the cost is merely that of the parents/siblings wishing to visit the disabled child who is already in hospital, then the visitors' costs may be covered either:

    • by a community care grant from the Social Fund (i.e. from the benefits agency); or failing this,

    • social services have power to make a payment to cover the cost using their powers under s.17 Children Act 1989; or failing this,

    • many hospitals have a charitable fund which may be able to provide limited assistance to help with such costs; again the social worker should be able to assist the family in accessing such funds.

Overnight accommodation for the parents

The hospital should make arrangements (particularly in relation to young disabled children) for their parents or carers to remain overnight with them during in-patient stays. The government has stressed that in such cases they should not be charged for the use of such facilities.[9]

Duties to carers

Hospital social workers are responsible for ensuring that carers are offered an assessment of their needs, under the Carers (Recognition and Services) Act 1995 and/or the Carers and Disabled Children Act 2000. The legal rights of carers under these Acts are considered separately (pp.237–40), but their needs (and the impact of their caring responsibilities on their ability to cope) must be considered during the discharge planning process. Guidance in the form of LAC (96)7 (at p.16) explains this duty in the following terms:

> The [1995] Act covers those carers who are about to take on substantial and regular caring tasks for someone who has just become, or is becoming, disabled through accident or physical or mental ill health. Local and health authorities will need to ensure that hospital discharge procedures take account of the provisions of the Act and that carers are involved once discharge planning starts.

Health services in the community

While surgery and other forms of acute medical treatment are normally provided in general or specialist hospitals (i.e. acute NHS trusts), many of the other NHS responsibilities for health care are delivered either by NHS community health trusts, primary care trusts, or via the primary care health workers. The type of service provided may include:

- physiotherapy
- speech and language therapy
- occupational therapy
- other early intervention habilitation programmes, e.g. conductive education
- short break/respite care in a community hospital or clinic
- general community nursing care
- the health visitor service provided in the disabled child's own home community
- paediatric and incontinence advice services (which are usually clinic based).

In addition, of course, the child's own GP will also provide primary care services. As we note above (p.90), research shows that parents of young disabled children value particularly highly those services which are designed to enhance their child's development.

In general the disabled child and his family can look to the social worker and their GP to help them access any of the services they believe they need. GPs are required by their contract to provide all necessary and appropriate medical services to their patients, including:[10]

I. arranging for the referral of patients, as appropriate, for the provision of any other services under the National Health Services Act 1977; and

II. giving advice, as appropriate, to enable patients to avail themselves of services by a local social services authority.

Accordingly GPs are obliged to help patients (including disabled children and their families) gain access to services provided by other branches of the NHS as well as putting them in touch with social services.

The obligation includes helping the family obtain a second opinion (i.e. from another consultant) concerning their child's medical condition. Families find that consultation with a different specialist or other health professional sometimes results in a new or refined diagnosis being given and the possibility of a different medical or therapeutic intervention. The experience of practising lawyers is that there is frequently a reluctance to agree to a second opinion being obtained (often for 'professional pride' or resource reasons). If a reasonable request for a second medical opinion is refused, then consideration should be given to instigating the formal complaints procedures (see p.254).[11]

Speech and language therapy

As we have noted elsewhere (p.27), research shows that it is crucial that all the statutory service providers co-operate in order to enhance the disabled child's ability to communicate. The obligation in relation to the provision of speech and language therapy or other equipment and assistance aimed at enhancing disabled children's communication is a shared obligation between health and education. Not infrequently therefore, both agencies look to the other to fulfil their obligations and in consequence the interests of the child suffer (see p.67 concerning the duty on agencies to co-operate). While we consider (p.126) the obligation of the education authority to provide speech and language therapy, the primary duty for these services is owed by the NHS, and this particularly so in the early years.

S.3 NHS Act 1977 makes specific reference to the obligation on the health service to provide facilities for 'young children' and accordingly health authorities must commission an adequate range of children's health-care services, including language and speech therapists.[12] These specialists are generally employed by community health NHS trusts and frequently based in child health clinics. If the need has not already been picked up by the trust, then a reference should be made for assistance via both the GP and social services. In particular, when carrying out an assessment of the child's needs, social services should refer the speech/communication need to the health authority (see pp.67–8) and ask for a positive input into the care plan. Where this is delayed or the therapy assistance is inadequate, then the appropriate response will generally be the use of the complaints procedures (see precedent letter in Appendix 8).

The widespread failure of the health services, as well as education and social services, to ascertain the wishes and feelings of children with profound impairments is well documented.[13] All too frequently this occurs due to thoughtlessness, but a shortage of therapists may also be a cause. As we have noted above, the general discretion of health authorities as to what services they fund is constrained by several factors, one of which being the requirements of the Human Rights Act 1998. Art.10 of the European Convention on Human Rights requires that everyone's right to 'freedom of expression' be safeguarded. Arguably, the right of a disabled child to therapies which enable them to communicate engages the obligation under Art. 10[14] and at the very least health authorities must positively consider this obligation when deciding what level of service it funds in this area.

Respite and short breaks

Frequently the care service that the household seeks is a 'short break' (sometimes called 'respite care'), whereby the carers can take a break from their responsibilities in caring for the disabled child and the child can have a break from his or her parents. The local authority responsibility for making such arrangements is considered at p.234 below. Where however the disabled child's impairments are substantial, it may be the health authority that has responsibility (and indeed it may be that only an NHS trust has the facilities to provide the necessary care). Unfortunately health authorities are sometimes reluctant to provide respite care and the family then becomes embroiled in a dispute between health and social services as to who should provide the care. In such cases, if the health authority is slow in making such assistance available (or refuses), then a complaint may be appropriate. A possible precedent letter in this respect is shown in Appendix 8. The NHS duties in relation to short-break care are also considered on p.167 below.

Primary care staff and carers

The importance of good collaborative working practices between social services and the NHS is emphasised in policy guidance issued on the Carers (Recognition and Services) Act 1995, as LAC (96)7. It stresses the role of the health services in supporting carers as well as the disabled people for whom they care, noting:

> 30. Primary care staff, including GPs and community nurses through their contact with users and carers, are in a good position to notice signs of stress, difficulty or rapidly deteriorating health particularly in carers. The provisions of the Act will help primary care staff to meet the medical and nursing needs of their patients who are carers. When making a referral for a user's assessment they should be able to inform the carer that they may also have a right to request an assessment and will be well-placed to encourage patients whom they consider will benefit most to take up the opportunity. Social services departments should make sure that primary care staff have relevant information about social services criteria and know who to contact to make a referral. GPs, nurses and other members of multi-disciplinary teams may be able to assist in an assessment of a carer's ability to provide and continue to provide care.

Social services in the early years

Although research has reported that families with young disabled children frequently have no contact with social services, it is crucial that contact is established at the earliest opportunity. We have seen how the services which the local authority can provide may make a difference to the quality of life of all family members and enable them to establish a positive and preferred way of living. If no contact has been made, a formal request for assistance should generally be made by the family. Where there is no immediate need for care services, then the approach may be for nothing more than registration on the register of children with disabilities. Contact in such cases may be made by writing a formal letter (Appendix 8).

Despite the research findings and government guidance emphasising social services' key networking role in relation to disabled children, practising lawyers find that an early approach of this kind sometimes results in an unhelpful response, not infrequently:

- Why have you approached us?
- What service do you think we ought to be providing?
- Since your need is primarily concerned with your son's/daughter's health (or education, etc. as the case may be) you should contact that agency directly.

The first and second statements disclose a clear failure by the authority to appreciate its planning and networking role, as well as expectations on the way assessments should be carried out. Social services should have procedures in place to ensure that parents are put in touch with the appropriate statutory and voluntary agencies so that a support network can be constructed which maximises the potential of disabled children and their families to have as full and normal a social life as possible. Assessments should also be needs led rather than determined by existing provision.

The third statement is unacceptable in that it conflicts with good practice guidance (concerning, among other things, the register of children with disabilities) and suggests that this is an authority which sees its responsibilities in a very narrow sense. It does not matter which agency is approached first. All the relevant agencies have a common responsibility to 'initiate discussions with the parents about services or procedures which might be beneficial to the child and family' and this assistance 'should include an explanation of what other agencies can provide, as well as information about the register'.[15]

The family has a right to receive a full service from whichever agency it approaches. It will generally not know who is responsible for what and who the key personalities are in the various authorities. It is the primary responsibility of social services to open these doors and to facilitate the provision of services by all these agencies. It is for this reason that a powerful obligation exists under s.27 Children Act 1989 which enables social services to bring pressure on health, education and housing agencies to ensure that each of these agencies fulfil their responsibilities to disabled children (see p.67).

The register of children with disabilities

As part of their duty to safeguard and promote the interests of disabled children,[16] social services are obliged to keep a register of children with disabilities.[17] Volume 6 of *The Children Act Guidance: Children with Disabilities* makes the following comments on the role of registers:

> 4.2 There is no duty on parents to agree to registration (which is a voluntary procedure) and services are not dependent upon registration. Registration can contribute positively to coherent planning of service provision for children with disabilities under the Children Act.

> 4.3 SSDs…will need to liaise with their education and health counterparts to achieve an understanding of disability which permits early identification; which facilitates joint working; which encourages parents to agree to registration and which is meaningful in terms of planning services for the children in question and children in general. The creation of a joint register of children with disabilities between health, education and social services would greatly facilitate collaboration in identification and a co-ordinated provision of services under the Act.

4.4 Whichever agency is the first to identify a child as having a disability whether it is the LEA, SSD or child health services they should initiate discussions with the parents about services or procedures which might be beneficial to the child and family. This should include an explanation of what other agencies can provide and information about the register. The registration of children with disabilities will be effective and productive only if parents and children are regarded as partners in the assessment process and as experts in their own right, from whom professionals may have much to learn.

As we have noted above, there is considerable scope for the imaginative use of registers, for instance, not only as a database to facilitate planning, but also as a means to target information appropriately to those who need it.

General advice and information

As part of their obligation to safeguard and promote the interests of disabled children, social workers must provide appropriate advice, guidance and counselling.[18] Frequently advice on some matters will be more appropriately obtained from other agencies, such as the Citizens Advice Bureau, law centre or solicitor with a legal aid contract to provide welfare and general benefits advice. However, social services do have a crucial networking role in this regard and in particular in relation to such matters as social security benefits, self-help user groups and general advice.

Social security benefits[19]

As has been noted above, research has shown that accessing social security benefits is a major cause of tension and distress among disabled children and their parents. Accordingly, the practice guidance reminds social services departments of their duty in such cases to explain what benefits are available and to 'ensure that families are receiving the benefits to which they are entitled and are referred, if appropriate, to the Family Fund Trust'.[20] The Family Fund Trust is a charity financed by the government whose object is to ease the stress on families who care for severely disabled children under 16. The fund provides information and grants. Contact and web address details are in Appendix 9.

Advice on self-help user groups

We have already noted the research results which have found that 'many families welcome introductions to support groups as a means of reducing social isolation, and gaining useful information and valued support'.[21] It is one of social services' functions to support the social integration of disabled children and their families by (among other things) ensuring that those families who express an interest in being put in touch with such a support group are so assisted. A list of useful addresses is provided in Appendix 9.

General advice (or how to access it)

When a disabled child is born, his or her parents will generally need advice on a multitude of matters about which they are unlikely to have had any previous experience; for instance, their rights to time off work to care for their child or to be with him or her in hospital.[22] Social services should be able to answer these common problems without having to direct the family to an outside advice agency.

Social services assessments

As we have noted above (p.63), the object of a social services assessment is to gather information concerning the disabled child's situation, so that a decision can be made about how best to help (both short term as well as to facilitate planning for the longer term). Guidance issued to social services emphasises that:[23]

> Assessments should be of a situation rather than of a specific person, or for a particular service. For disabled children in particular, there is a risk that assessments may be focused around assessing the child's problems, or assessing the child for specific services, rather than assessing the child's overall situation and needs.

> Services for disabled children are often fragmented between different agencies. Different perspectives, values and professional languages can complicate working together across agency and discipline boundaries. Young disabled children often come sequentially to the attention of health workers, then education and then social services.

In general, however, the social services assessment obligation in relation to a disabled child will become more substantial as he or she grows older, as the social handicap caused by the impairment becomes more acute. Accordingly a detailed analysis of the assessment duties is considered in Appendix 3.

The provision of services

The Children Act 1989 requires social services departments to make available an array of services in order to safeguard and promote the interests of disabled children. The potential range of these services is considered in greater detail on pp.232–37, but in the context of disabled children in their early years these may include:[24]

- social, cultural, or recreational activities
- respite/short break care (and see p.93 above where the value of home-based respite care is emphasised)
- counselling
- home help (which may include laundry facilities)
- travel assistance
- assistance to enable the disabled child and his family to have a holiday.

The Children Act emphasises that services may be provided to other family members if necessary in order to safeguard and promote the welfare of the disabled child. An example of this (given in good practice guidance) arises where the parents of a child with multiple disabilities may find attendance at a local clinic impossible without daycare arrangements for the child's brothers and sisters. In such a situation the guidance advises that it is the responsibility of the social services department to make such arrangements.[25]

The social services co-ordination role

The various duties on social services and the NHS to work together are considered at p.67 above. However, in relation to the NHS (and in particular their outpatient care functions) this has been reinforced by specific guidance which requires social services departments to:

> liaise closely with their child health services counterparts not only to encourage their parents to share in recording their child's development and health care needs, but also to ensure that where children in need are identified parents and child can contribute to decisions on the type of care and support provided to the family.[26]

Thus, if for any reason there is a problem accessing any such community based health care and the GP has failed to act as the facilitator, the social worker has a responsibility to help resolve the impasse. The social services authority have, for this purpose, considerable joint working powers (considered at p.67 above).

The education department's role in the early years

S.14 Education Act 1996 places a duty on local education authorities (LEAs) to provide sufficient primary and secondary schools for all pupils in their area. In respect of children who have significant learning difficulties, this duty is amplified by Part IV of the 1996 Act to make specific arrangements for children who have 'special educational needs'.

The Act lays down detailed procedures that must be followed by schools and LEAs in order to ensure that children with such needs receive appropriate educational support. Since these procedures are generally applied to children over compulsory school age (i.e. over five), they are primarily considered in Chapter 6, 'The School Years'. However, if the educational or developmental progress of a child under five gives rise to concern, then the Act makes provision for the educational needs to be assessed at that time.

The Act obliges LEAs to identify the special educational needs of children for whom they are responsible (aged two or over) and to make arrangements for these needs to be met (s.321). In relation to such children, once the nursery class, school or LEA has become aware of the child's special educational needs, then the duty to follow the detailed special educational needs procedures arises (see p.127 for detail as to what this entails).

It will generally be in the interests of a disabled child who is likely to have significant learning difficulties to be assessed under the special educational needs procedures as soon as possible. This will ensure that his or her needs come to the notice of the LEA at an early date, so that any special facilities or services are made available without there being unnecessary delay in the crucial early years. A disabled child's parents are entitled to request such an assessment and the LEA must in general comply with such a request (s.329). A precedent letter for such a request is contained in Appendix 8.

While the obligation to initiate such assessments rests with LEAs for all children aged over two, they may only be undertaken in relation to a child under that age with the consent of his or her parents (s.331).

The Department for Education's *Code of Practice on the Identification and Assessment of Special Educational Needs*[27] explains (at para. 5.4) that for a child under two to be referred to the LEA:

> It is probable that any special needs will have been first identified by his or her parents, the child health services or the social services. The child is likely to have a particular condition or to have a major health problem which has caused concern at an early stage. Assessment of children under two need not follow the statutory procedures which are applicable to assessments of children who are aged two or over.

The Code of Guidance suggests (at para. 5.5) that for such young children educational assistance may take the form of home-based programmes such as Portage[28] or peripatetic services for children with hearing or visual impairment.

Health and social services educational responsibilities for children under five

Where a health authority or hospital is involved in the provision of health care for a child who is under the age of five, then if it believes that he or she 'probably has' special educational needs, then it must (by virtue of s.332 of the 1996 Act):

- advise the child's parents of its opinion and that it (i.e. the health authority or NHS trust) is obliged to notify the LEA of this fact

- after discussing the matter with the parents, the health authority or NHS trust must then bring the child's special educational needs to the attention of the LEA.

The Code of Practice emphasises the importance of such an early liaison between health and education, noting (at para. 5.11) that 'for children under five very early contact with child health services will be important in order to ensure that there is no physical cause for the difficulty in question (such as a hearing or visual impairment) or to secure advice on the possible cause and the effective management of difficult behaviour'. In similar vein the Code of Practice (at para. 5.12) notes:

> All services providing for young children, such as playgroups and daycare facilities or other provision run by social services, child health services or voluntary organisations, should have information from the LEA on local procedures for the identification of 'special educational needs'.

> Liaison between the LEA and the relevant social services departments should ensure that there is clarity about how best to express concerns and about the information required in order to make a referral positive and constructive.

When a child under five is referred to the LEA by social services or the health services, then the guidance[29] stresses that 'there should be agreed procedures for acting speedily in order to ascertain whether the child's needs require specific intervention by the LEA'. In the first instance the LEA may wish to invite a preschool adviser or educational psychologist to discuss with the service in question how best to take the matter forward. At this stage advice may be all that is required. In some instances referral to a child development centre or team may be the best way forward in order to clarify the nature of the child's difficulties. In other cases it may be clear that a child's difficulties warrant a statutory assessment.[30]

Planning ahead

Education

Parents of disabled children who wish their child to go to mainstream school, frequently find that they have to start planning very early to ensure that appropriate supports are put in place and the chosen school and its staff adequately prepared. As we have seen, children and their parents find that they can often not take it for granted that such provision will be planned for and put into operation.

Where a child's learning difficulties are such that the parents believe it may not be possible for his or her special educational needs to be met within one of their LEA's mainstream schools, then they should take steps as soon as possible to investigate what provision may be available (both from the LEA and elsewhere). While the Code of Practice advises that LEAs must give parents information about the full range of provision available in their maintained and special schools 'at the earliest opportunity' (para. 3.11(iv)), in practice it frequently takes parents considerable time to find out about alternative schools and also to visit and assess their suitability. The sooner these enquires are commenced the better.

Notes

1   The Times, 20 July 1999; 2 CCLR 285.
2   The Health Ombudsman reached a similar conclusion in a complaint against Leeds Health Authority, see Health Service Commissioner Second Report for Session 1993–94; Case, No. E62/93–94 (HMSO) and in particular L. J. Clements, *Community Care and the Law*, 2nd edn (LAG, London, 2000), Chap.6, 'Legal Action'.
3   (1998) 1 CCLR 150.
4   Executive Letter EL(95)97.
5   [1995] 2 All ER 129, CA.
6   And quite probably Part III Disability Discrimination Act 1995, see p.257.
7   Department of Health 1994, p.4, obtainable from the Department of Health, PO Box 777, London SE1 6XH; fax: 01623 724 524; e-mail: doh@prologistics
8   Para. 13.11, *The Children Act 1989: Guidance and Regulations, Vol. 6, Children With Disabilities* (HMSO, London, 1991).
9   Para. 4.9, 'Welfare of Children and Young People in Hospital' HSG (91)1.
10 Schedule 2, para. 12 National Health Service (General Medical Services) Regulations 1992 (as amended).
11 GPs have, in addition, a contractual obligation to seek second opinions in appropriate cases under Schedule 2 para. 12(d) National Health Service (General Medical Services) Regulations 1992.
12 See for instance, Department of Health *Providing therapists' expertise in the new NHS developing a strategic framework for good patient care* (HMSO, London 1997).
13 See p.27 above and see Department of Health Social Care Group *Disabled Children: Directions for Their Future Care* (HMSO, London 1998) which noted at para. 10.3 that: 'Typically, the section of the form headed "child's view" was left blank or the social worker made comments such as "She is unable to verbally communicate therefore her view is not available"'; and at para. 10.4 that many young disabled people did not have access to a communication system which suited their needs.
14 While the jurisprudence of the European Court of Human Rights may not have developed to a stage where it would find that Art.10 created a positive right to a therapist, it is quite possible that domestic courts will make this development. The Department of Health appears to accept such a

proposition; it quotes with approval (at para. 3.125, Department of Health, *Assessing Children in Need and their Families: Practice Guidance*, (HMSO, London, 2000), the assertion made by Jenny Morris that 'disabled children have the human right to take part in play and leisure activities and to freely express themselves' : J. Morris, *Accessing Human Rights: Disabled Children and the Children Act.* (The Who Cares? Trust, London, 1998), p.20.

15   *The Children Act 1989: Guidance and Regulations, Vol. 6, Children with Disabilities* (HMSO, London), para. 4.4.

16   S.17 and para. 1 of Schedule 2.

17   Para. 2 of Schedule 2; *The Children Act 1989: Guidance and Regulations, Vol. 6, Children with Disabilities* (HMSO, London), see also para. 4.2.

18   Schedule 2, para. 8(a) Children Act 1989.

19   A detailed analysis of the entitlement of disabled children and their families to social security benefits is beyond the scope of this book. For comprehensive (annually updated) details of entitlements, see Disability Alliance, *Disability Rights Handbook* (Disability Alliance, London). Disability Alliance, Universal House, 88 Wentworth Street, London E1 7SA tel: 0207 247 8776.

20   S.17(1) and para. 8(a) Schedule 2 Part I Children Act 1989; see also *Assessing Children in Need and their Families: Practice Guidance*, op. cit. Para. 3.121.

21   Jenny Morris, *Assessing Children in Need and their Families: Practice Guidance* (HMSO, London, 2000), para. 3.124.

22   Under s.57A Employment Relations Act 1996 an employee is entitled to take a reasonable amount of time off work:

   •   to provide assistance on an occasion when a dependant falls ill, gives birth or is injured or assaulted

   •   to make arrangements for the provision of care for a dependant who is ill or injured

   •   in consequence of the death of a dependant

   •   because of the unexpected disruption or termination of arrangements for the care of a dependant or

   •   to deal with an incident with his or her child which occurs unexpectedly in a period during which an educational establishment which the child attends is responsible for him.

23   Policy Guidance Framework for the Assessment of Children and their Families (Stationery Office, London, 2000) at paras. 3.20 and 3.23 respectively.

24   Schedule 2 para. 8(a) Children Act 1989.

25   *The Children Act 1989: Guidance and Regulations, Vol. 6, Children with Disabilities* (HMSO, London), para. 10.3.

26   *The Children Act 1989: Guidance and Regulations, Vol. 6, Children with Disabilities* (HMSO, London), para. 10.3.

27   See p.127 below where this guidance is considered in greater detail.

28   Namely a planned approach to home-based, preschool education for children with developmental delay, disabilities or any other special educational needs; see reference to the National Portage Association, Appendix 9.

29   Department for Education's Code of Practice on the Identification and Assessment of Special Educational Needs, para. 5.15.

30   For details of what such an assessment requires, see p.127 below.

CHAPTER 6

The School Years

Introduction

In this chapter we shall consider the experience of disabled children and those close to them during the child's school-age years. Many of the issues which become significant in their lives during this period will already have been evident in some form in the early years. As time goes on at least some of these experiences are likely to become integrated into an established way of living. Some of the issues may have less impact simply because families are familiar with them and have found a way of coping. Over time or at specific points, others can become magnified or assume a greater significance. As we have already suggested, there are many distinctive aspects associated with the experience of having a very young disabled child in the family. Nevertheless, when children are very young, families with disabled children have a significant amount in common with those of households with other young, dependent children. As the children get older, however, the divergence in need, opportunities and lifestyles between disabled and non-disabled children and their respective families may become increasingly marked. In this chapter, we shall focus on:

- increasing autonomy and choice for the growing disabled child
- getting a decent education
- leisure and social life
- the personal, material and practical needs of individuals and families.

It is important to recognise that all of these areas are interrelated and success in making headway in one area may well depend upon offering relief or support in another. For example, parents may wish to meet the sometimes con-flicting needs of their disabled and non-disabled children to develop leisure interests, friendships and social activities. Their ability to do so may be affected by the size of the family income, the level of family support services which they have been offered, including sitting-in provision and short-term breaks, whether they own a car, and so on. As many researchers and practitioners have recognised, this makes it crucial to consider flexible packages or menus of services which take into account the needs of all individuals in the households and families concerned (Ball 1998; Beresford *et al.* 1996; Russell 1996; Social Services Inspectorate 1998). In addition, the significance of key themes raised in Chapter 3 can be seen again. The co-ordination, organisation and delivery of services, families' access to information and their ability to negotiate the maze successfully, the availability of advocates or key workers, etc. all have a bearing on the choices that growing children and their families have about the way they live their lives.

Increasing autonomy and choice for the disabled child

While the question of growing independence and individual identity is an issue of importance for children of all ages, it becomes increasingly significant as the child matures. Notwithstanding the diversity of such experience among non-disabled children, there is a general expectation that as they grow they will gradually broaden their horizons to include within their social world a greater number of people and situations in addition to their parents, their immediate family and home. Within varying limits, they will take a greater degree of respon-sibility for themselves and their actions. They are also likely to be able to make their voices heard more.

We suggested in earlier chapters that it has been increasingly recognised that too little attention has been paid to these aspects of disabled children's develop-ment and that there is a corresponding need to create opportunities which enable them to have comparable aspirations and experiences to those of their non-disabled peers. We also recognised that the means and routes to achieving the experience may need to be very different. The notion that disabled children should have 'independence' is not new, but in the past this has sometimes been limited to the idea of individual skill acquisition on the part of the disabled child. While acquiring useful skills or enhancing, for example, individual motoric and cognitive development may be positive, there has been a strong challenge to the assumption that autonomy, choice and having a say about your life should be the preserve only of those who can achieve certain levels of functional independence (Morris 1993).

Because of their need for support and assistance and sometimes because of difficulties in communication, disabled schoolchildren have a far greater chance than their non-disabled peers of having someone make decisions on their behalf, of not being consulted about major questions that affect them and of having a more restricted and confining social and personal life (Beecher 1998; Beresford 1997; Russell 1998). The process of being heard in your own right accords value to the things that you think and feel, gives others information to act on and can make a vital contribution to growing maturity.

Concern over this has resulted in a growing body of work which emphasises disabled children as individuals in their own right, seeks to give voice to their experiences and preferences and helps them and their families to find practical ways of moving forward. Perhaps the most important thing to stress is the variety of approaches that are necessary and desirable if individual disabled children are to be consulted effectively and enabled appropriately to increase the degree of autonomy and choice that they can have in their lives. Within the growing body of practice and research which focuses on these aspects of children's experience and potential, there are many examples of good practice which can be adapted or developed to fit the needs and circumstances of particular children or the settings of practitioners wishing to provide a more responsive service (for example, Beecher 1998; Beresford 1997; Chailey Young People's Group 1998; Leighton project 1998; Marchant and Page 1992; Minkes et al. 1994; Morris 1998d, 1999; Russell 1998; Ward 1997).

It is evident and very basic that if disabled children are to develop the possibility of expressing opinions, needs and preferences they, like others, must have a way of communicating. For some children this is straightforward, while for others it presents a major barrier in their lives. The past few years have seen an increasing emphasis on the importance of finding methods of communication which work effectively for every child and an acceptance that for children with complex impairments this can often entail the use of multiple systems and approaches. The contribution of skilled specialists such as speech and language therapists as well as the co-operation and commitment of everyone in a child's environment are essential if children are to be encouraged and enabled in this most central area of their development.

It is widely accepted that we need to think broadly and creatively about developing environments (and people in them) that are receptive to the variety of ways in which children make their observations and preferences known and which maximise and extend the possibilities for their doing so. As well as speech and formal communication systems such as Makaton, British Sign Language and Bliss, it is important that we regard, for example, body language, facial expression, 'pointing' with head and eyes as legitimate ways of communicating which can be central to a child's development and well-being. In addition, recent years have opened up the possible use of a range of more 'high tech' communication aids such as computers and voice synthesisers, sometimes in combination with more 'low tech' approaches. Some children's initiatives and responses are so fine-grained or difficult for the untutored eye to appreciate that they will need and benefit from someone acting as their individual enabler or interpreter at least some of the time. In practice, this often turns out to be someone who lives or works closely with the child. As part of creating a receptive environment it is important that this knowledge about individual children's ways of communicating is shared in detail so that possibilities for meaningful expression are extended and margin for error in understanding reduced. It is clear, however, that systems of communication are only effective if people in contact with a child believe that it is important to make use of them. As Russell (1998, p.23) suggests, 'In some instances, disabled children may not be heard because it is assumed they will have nothing to say.'

If we assume a willingness to hear, see and understand what disabled children may wish to convey, including their evaluation of any services they receive, there is a variety of approaches that can aid the process once a system of communication is becoming established. Beecher (1998) and Russell (1998) provide helpful overviews of key research, approaches to practice and projects in action. Again, the importance of having available a range of approaches cannot be stressed too strongly. While it is impossible to generalise about meeting the individual needs of disabled children, there are key issues and suggestions which repeatedly appear in the literature concerned with approaches that extend disabled children's opportunities to act on their worlds. For example, the importance has been stressed of having a range of age-appropriate and child-centred media available for exchange of information and opinion. Children may show what they wish to convey through play, use of pictures, stories, art, music and drama, as well as direct verbal and non-verbal conversations. Advocacy, self-advocacy and other forms of representation also offer opportunities for some individuals and groups. 'Buddying' and other peer support arrangements between different combinations of disabled and non-disabled children, either one to one or in groups, have proved helpful. Such initiatives can provide a supportive framework for children to spread their wings, learn from the experience of others and develop their own ideas. They may also provide a structured way of making new friendships or social networks in addition to those generated by family. In some services, key workers and enablers may ensure that work related to individual children's needs is co-ordinated and that their experience is heard in whatever form is appropriate.

It would seem a great pity if such positive initiatives on children's autonomy were taken to indicate an implied and general criticism of parents and their role. Because a very great deal is asked of parents of disabled children and because they are often thrown into a closer and more protracted relationship with their sons and daughters, there is a danger that they may too easily become prime suspects when questions are raised about the quality of their sons' and daughters' childhood experience. If the child's experience is rather restricted, some may be tempted to draw too hasty conclusions about the ability and intentions of parents (Read 2000). While some disabled adults recall their families as confining and difficult, there are others who remember their parents as valued allies who supported them to make important gains which often flew in the face of more conventional and lower expectations. Some, unsurprisingly, describe a mixture of experiences (Reisser 1992; Thomas 1999). As with non-disabled children, the quality of family life varies. As we have seen, however, one important difference between the two groups is that much more is routinely asked of parents of disabled children and often in circumstances where they have fewer resources than other families. It would seem very harsh indeed to judge any parents as having offered too restrictive an upbringing to their child without asking questions about what they might have wished for and been able to achieve had they had the resources which allowed both adults and children greater freedom of choice and room for manoeuvre. It is important to acknowledge that the independence, however limited, which many children achieve comes as a direct result of their parents' hard work and perseverance. It is also crucial for us to appreciate that in the face of a lack of service provision, parents often feel that they have to become their child's sole advocate. Any practitioner or service provider needs to be sensitive to the dangers of appearing to set the child's need and right for autonomy in opposition to parents' often strong sense of responsibility. Drawing on the knowledge of all family members to learn lessons from the past and to plan for the future is an essential feature of good practice.

Getting a decent education

In the UK, the beginning of what was to become a sea change in thinking about the education of disabled children occurred during the late 1970s and early 1980s. At that time a small but growing number of academics, practitioners, policy makers and parents began to challenge the established wisdom that it was both necessary and desirable for disabled children to be educated in separate or segregated institutions (Barton 1986; Booth and Potts 1983; Booth and Swann 1987; Family Focus 1984; Walker 1982). The movement arguing first for the 'integration' and later for the 'inclusion' of disabled children in mainstream settings gathered strength in the 1980s and 1990s with the concept gaining increased official recognition and support across that period (DfEE 1998).

Among other things, it was argued that a segregated education system reproduced and maintained the disadvantaged position of disabled children and young people in a variety of ways. It was seen to play a major part in ensuring that disabled children started on a course of segregation and unequal opportunities that would continue for the rest of their lives. It was reported that the schooling they were offered was frequently of inferior quality and narrower dimensions and that this ensured that the majority were unprepared for employment and autonomy in adult life. Early campaigners pointed out that there was no reason why support services most often associated with special education could not follow disabled children where necessary and allow them to be supported in a mainstream setting. As time went on, it was more frequently emphasised that the major challenge was how the education system as a whole and schools within it might change in fundamental ways in order to meet the needs of a more diverse range of children and be the richer for it (Booth 1999; Reisser and Mason 1992). In the 1990s, as more children, parents and teachers had practical experience of working on these issues, a range of material became available which began to identify the factors which made for successful and positive inclusion in education. Sebba and Sachdev (1997) provide a clear and accessible review of research and practice in this area.

As one would expect, the reactions of disabled children and adults and their families to these shifts in thinking and to experiences of inclusive and separate education has been mixed. Shaw (1998) reports a strong commitment on the part of both disabled and non-disabled pupils to the principle and practice of inclusion, together with concerns about whether the necessary changes are always in place in the education system which make it work for the pupils concerned. The views of parents in Dobson and Middleton's study (1998) are not untypical of those reported by others. Parents whose children had less complex and severe impairments were happier with the principle of mainstream provision, but nevertheless described continual problems over ensuring that adequate and appropriate supports and facilities were provided. Within mainstream education their children could find themselves excluded from taking part in some activities which were timetabled for everyone else. The necessary organisational arrangements and resources were not always in place and some teachers did not have the required skills to meet the children's educational needs. Other parents whose children were in special schools were unhappy about the distances they were transported and the way these arrangements isolated their sons and daughters from others in the neighbourhood. They also found that they had repeated requests for contributions for school events, funds and trips.

Parents of disabled children have to make difficult choices about what they genuinely regard as being in their child's interests at any particular time. They have to consider the information they have, take all circumstances and human and material resources into account and decide what seems to them the best option. The choices they make have to be pragmatic to some degree, but this does not mean that decisions are not driven by strong moral or ethical considerations. Parents' determination to minimise their disabled children's disadvantage, maximise their room for manoeuvre and strive for what they regard as the best achievable option have been repeatedly reported (for example, Beresford 1994; Dobson and Middleton 1998; Read 2000). Some parents make a considered and positive choice in favour of mainstream school. Some parents genuinely believe that there are some forms of specialised provision that make a distinctive, high quality and desirable contribution to their children's development and well-being (Read 1996). Others may have a commitment in principle to inclusive education but cannot see how it can be made to work for their child's benefit as things stand. It is not uncommon for parents to feel that they have to trade off some desirable things to get others. In Chapter 8 on living away from home we deal with the issues and experiences related to placement in a residential school.

Information can make a very great difference to the basis on which parents make these difficult decisions and to the confidence they feel about them. As we have already seen, however, families often find themselves without adequate information. Parents should expect to be able to have informed discussions about a range of educational provision with those practitioners with whom they have contact. It is also reasonable for them to expect to be able to visit different schools in order to ascertain how they think their child's needs could be met in a particular setting, whether in the mainstream or special education sector.

Some families may feel that the information provided by their local education authority is very sound and that they are satisfied with the choices of schooling they have seen. However, some may feel they need additional or different information than that readily on offer. They may find it helpful to know that a number of voluntary organisations and groups give information and advice to parents over these crucial issues and some have helplines. Two organisations specialising in advice on education are the Advisory Centre for Education (ACE) and the Independent Panel for Special Education Advice (IPSEA). Their addresses and contact numbers can be found in Appendix 9. As increasing numbers of households are either connected to the internet or have access to it elsewhere, more parents use it to search for information about education and other matters and to make contact with families or organisations sharing similar experiences or concerns.

The specialist organisations which we have mentioned can also help children and their parents with a further problem that is identified consistently in research: the complexities of the statementing process by which a child's special educational needs are assessed and provision made accordingly. In other words, even when parents feel well informed or clear about what they would regard as a good choice of education or a particular school for their child, they may find that the process of achieving it is not easy. In the 1990s, a series of reports and studies highlighted the fact that parents find the procedures lengthy, complex and alienating (Audit Commission 1992; Association of Metropolitan Authorities 1994; Beresford 1995; Spastics Society 1992). It was also argued that there was a significant gap between the rhetoric of individualised, needs-led assessment and a reality which was provision focused (Swann 1987). Despite the introduction of a revised code of practice in the early 1990s (DfEE 1994) and the setting of time limits for the procedures involved, the process undoubtedly remains perplexing and stressful for very many children and their parents. Those who wish to challenge any aspect of the assessment or related decision making may find it particularly taxing and frustrating.

Parents may be aware one way or another that they are operating in territory which is more familiar to the professionals and this places them at a disadvantage. Despite the fact that legislation and guidance emphasise the importance of practitioners working in partnership with parents, many service users do not experience it this way and find the whole business anxiety provoking and intimidating. Many people are simply unused to the language which professionals employ in their reports and discussions and may find it difficult to frame their own ideas and intervene effectively in a set of unfamiliar procedures. As has been observed, for those whose mother tongue is not English and who may have had less exposure to the services involved, the problems can be magnified, leaving them very disadvantaged indeed (Baxter *et al.* 1990).

The Code of Practice (DfEE 1994) prescribes the designation of a 'named person' who is available to advise children and their parents as they proceed through statementing and other associated procedures. This is a person independent of the local education authority (LEA) who has the potential to help families unfamiliar with the process and to make sure they are enabled to represent their child's interests in the most effective way. The named person may be, for example, from an appropriate voluntary organisation in the area. Parents may also nominate someone of their choice who is not on the LEA list of suggested people. Having the support of someone who is familiar with the procedures but independent of the LEA may be particularly important for those parents and children who wish to question some aspect of the assessment and recommendations of the professionals involved.

In addition to the 'named person', the LEA has to designate an officer employed by the authority who is the point of contact for the family. We have no wish to undermine the efforts of those in this position who take a proactive and positive role in relation to families and we recognise that in some authorities such officers act as a helpful consultant and a valuable guide through the maze. In others, however, their approach is at best rather minimalist, making sources of alternative advice and support crucial.

Leisure, play and social life

Within the general population there are probably greater expectations than ever before about the provision of opportunities for leisure and play. There has been an expansion of leisure and holiday facilities for both adults and children, though the distribution will vary from one geographical area to another and there will be substantial variation of access between income groups (Williams 1993).

In addition to these changing expectations in relation to the standards of formally provided facilities, the informal leisure and play activities as well as the friendship and social life that are associated with them form an important element of childhood, contributing significantly to children's personal development (Association of Metropolitan Authorities 1994; Cavet 1998).

These enjoyable childhood experiences are as formative and important for disabled children as their non-disabled peers and yet there is evidence that there are far fewer play, leisure and social opportunities available to them (Beresford *et al*. 1996). Beresford *et al*. (1996) and Cavet (1998) provide useful reviews of some of the factors which contribute to this worrying state of affairs.

Children often form friendships that are based around contacts made at school. Disabled children who attend special schools some distance from home may not maintain contact so easily out of school hours unless they have assistance from adults to enable them to do so. For example, research has indicated that some disabled children have informal play contacts only once a week (Sloper *et al*. 1990). In addition, as Beresford *et al*. (1996) point out, children mostly choose to play with peers who are at the same developmental level as themselves. The widening developmental gap between children with learning difficulties and their non-disabled peers may in part account for the diminishing social contact between them as they get older compared with frequency of informal contact at a younger age.

Beresford *et al*. (1996) also point out that the family plays a crucial mediating role in relation to the child's social life. Arranging play and leisure for children who are not best placed to find it for themselves spontaneously often requires money, transport, time and energy. We have already seen that many families are hard pressed to meet everyone's needs, frequently on very low incomes and do not always have transport.

In addition, there are other environmental factors within and outside the home which create barriers to leisure, play and social contact. The built environment and facilities within it are not always accessible or safe for the disabled child. There have been improvements, however, and some have argued that the provisions of the Disability Discrimination Act will enable a continuation of this trend (Cavet 1998). As we saw in Chapter the houses and flats in which families live are frequently unsuitable for disabled children and their carers and this can act as a further impediment to ordinary, shared childhood activities. Children and their families sometimes also encounter negative attitudes or a lack of positive awareness on the part of the general public and providers of leisure and play facilities and this can make outings unpleasant or cause them to limit what they do (Association of Metropolitan Authorities 1994; Beresford 1995). Having continually to battle, challenge or make out a case can sometimes feel as if all the fun has been taken out of the outing and the purpose therefore defeated.

If this is the case, it is small wonder that some parents and children opt to make use of the quite wide variety of specialist and separate leisure activities and facilities provided for disabled children alone. While there has been considerable debate about the importance of avoiding ghettoisation and ensuring that mainstream community facilities routinely include disabled children (Jigsaw Partnerships 1994), Cavet (1998) points to the arguments for disabled children and young people making the positive choice (as long as that is what it is) to associate with each other. She gives the example of the role that deaf clubs play in promoting and sustaining a positive deaf culture and identity. She also highlights the importance of ensuring that leisure activities are culturally appropriate for the child or young person concerned.

Beresford *et al.* (1996) and Robinson (1996) draw attention to the part that short-term breaks and befriending schemes can play in extending the child's social world and creating enjoyable opportunities for contact with additional adults and children who are both disabled and non-disabled. Child support workers or children's personal assistants can also play a positive role. These services may be centred on the family home or elsewhere. Support workers or befrienders may do something enjoyable with children at home or take them out. They may accompany them to specialist provision or enable and assist access alongside other children to a community facility. Participation in a family link scheme provides another example of an opportunity for extending social contact outside the child's own family. Increasingly, whatever the arrangement, there is an assumption that, like any child, the disabled schoolchild should be consulted about preferences and experience of breaks and play provision (Beresford *et al.* 1996; Minkes *et al.* 1994).

Having acknowledged the importance of play, leisure and social contact in relation to all children's development and well-being, it clearly has to be unacceptable for disabled children to have a more impoverished childhood than others in this respect. Good practice therefore demands that we use the measures we have at our disposal to create the chances they need which are so often not available. The Family Fund, the Chronically Sick and Disabled Persons Act, and s.17 of the Children Act can all have calls made upon them to improve these opportunities for children and their families.

Personal, material and practical support needs of individuals and families

By the time a disabled child is of school age, everyone involved has often become accustomed to the situation and developed their own ways of coping and keeping going. The fact that the situation is not new may mean that many children and families are left to soldier on without their needs for practical, personal and family support being reassessed to take account of the ways in which people and circumstances change.

When researchers explore the experiences of such disabled children and their families, they often pay tribute to the ways those involved manage a workload which is by anyone's standards complex and demanding. The question 'How do they do it?' is frequently posed. Substantial attention has been paid by researchers both to the positive and characteristic coping strategies that families establish (Beresford 1994) and to the personal and practical costs of dealing with so many demands for a protracted period (Beresford 1995; Philp and Duckworth 1982; Russell 1998).

We neither wish to minimise the importance of coping strategies that those involved develop, nor detract in any way from families' achievements in this respect. We believe strongly, however, that the positive features of their lives and the rewards they describe should never be mistaken for an absence of need or used to justify a lack of services. Everyone should undoubtedly remain impressed with the way that the majority cope, but we need to remind ourselves frequently of some of the ongoing costs which may put those concerned in jeopardy. Good practice should focus on and bolster their positive aspirations and achievements at the same time as providing integrated family services which help them to avoid some of the danger zones. The approach to such service provision and the needs which it can address are discussed in some detail in Chapter 3.

Beresford (1994) describes how 'keeping going' becomes a way of life in families with disabled children. Those coming in from the outside can see the stresses, but frequently not the features that parents regard as positive. She argues: 'Until research can look at the child as the parents do, we will never fully understand how parents manage and what keeps them going' (Beresford 1994, p.67). When parents define the things that ensure they carry on providing high levels of care and assistance, they tend to talk about love for the child combined with their assumptions about what naturally comes with the territory of being a mother or father (Beresford 1994; Read 2000). Helping your children to develop and taking pride and pleasure in their achievements, as well as taking satisfaction from meeting a challenge and winning some ground, are often reported as very important. As Russell (1998) warns, however, many families are only just managing. The demands are often so great, their circumstances so fragile and human and practical resources so limited that an unforeseen crisis or change of circumstances can upset the equilibrium.

We have also referred previously to research which reports that in many households, these issues become even more pressing as time goes on (Beresford 1995). As we have seen, for example, the logistics of assisting and caring for older and larger children can become more complicated and demanding, particularly when suitably adapted accommodation and equipment are not available. Parents report that challenging behaviour creates more management problems and greater restrictions in family activities. Over time, the toll on the health of main carers caused by physically strenuous work such as lifting growing children can be considerable. Limited income over a longer term period leaves less margin for error and room for manoeuvre. Other children do not stand still either. Interests may diverge and additional demands need to be met by already overstretched parents.

The long-term and taxing nature of some of the problems faced by the individuals and families concerned make it crucial for them to have their needs reviewed or reassessed at regular intervals, taking account of the range of issues which were identified in Chapter 3. In addition to the fact that the provision of some community-based services can undoubtedly raise the standard of living of all family members quite substantially, it is also important to consider whether they may play a part in enabling some children and their parents to continue living together. While further research is needed to establish what are the issues and circumstances which trigger the separation of substantial numbers of disabled children from their families of origin (see Chapter 8), it would be surprising if the stress and workload which many manage long term were not contributory factors in some cases at least.

LEGAL COMMENTARY

Introduction

Regrettably many disabled children reach their school age years having had little or nothing by way of specific assistance from the health, social services and education authorities. It is however during their school years that the provision of practical help and appropriate services can often have the most profound influence in ensuring that disabled children not only have the best opportunity of maximising their potential in terms of intellectual achievement but also in terms of social integration.

While typically it will often have been the health services which had most contact during the 'early years', unsurprisingly it will generally be the education department that is the lead organisation during the school age years. Clearly this will not always be the case. Some children with severe and complex impairments or major health problems may have significant contact with health and social services, too. As we have noted, however, it does not follow that children and their families with substantial and complex support needs receive services to meet those needs.

Education

Most children with physical impairments do not need any special educational assistance. What they do require however is education in a non-discriminatory environment which respects their 'differentness' and provides them with true equality of opportunity. While schools are not covered by the substantive provisions of the Disability Discrimination Act 1995,[1] the Act inserted into the special educational needs legislation an obligation upon schools to include in their annual reports information concerning:[2]

- the arrangements for the admission of disabled pupils
- the steps taken to prevent disabled pupils from being treated less favourably than other pupils
- the facilities provided to assist access to the school by disabled pupils.

Historically, as we have noted earlier, disabled children's educational needs were often poorly served by local education authorities. All too frequently disabled children were categorised according to their impairment and then dispatched to a 'special school' for 'the handicapped' or 'the blind' or 'the deaf', and so on. Concern about such ghettoisation and the generally inferior nature of the education provision led to the Warnock Report in 1978[3] which in turn resulted in radical reform in the guise of the Education Act 1981. The 1981 Act introduced many positive reforms, not least:

- the emphasis on 'inclusive education', namely a general presumption in favour of disabled children being educated within the mainstream of educational provision
- that where necessary disabled children should be provided with individually tailored 'statements' detailing their special educational needs. The statements spelt out with considerable precision the educational services required by the child. Once finalised, the local education authority (LEA) was legally obliged to provide the services specified in the statement.

The 1981 Act contained, however, various imperfections, most obviously the complex and bureaucratic nature of the statementing process and the length of time it took to complete the procedures. Such was the problem of delay that not infrequently a statement of a child's special educational needs was only concluded when the child was about to leave full-time education; most of the child's childhood having passed while the process and arguments lumbered on, with the statement emerging when it was no longer of any use or relevance. Progressive reform of the legislation (the relevant Act is now the Education Act 1996) and guidance[4] has sought to remedy the problem of delay, but the complex and technical nature of the process remains.

The special educational arrangements made for disabled children vary widely throughout the UK, with some excellent authorities. However many are slow to come forward with appropriate provision. While regrettable, this is perhaps hardly surprising given that the potential expenditure in relation to the needs of an individual child may be substantial. For instance it may require, on occasions, the local authority to pay for the child's place:

- in an independent school (even if no statement of special educational needs has been made)[5]
- in an overseas institution under s.320 Education Act 1996.

Where a child's physical or mental impairments are such that they do result in learning difficulties, then it is essential that the special educational needs procedures detailed by the 1996 Act are triggered as soon as possible. Since the scheme is complex, parents not only need to acquire an understanding of the rights the legislation gives to their children but also to make contact with specialist organisations, local groups and possibly lawyers who can help them access these rights. In terms of national organisations, the Advisory Centre for Education (ACE) for instance, publishes a practical handbook on special education rights and provides a telephone advice line; as does the Independent Panel for Special Education Advice (IPSEA) (Appendix 9).

Where legal proceedings become necessary, legal aid will frequently be available. In the first stages (when advice and guidance from the lawyer is being sought), the legal aid means test depends upon the parents' financial circumstances,[6] whereas once legal proceedings are initiated the means test is based upon the child's financial circumstances and accordingly is generally available without contribution. Advice as to suitable solicitors is best obtained by making contact with other families in the locality who have experienced similar problems or, failing this, from the Citizens Advice Bureau, or a national organisation such as ACE or IPSEA. If there is no local expert, it may be appropriate to contact a lawyer from outside the area who has a proven expertise in this field.

Speech and language therapy and other aids/assistance to communication

As we have noted elsewhere, the opportunity to learn language and the means to communicate are a crucial part of any child's development. In addition, the importance of ensuring that the disabled child is enabled to communicate his or her wishes and preferences cannot be over-emphasised. All too often, however, the necessary assistance to enable this to happen is inadequate, if not simply overlooked.

At p.101 above we considered the obligation on the health services to provide speech and language therapy assistance; such assistance can however also be the responsibility of the LEA in certain situations. In this respect, the Code of Practice[7] makes the following points:

> 4.34 Speech and language therapy may be regarded as either educational or non-educational provision, depending upon the health or developmental history of each child. Prime responsibility for the provision of speech and language therapy services to children rests with the NHS. This applies generally and also to any specification of such services in a statement of special educational needs, whether in Part 3 as educational provision or in Part 6 as non-educational provision. [Health authorities and primary care trusts] are responsible for purchasing therapy services through the contacts they make with providers of health care (NHS trusts). The NHS provides a professionally managed speech and language therapy service, covering pre-school, school-age and adult groups and which has close links with the other child health services.

> 4.35 Where the NHS does not provide speech and language therapy for a child whose statement specifies such therapy as educational provision, ultimate responsibility for ensuring that the provision is made rests with the LEA, unless the child's parents have made appropriate alternative arrangements. Schools, LEAs and the NHS should cooperate closely in meeting the needs of children with communication needs.

In *R v Harrow LBC ex p M* [1997][8] the disabled child was assessed as requiring, as part of his special educational needs, speech therapy and language therapy as well as occupational therapy and physiotherapy. The court noted that in general these would be provided by the health authority, but since in this case the health authority did not arrange all of the provision required, the court held that the education department was liable to arrange it. While a statement of special educational needs may require an LEA to provide such therapies (albeit that they are the primary responsibility of the NHS), in *Bradford MC v A* [1997][9] the court held that a statement of special educational needs cannot require the provision of basic nursing care.

The special educational needs procedures

The present procedures for responding to a child's special educational needs are based upon certain 'fundamental principles' which are spelt out in a code of practice issued by the Department for Education in 1994, *Code of Practice on the Identification and Assessment of Special Educational Needs*. These principles stress the need for children to have effective assessment and services at the earliest opportunity, and that where appropriate they receive their education alongside their peers in mainstream schools. A copy of the 'principles' is annexed at p.243 below.

LEAs are obliged to have regard to the Code and courts pay it especial regard when making decisions. The government has issued for consultation a revised code which it intends to finalise in the 'Spring 2001' and bring into force on the 1st September.[10] The present Code and many other special educational needs documents and booklets can be accessed directly on the internet [www.dfee.gov.uk/sen/publicat.htm], or ordered (free of charge) from DfEE Publications (see Appendix 9 for contact details). Many of the publications are also available in Braille and on audio tape.

The Code recognises that there is a continuum of needs among children with learning difficulties and that while about 20 per cent of all children need special provision at some stage of their education, only about 2 per cent will require a statement of special educational needs. Accordingly it advocates a phased response from stage 1 (relatively low level needs) to stage 5 (highest needs including the provision of a statement).

The first three stages of the phased response advocated by the Code are based in the child's school, which will, as necessary, call upon the help of external specialists. At stages 4 and 5 the LEA shares responsibility with the school (Figure 6.1).

While there are many cases where this staged response works well, all too often significant resources are only provided if the child obtains a statement of his or her needs. Therefore statementing is the goal of many parents of children who experience learning difficulties. S.324(5) of the Education Act 1996 obliges LEAs to 'arrange the special educational provision specified in the statement'.

Special educational needs assessments

Under s.321 of the 1996 Act, LEAs are obliged to identify all children in their area who have special educational needs aged between 2[11] and 16 (and up to 19 in certain situations).[12]

In a rather circular way, s.312 of the Act defines a child as having 'special educational needs' if he or she has a 'learning difficulty which calls for special educational provision to be made for him' or her. It then states that a child has a learning difficulty as follows:

- if she has a significantly greater difficulty in learning than the majority of children of her age

- if he has a disability which either prevents or hinders him from making use of educational facilities of the kind generally provided for children of his age in schools within the area of the LEA

- if he is under the age of five and likely to fall into one of these categories when over five or is likely to unless special education provision is made (see pp.107–108 above).

Assessment and the statutory time scales

Where a child's special educational needs are such that they cannot satisfactorily be met under stages 1 to 3 of the procedures, then his or her parents (or the LEA of

---

Stage 1: Class or subject teachers identify or register a child's special educational needs and, consulting the school's SEN co-ordinator (the member of staff who has responsibility for co-ordinating SEN provision within the school), take initial action.

Stage 2: The school's SEN co-ordinator takes lead responsibility for gathering information and co-ordinating the child's special educational provision, working with the child's teachers.

Stage 3: Teachers and the SEN co-ordinator are supported by specialists from outside the school.

Stage 4: The LEA considers the need for a statutory assessment and, if appropriate, makes a multidisciplinary assessment.

Stage 5: The LEA considers the need for a statement of special educational needs and, if appropriate, makes a statement and arranges, monitors and reviews provision.

Figure 6.1 Phased responses to educational needs

its own volition) can institute action with a view to the child's needs being formally assessed. There is of course no need for the LEA or parents to wait until stages 1 to 3 have failed before initiating the statementing procedures.

The assessment process follows detailed procedures laid down in the Act, the Code and the Education (Special Educational Needs) Regulations 1994. These stipulate that the decision as to whether to assess or not should be made after a thorough consideration of all the facts and within six weeks of receiving the request unless circumstances make it impossible. If the parents' request for an assessment is refused, they can appeal against the refusal (ss. 328–9 Ed·.cation Act 1996) to an SEN tribunal (see below). If the LEA decides to assess, it must send to the parent a formal notice setting out:

- the proposal to assess and the procedure to be followed (including a named officer for liaison)
- the parents' rights to make representations about the assessment proposal (within 29 days).

Where the LEA has initiated the assessment process, the parents are entitled to object. However, although the local authority must consider representations it can nevertheless decide to proceed (unless the child is under two years of age) – there is no right of appeal against such a decision. In general parents will welcome the assessment and accordingly, in order to expedite matters, they can reply promptly confirming agreement and asking that the process be expedited (i.e. there is no need for the LEA to wait for the expiration of the 29-day period).

Once a local authority has decided to proceed, the process is subject to fixed time limits:

- ten weeks for the making of the assessment
- two weeks for the drafting of the proposed statement
- eight weeks for the finalising of the statement (i.e. the period from the issue of the proposed statement to the issue of the final copy of the statement).

The law sets out in detail how the assessments are to be carried out, including the need to obtain advice from the child's parents, from the educational, medical and psychological services, as well as from the social services department and any other advice which the authority considers appropriate for the purpose of arriving at a satisfactory assessment(para 3.121 SEN Code).

Special educational needs within mainstream schooling

There is a general obligation to ensure that children with special educational needs receive their education in mainstream schools, provided this is compatible with:

- the child receiving the special educational provision which his or her learning difficulty calls for[13]
- the provision of efficient education for the children with whom she/he would be educated
- the efficient use of resources (s.316 Education Act 1996).

Co-operation with social services and the NHS

The LEA can request help from any health authority or social services department in the exercise of its duties towards children with social needs. Provided the request is reasonable and compatible with their own statutory duties and obligations, they must comply with the request (s.322 Education Act 1996).

Code of Practice: guidance on the preliminary stages

LEAs are under detailed procedural obligations to ensure that parents are properly informed of their rights and assisted during the statementing process. These duties are spelt out on pp.3.9–3.21 of the 1994 Code of Practice, which is summarised below. A full copy of this section of the Code is contained in Appendix 4. LEAs must ensure the following:

1.   Parents are provided with information concerning:

     • the assessment process, its timescales and their rights

     • the named LEA officer: namely the LEA employee who liases with the parents over all arrangements in the assessment and statementing process

     • the named person: namely the person (generally independent of the LEA) who supports and advises parents in their dealings with the LEA.

2.   They involve all other relevant agencies, such as social services and health.

3.   They respond to parent instigated requests for special educational needs assessments (including in cases where the child is in an independent school).

The statement

If, after assessment, the LEA decides not to make a statement, the parents must be informed in writing and they are entitled to appeal against the refusal (s.325, Education Act 1996). The appeal is heard by the SEN tribunal (see below).

If the authority decides to make a statement, it must send the parents a copy of the proposed statement within two weeks of the date on which the assessment was completed. Attached to the proposed statement should be all the evidence and assessment reports that the LEA considered in drawing it up. A copy of a draft statement is shown in Appendix 4.

If the statement is accepted (the parent agrees with the LEA's description of the child's needs and feels that the necessary additional support, special equipment, etc. are appropriately recorded in the statement) then the LEA is informed and the duty to provide for the needs arises.

If the statement is not agreed, the parent is required to make representation (and arrange a meeting with the LEA within 15 days). The parent must notify the LEA of this requirement within 15 days. After meeting the local authority, the parent has 15 days within which to seek a further meeting with any or all of the people who provided the local authority with advice (in preparing the proposed statement) and after the last of any such meetings the parent has a further 15 days in which to submit comments on anything in the statement with which he or she disagrees.

Within eight weeks of issuing the proposed statement, the LEA must consider all representation received and then notify the parent that either:

- it has confirmed the statement of special educational needs unchanged (or in a modified form)
- it has decided not to make a statement.

In either case the parents are entitled to appeal to the SEN tribunal.

Naming a school

When the LEA serves the proposed statement it leaves blank Part 4, the section entitled 'placement'. This enables the parents to express their preference. Under s.324 paras. 3–5 Schedule 27 of the Act, LEAs are obliged to agree to the statement naming the school of the parents' choice provided:

- it is appropriate to the children's needs
- it is compatible with

  (i)   the interests of other children also in the school

  (ii) the efficient use of the LEA's resources.

Practising lawyers find that LEAs are generally reluctant to agree to a school being named which is outside their area, most obviously because it is likely to entail considerable expense. Parents should accordingly anticipate LEA objections to any proposal which would involve substantial expenditure and be prepared to persevere in the face of such resistance, to ensure that their child receives the most appropriate provision. LEAs are under an obligation to provide parents with:

- information about the full range of provision available in maintained mainstream and special schools within their area (see the Code of Guidance at p 3.11(iv) copied above), at the earliest possible stage

- a list of these schools when they serve the proposed statement (p.4.47 of the guidance).

However, it is not infrequently the case that parents need more time to decide whether or not to insist upon a named school. In such situations they should request additional time to consider this matter (i.e. an extension of the 15-day period). The Code states, at p.4.47:

> If the parents make representations in favour of a non-maintained special school or an independent school, an officer of the LEA should discuss with them why they believe that school should be named. If naming the school in question would provide the child with residential education, the LEA should discuss with the parents why they feel such provision is necessary to meet the child's special educational needs and, if appropriate, may choose to involve the social services department in discussing the child's wider needs with the family. If parents have not visited the school and wish to do so, an officer if the LEA should help arrange such a visit.

Special Educational Needs Tribunal

Where the parents disagree with all or part of a statement (or challenge the LEA's refusal to prepare a statement) and the dispute cannot be resolved, then there is a right of appeal to the Special Educational Needs tribunal. When notifying parents of its decision (concerning the statement) the LEA will also send a copy of a useful publication *Special Educational Needs Tribunal, How to Appeal*. The booklet contains the form that must be used if an appeal is to be made and the form must be lodged with the tribunal office within two months of the decision date (see Appendix 9 for contact details). The tribunal has a helpful website which contains the text of the booklet and an explanation as to what can and cannot be appealed and details of alternative remedies (such as representations to the Department for Education and Employment and the use of the local ombudsman).

The tribunal is composed of a legally qualified chairperson and two lay people, one of whom must have knowledge and experience of children with SEN and the other of local government. There is a fixed timetable for appeals (the copying of the appeal to the LEA, the LEA's response, the parents' reply, the notification of the tribunal date, etc.). Tribunal hearings must in general be heard within four to five months of the parent notifying them of the appeal. If the appeal succeeds the LEA is obliged to implement the direction of the tribunal as soon as possible. While parents are able to represent themselves before the tribunal, this is a stage at which it is generally advisable to seek advice and assistance (if not representation).

Annual reviews of statements

Once finalised, LEAs must review the statement every 12 months. If on review the LEA decides to amend the statement (or cease to maintain a statement) there are detailed procedures laid down for this process and the parents have a right of appeal to the SEN tribunal. The annual reviews are of particular importance as key transition stages are approached, and particular obligations exist in relation to the review which takes place after the young person's fourteenth birthday. (These are considered in detail on p.155.)

Social services

In addition to their obligation to provide care services, social services are the key networking agency to whom the family should be able to turn as and when they experience difficulties. If the problem relates to health care or an unmet educational need, then it is the duty of social services to intercede with the health body or their colleagues in the education department in order to ensure that the matter is resolved. If however the problem concerns matters such as the need for general advice (including welfare benefits advice), counselling, homecare services, transport, day centre or other recreational needs, respite care, home adaptations or appliances, then the social services department must decide whether it should make the necessary assistance available.

The first step in this process will almost invariably be an 'assessment'. At p.62 and 229 above we consider the legal and good practice requirements for the assessment process, and at p.231 above we describe the subsequent care planning process which culminates in the provision of care services.

As we have seen, research as well as Department of Health policy[14] has identified a number of services frequently mentioned by disabled children and their families as being of particular importance. Some of these have already been considered, including the importance of the family having a named social care manager, a keyworker to co-ordinate the relevant professional support services, access to an advocacy service (p.46 and 61) and the need for authorities to publish clear criteria for entitlement to their services (p.65). Other services mentioned include access to interpreters and home adaptations,[15] as well as aids and equipment,[16] laundry service,[17] respite care/short-term break services,[18] transport,[19] homecare and support workers. As we have noted above, the research also highlights not only the importance of support for informal leisure and play activities, but also that such activities do not necessarily occur spontaneously, often requiring money, transport, time and energy. Social services have substantial powers under both the Children Act and the Chronically Sick and Disabled Persons Act 1970 to provide and fund the necessary support (see p.232). Both these Acts can also be used to fund adaptations to the built environment to provide the child with safe access to leisure and play activities; in addition disabled facilities grants may, in certain situations, be used for such purposes (p.262).

The needs of every disabled child and his/her family are of course unique and vary with time. In the early years the need to access an upstairs bathroom may be met by being carried by a parent. As the child grows this will cease to be both tenable and appropriate and a stair lift, a through floor lift or adaptations to construct ground-floor facilities may be required. As we have noted above, needs change, particularly during the school age years, and on each occasion a reassessment will be necessary.

The social services department must not only consider the needs of the disabled child, but also the needs of the wider family and in particular carers. In relation to carers, the social services obligations are twofold: the duty under statute to assess and respond with appropriate assistance (p.64); a duty at common law to take steps to ensure, so far as is reasonable, that they do not come to harm as a result of their caring tasks.

Health risks for carers

The health risks to which carers are exposed are rarely given the consideration they deserve. Local authorities are of course required to take all necessary steps to avoid their staff being exposed to injuries through 'manual handling' (i.e. in lifting heavy or inappropriate objects). If the manual handling cannot be avoided altogether (for instance, by the use of a hoist) then the authority is required to take steps to reduce the dangers so far as is feasible by, for instance, carrying out a risk appraisal and staff training on safe lifting techniques, etc.[20]

While local authorities are only under a statutory duty to take such action to protect their staff, they are frequently under a common law duty to take action to ensure that carers and disabled children are not exposed to equivalent risks. The risks posed by caring are well documented. Almost four out of every ten accidents reported in the health care sector arise from manual handling.[21] Over 50 per cent of carers have suffered a physical injury such as a strained back since they began to care. An equivalent number receive treatment for a stress-related illness at some time during the same period.[22]

Where the local authority has carried out a community care assessment and is aware of the carers' caring tasks, then it will almost certainly owe the disabled child and the carer a 'duty of care'. It will need therefore to take steps to warn of the risks and use its expertise to minimise the dangers (for instance, in providing appropriate aids and adaptations to reduce the risks as well as providing information and training). In the Department of Health guidance *Disabled Children:*

Directions for their Future Care (1998) attention is drawn to the importance of ensuring that carers are provided with appropriate training in relation to a range of areas, from simple first aid basic life skills to specific training connected with the child's particular impairment (para 9.12).

It should also be appreciated, that if the caring task imposes a risk on the carer, then this will impair his or her 'ability to provide and continue to provide care', which is, of course, of direct relevance to the Carers Act assessment duty (see p.237).

Health Services

Department of Health research[23] has, as we have noted, identified a variety of health services which are frequently mentioned by disabled children and their families as being of particular importance. A number of these are considered in Chapter 5, including good access to primary care, with a named GP and support from a health visitor; contact with a community paediatrician and paediatric community nursing team; access to incontinence advice; the opportunity of respite care and access to good quality physiotherapy, speech therapy, occupational therapy and conductive education services. Other important services include the use of a range of laundry services (p.237) and access to equipment on loan.

The Audit Commission[24] has identified as one of the five key impediments to inter-agency working the problems involved in organising aids and appliances. Research suggests[25] that although most health and local authorities attempt to create joint equipment stores and consider such a joint facility to be essential, in practice the supply of equipment is a problem. A major cause of the confusion in this area relates to the overlapping responsibilities of health and social services for providing items such as hoists, walking aids and incontinence equipment. In general, therefore, where an item of equipment is required and an inter-agency dispute arises as to its provision, a joint complaint should be made (p.76), emphasising the joint working failure of the two authorities (p.67).

Wheelchairs

Wheelchairs may be obtained from NHS trusts for temporary use on discharge from hospital. In general the disabled person will be referred to an occupational therapist, physiotherapist or consultant for assessment as to the most suitable wheelchair. If the patient has difficulty using a manual wheelchair, the trust can supply an electric model (including one for outdoor use if appropriate).[26] The NHS operates a 'wheelchair voucher scheme' that gives users the option of purchasing from an independent supplier or from the wheelchair service. In either case the user can top up the voucher cost (which covers only the cost of a 'standard' wheelchair to meet the user's needs) to enable a more expensive model to be acquired. However, if the chair is purchased from an independent supplier it is owned by the user who is responsible for its maintenance and repair, whereas if the 'wheelchair services' option is chosen, the trust retains ownership but is also responsible for maintenance.[27]

Notes

1   At the time of writing the government is consulting on the terms of the proposed 'Special Educational Needs and Disability in Education Bill' which contemplates a limited extension (for disabled students) to the protection of the 1995 Act.
2   Education Act 1996, s.317(6).
3   The *Report of the Committee of Enquiry into the Education of Handicapped Children and Young People* (HMSO, London, 1978).
4   The relevant guidance being issued by the Department for Education, as *The Code of Practice on the Identification and Assessment of Special Educational Needs* (HMSO, London, 1994).
5   See *R v Hampshire Education Authority ex p J* [1985] 84 LGR 547 and *R v Hampshire Education Authority ex p W* [1994] ELR 460, QBD.
6   Frequently the lawyer will however be prepared to provide a free initial 'diagnostic' interview, and as part of this to explain very precisely what the sort of implications may be (if any) of pursuing the legal issues further.
7   Op. cit.
8   [1997] ELR 62. See also *R v Lancashire CC ex p M* [1989] 2 FLR 279. CA where the Court held that in most cases speech and language therapy provision constitutes special educational provision and is thus the responsibility of the LEA under s.324 (5)(a)(i) Education Act 1996, but cf. *R v Isle of Wight Council* [1997] ELR 279.
9   [1997] ELR 417.
10   Available at: http://www.dfee.gov.uk/sen/standard.htm
11   The rights of children aged under five are considered at p.108 above.
12   Where the school is maintained (or the schooling funded) by the LEA, see p.159 below where this obligation is considered in greater detail.
13   At the time of writing the government is consulting on the terms of the proposed 'Special Educational Needs and Disability in Education Bill' which may remove this requirement.
14   Department of Health Social Care Group *Disabled Children: Directions for Their Future Care* (HMSO, London, 1998), para. 7.1.
15   See p.5 and 101 in relation to grants to support the cost of adaptations, see p.236.
16   See p.236 for social services provided equipment and p.100 for health care equipment see.
17   See p.237.
18   See p.234.
19   See p.236.
20   Regulation 4, Manual Handling Operations Regulations 1992 SI No. 2793.
21   Health and Safety Executive Guidance HS(G)104 para. 89.
22   M. Henwood *Ignored and Invisible? Carers' Experience of the NHS* (Carers National Association, DoH, London, 1998) cited in *Caring about Carers: A National Strategy for Carers, LASSL (99)2.*

23   Department of Health Social Care Group *Disabled Children: Directions for Their Future Care (HMSO, London, 1998), para. 7.1.*

24   Audit Commision, *United They Stand* (London, HMSO, 1995).

25   L. Clements and P. A. Smith *'Snapshot' Survey of Social Services' Responses to the Continuing Care Needs of Older People in Wales* (Cardiff Law School, Cardiff, 1999), para. V.8.

26   HSG (96)34.

27   HSG (96)53.

CHAPTER 7

Becoming an Adult

Introduction

In previous chapters we have stressed the importance of gradually creating opportunities for disabled children to develop an appropriate degree of independence and autonomy. We have suggested that a range of supports and services may need to be available if disabled children and those close to them are to have experiences comparable in this respect to those enjoyed by non-disabled children and their families. The life that someone has as an adult will depend in part at least on the groundwork laid throughout childhood.

While our emphasis so far has been on the fact that becoming an adult begins the day you are born, we shall concentrate in this chapter on particular issues related to the transition from childhood to adulthood. In Chapter 3, we identified this period as one of the critical transitional points in the lives of young people and their families. It is a time when a range of legal and organisational arrangements change, new information needs to be accessed and new plans formulated and put into operation. All the evidence we have indicates that this may turn out to be a particularly hazardous time in the lives of those concerned. This is partly because of what has gone before and partly because of specific features associated with this point in the lifecourse. All the indications are that unless very positive and proactive steps are taken, certain things may happen by default or design which do not augur well for both the young people concerned and their families. In this chapter, we consider:

- what it means to become an adult
- key findings from research on disabled young people's experience of progressing towards adulthood

- representation, support and information
- service provision and planning for transition to adult life.

What it means to become an adult

In a paper on the dynamics of transition to adulthood for both disabled and non-disabled young people, Riddell (1998) argues:

> Development from childhood through adolescence to adulthood is at one level a process of biological change and as such is not merely a social construction. At the same time, it is evident that within different cultures and at different historical periods the social construction of childhood, adolescence and adulthood changes markedly (Aries 1973). This implies the existence of a state of interaction between biology and culture so that the physiological and emotional process of maturation is overlaid by a range of cultural expectations which will be subject to change over time and will be influenced by the wider economic context. (Riddell 1998, p.193)

She proceeds to describe the ways in which adulthood in modern industrialised societies is construed as a central social status. The achievement of this status entails the crossing of certain age-specific thresholds and this, in turn, carries with it both rights and obligations. Examples of the thresholds she describes include criminal responsibility, sexual consent, voting rights, conditional or unconditional marriage rights and the giving of medical consent. Obligations may include paying income tax when employed, attending for jury service and so on.

Riddell's analysis raises a number of important issues which can inform our discussion on the process of transition to adulthood for disabled young people. First, she indicates the diversity of social and cultural experiences, expectations and practices that may be associated with progression to adult status. This would lead us to be circumspect about the yardsticks we use for measuring the degree to which any young person has moved towards adulthood. In other words, we should be hesitant about assuming that models which may in fact only be relevant to specific ethnic and social groupings are universally applicable. For example, without qualification, a young person's living separately from the family of origin prior to marriage cannot be used as an indicator of progression to adult status. In addition, the extent to which such arrangements prove possible, even when regarded as desirable, may be influenced in the UK, for example, by matters such as youth unemployment and policies on eligibility to state benefits.

Second, Riddell draws to our attention the significance often attributed to normative biological maturation. When this is regarded as a key indicator, there are clearly implications for those whose development may not be defined as falling within the normal range or who are living with impairment. There may be a dominant and widespread assumption that access to the rights and obligations associated with adulthood is contingent upon having a particular physiological and intellectual status. Riddell's general discussion of the dynamics of transition reminds us that definitions of childhood, adulthood and transition are by no means straightforward. It also begins to signal some of the ways in which the legal markers of adulthood, however variously defined, may be withheld from disabled young people and just how difficult it may be for them to attain some of the orthodox benchmarks of adult status.

Our view is that even though the dominant templates used by the majority to define progression to adulthood do not always sit easily with the needs and circumstances of disabled young people, there can be no assumption that they should be deprived of those experiences and aspirations frequently associated with an adult way of life. While these things may be difficult to achieve for some, we should nevertheless start from the premise that there are some basic rights which all adult citizens should enjoy unless a case can specifically be made to the contrary. Good policy and practice should therefore be directed towards supporting and enabling young disabled people and their families to work towards having choices that are within the range regarded as ordinary for the general population.

Disabled young people and transition to adulthood

Quality of life

There is now a substantial body of empirical research and other literature that indicates the extent of the limitations on their quality of life experienced by many disabled young people and those close to them as childhood is left behind (for example, Barnardo's Policy Development Unit 1996; Baxter *et al.* 1990; Beresford 1995; Corbett and Barton 1992; Flynn and Hirst 1992; Hirst 1987; Hirst and Baldwin 1994; Hirst, Parker and Kozens 1991; Morris 1999b; Social Services Inspectorate 1995a; Thompson, Ward and Wishard 1995).

As Hirst and Baldwin (1994) point out, concern over disabled young people's quality of life and experience in adulthood is by no means new. Since the early 1960s, research and official reports have repeatedly raised serious questions about the quality of health, education and social support services available to them in the post-school period, as well as drawing attention to widespread inequalities in access to the labour market (Court 1976; Ferguson and Kerr 1960; Walker 1982; Warnock 1978; Younghusband *et al.* 1970).

Hirst (1987) summarised the findings of his study of the careers of 274 disabled young people between the ages of 15 and 21 as follows:

First, the vast majority of young people in this sample can look forward to an occupational role which is both undervalued by and segregated from ordinary adult society. Secondly, they face long-term dependence on the social security system, incomes close to the official poverty line and low living standards. Thirdly, and as a consequence, they will have few opportunities to develop control over and responsibility for their own lives. The net result will be that these young people will suffer restricted activities and choice not only in their vocational activities but also in their living arrangements and social lives. Young people with disabilities are particularly dependent for the quality of their adult lives on the services provided for them. Those services need to extend the range of options available to young disabled people and enable them to exercise their own preferences. (Hirst 1987, p.73)

More recent research confirms that substantial problems continue to exist for large numbers of the young people and adults concerned. Beresford's survey in the mid-1990s of 1100 households with a disabled child up to the age of 14 years explored the nature of a wide range of needs on the part of both parents and their sons and daughters. The study indicates some trends which are pertinent to the issue of transition to adulthood. She found that as children grew older, there was a greater likelihood of their having unmet needs for services. Similarly, the extent to which parents' needs remained unmet also increased with the child's age. Parents of older children not only needed more financial support and assistance with day-to-day caring tasks, but they also wanted help with planning their child's future. Children with more severe impairments had more unmet needs than others, as did their parents (Beresford 1995). In summary, as many children grew older, they and their families often had increased needs which were not being met by adequate interventions and supports.

Hirst and Baldwin's (1994) study of around 1000 young people in adolescence and young adulthood is generally regarded as one of the most comprehensive pieces of research on the topic and therefore merits detailed consideration. It set out to investigate the extent to which disabled young people manage to attain an independent adult life more or less easily than young people in general. It did so by comparing the circumstances and lifestyles of disabled and non-disabled young people. The study also investigated differences in experience of adulthood among disabled young people according to type and severity of impairment.

Hirst and Baldwin report that while transition to adulthood remains a very difficult time for disabled young people, the experience was not uniformly bleak for everyone. Quite substantial numbers were progressing towards adulthood in ways that did not diverge significantly from their non-disabled peers. They had a measure of independence, age-appropriate social activities, a good image of themselves and some sense of personal control over their lives. Some were in paid employment.

Sadly, however, the study also reveals other experiences which give rise to considerable concern. It reports that between 30 and 40 per cent of the disabled young people were likely to have great difficulty in attaining a degree of independence in adult life comparable to that of their non-disabled peers. Hirst and Baldwin highlight a number of key findings:

- Disabled young people were less prepared for and less likely to be living independently of their parents than young people in general.

- Achieving independence through employment was difficult for most disabled young people who were half as likely as their non-disabled peers to be in paid work.

- While financial independence increased with age for all the young people, many of those who were disabled faced long-term dependence on the social security system, incomes substantially below those of young people in general and restricted personal spending. Fewer disabled young people controlled money from their social security benefits. Where they did, it was often regarded as a contribution to their keep, thus restricting the income over which they had direct control.

- Although most disabled young people recorded positive views of themselves and a degree of autonomy, they were more likely than their non-disabled peers to report feelings reflecting a poor sense of their own worth and abilities and a limited sense of control over their lives. Disabled young people who had attended special school and had no post-school provision were at greatest risk of feeling worthless and helpless.

- Although most disabled young people had social and friendships networks, their social lives and use of leisure were more limited and more likely to be dependent on their parents than non-disabled young people. Non-disabled young people tended to have a wider circle of friends, closer friendships and more frequent contacts. Generally lower participation by the disabled young people in ordinary social activities was offset to some degree by participation in clubs, including those exclusively for disabled people.

- The medical care for the disabled young people was provided more in hospital outpatient departments or clinics rather than through GPs. There was, however, a lack of adequate provision to keep their health needs under review following discharge from paediatric services. There was widespread uncertainty about the ways in which disabled young people could take responsibility for their own health.

- Despite their health needs, there was a lack of continuity in the provision for disabled young people of therapy or paramedical services in the post-school period.
- Few of the disabled young people had had recent contact with a social worker. (Hirst and Baldwin 1994, pp.109–110)

Hirst and Baldwin also point out that the circumstances, lifestyles and aspirations of the disabled and non-disabled populations diverged more as they got older, largely as a result of unequal access to employment and therefore independent income. As the young people went through their late teens and entered their twenties, the existing gap widened to the extent that it was unlikely that the disabled young adults could ever catch up.

This study also draws our attention to the particularly disadvantaged position of young people living with severe and multiple impairments. Their access to experiences which others could regard as ordinary was severely limited and their lives were described as 'marginalised and isolated'. Hirst and Baldwin refute any suggestion, however, that there is an inevitable connection between severity of impairment and these quality of life outcomes. They point out that there were substantial differences in the experiences of those living with severe impairment and that these reflected inequalities in the support and opportunities made available to them rather than their functional abilities.

Barriers to opportunity

We are not suggesting that the nature of impairment is an insignificant factor in young people's lives but rather that the restrictions which many experience are not a necessary consequence of it. Such restrictions can be mitigated and thus the quality of life substantially enhanced by the introduction of appropriate supports and opportunities.

Others share Hirst and Baldwin's notion that the degree of autonomy to which a disabled young person may aspire has to be understood with reference to a complex relationship between impairment, social disadvantage and available opportunities. Barnardo's Policy Development Unit (1996) emphasises the way in which social forces and institutional structures present the young people concerned with social, economic and physical barriers that deny them equal opportunities and citizenship. They argue that the situation is significantly worse for those from minority ethnic groups and for young women. They specify how young people and their families are trapped by current limitations on community care services:

Current community care policies assume that young people with disabilities will stay at home and that parents will continue to act as the main care givers. Options for supported living or alternative forms of personal care remain limited, and while this situation exists parents are not going to feel confident in relinquishing their responsibilities. (Barnardo's Policy Development Unit 1996, p.61)

The absence of supported living and personal assistance services is significant in that it may inhibit the extent to which disabled young people can take control of their own lives and broaden their horizons beyond their immediate family. It also has the effect of keeping the young person and other family members in a protracted and close relationship which may prove demanding and restrictive in at least some respects for all concerned. We do not, of course, wish to undermine or be critical of close familial and other relationships that are important to those involved. Rather, we are suggesting that whatever disabled young people and their families might otherwise wish, force of circumstances and unmet needs combine to define the parameters of their relationships in particular ways. This is, however, only one element of a series of interlocking factors which restrict disabled young people and adults. In many cases, the disadvantage experienced in one area will have a knock-on effect on others.

The question of restricted employment opportunities provides another useful example of the way in which a number of interrelated factors together operate as barriers or disincentives. It is evident how the circle becomes tightly closed and employment placed beyond the reach of many young people. Having a job is one of the most significant single issues in any adult's life. Over two decades, research has consistently indicated that economically active disabled people face greater barriers than their non-disabled peers in relation to employment opportunities (Anderson 1995; Barnes 1991; Gooding 1994; Lonsdale 1990; NACAB 1994; Thornton, Sainsbury and Barnes 1997). As a group, disabled people are more likely to face unemployment and to be among the long-term unemployed. When they have jobs, they are more likely than comparable workers in the general population to be in low paid, low status positions.

These disadvantages cannot be explained wholly in terms of their functional abilities. Disabled young people have frequently had a more restricted education than others and have often been afforded fewer training opportunities. In addition, there has been reluctance on the part of employers to comply with even the very limited legal obligations established in relation to the employment of disabled people in the post-World War II period, let alone contributing to the creation of equal opportunities. There have been many reported experiences of discrimination in recruitment and in the workplace (Morris 1999b). That employers might be required to make reasonable adjustments to the workplace and to working practices is a measure only recently introduced by the Disability Discrimination Act 1995. It still remains to be seen what effect it will have on the employment opportunities of the majority of disabled adults.

In addition to the related issues of education, training and the workplace, young people may find that the vexed question of transport has a bearing on whether they are able to be economically active. Without appropriate transport, getting to the workplace or doing so without undue difficulty and fatigue, may prove to be a significant barrier. Frequently, family and friends may be the only source of support in this respect.

The means testing of certain services, as well as the loss of key benefits, can also make employment non-viable for some groups of people. For example, the fact that funding of personal assistance through the Independent Living Fund is means tested creates a barrier to employment for those with high support needs. It can simply leave them with take-home pay that is not substantially above the income support level. (Kestenbaum 1998; Morris 1999b). Some people with learning difficulties who use supported housing schemes have also been found to face barriers to employment because of the fact that it is almost impossible for them to earn enough to meet the rent for such schemes. For many, being a service user of supported housing is contingent upon being in receipt of housing benefit (Morris 1999b; Simons 1998).

It is evident then that the barriers and disincentives to employment may prove insurmountable for many disabled young people. As we have already suggested, however, for those who are not in paid employment there are considerable personal and financial consequences. People are often accorded and in turn accord themselves value and esteem from being in paid work. The workplace provides a location for making and maintaining social contacts. The working day and the working week give a structure and routine which many people need and value. Finding purposeful activity, social contacts and self-esteem in other ways is extremely important but not always straightforward. In addition, disabled people who are without jobs face restrictions in income combined with high costs of disabled living and therefore limited access to goods and services (Bertoud, Lakey and McKay 1993). As we have seen in earlier chapters, the same is true of the household as a whole if the disabled young person is living with his or her family of origin. It is all too easy to see how financial pressures on the whole family may make it difficult for the young person to be allocated a distinct and separate income which they control themselves.

A further problem encountered by many disabled young people and those close to them is in part related to some of the barriers and difficulties that we have already described, but nevertheless deserves consideration in its own right. As the young people approach adulthood, there is a tendency for services to fragment, become even more difficult to access than before or become completely unavailable. The transition from children's to adults' services is fraught with problems and there is a danger that many young people and their families fall through the net. The type of inter-agency co-operation and planning that we consider later in this chapter is frequently not undertaken in a way that would safeguard the future interests of the service users concerned.

As we have suggested earlier, many children and their families have substantial unmet needs for services that are essential to their well-being. Nevertheless, for some, the fact of being in the school system and having a statement of their special educational needs means that at least some information and services come their way. These may not be easily replaced when the young person leaves school. For example, once paediatric services no longer have responsibility, appropriate medical and health-care services may prove fragmented and difficult to access. Young people who have complex health-care needs may require services and treatment from a variety of practitioners within the health service and this provision is frequently unco-ordinated. Within the health service, practitioners who take specialist or lead responsibility for ensuring that young disabled people's needs are met are still rare, as are organisational arrangements set up to deal with the problems of transition (Morris 1999b). Many young people find that physiotherapy and speech and language therapy cease to be available once they leave school. They and their families may also find themselves unsure about their rights in relation to provision of essential equipment as well as the procedures for obtaining it.

The provision of social care and support services may also present problems. As we have seen, in many local authorities there is no register of disabled children to aid service planning or to target those who are reaching key points which make them vulnerable to having unmet needs. Within social services departments, the progression from children's to adults' services is frequently far from seamless. In addition, even when local education authorities comply with the statutory requirement (described later in this chapter) to notify social services when children with a statement pass their fourteenth birthday, there is evidence that this by no means guarantees that the young people concerned will have an assessment of their needs for community care and support services.

Adequate health and social care services are essential in their own right. In addition, we have also seen that for many disabled young people there is a clear and undeniable association between the nature of services with which they are provided and the degree of autonomy and quality of life that they are able to attain as they progress towards adulthood. This makes the gap between children's and adults' provision, as well as the falling away of some services, extremely significant and deserving of the attention of those involved in policy and practice. It also indicates how fragile is the position of young people and their families at this point and underlines the need for extremely positive and proactive steps to be taken to counter the potentially damaging effects of the organisational arrangements as they frequently operate.

Representation, support and information

Some organisations have recognised the need to develop focused or special projects in order to make a significant difference to young disabled people's experience of transition to adult life and have developed guidance for good practice (e.g. Morris 1999a). Some young people and their families are fortunate enough to have access to such projects or to agencies attempting to adhere to good practice guidelines. Many, however, do not. The importance of this time, the barriers faced by all concerned and the negative consequences of not accessing services which assess and meet need, make it extremely important for as many young people and their families as possible to have access to advocates and keyworkers as well as sources of direct information. In other words, it is a time when people are likely to need all the human and information resources they can muster if they are to find their way through the maze and get a result they regard as successful.

- *Getting Your Rights: A Guide for Young Disabled People.* Barnardo's (Barkingside: Barnardo's; available as text or audio cassette).

- *Move on Up: Supporting Young Disabled People in their Transition to Adulthood.* Jenny Morris (Barkingside: Barnardo's, 1999).

- *Growing Up: A Guide to Some Information Sources Available to Young Disabled People and their Families.* Wendy Beecher (London: Council for Disabled Children, 1998).

- *After Age 16 What's New? Services and Benefits for Young Disabled People.* Family Fund (York: The Family Fund; free to disabled young people and their families on request).

- *Making Connections. A Guide for Agencies Helping Young People with Disabilities Make the Transition from School to Adulthood.* DoH (Wetherby: Department of Health Publications Centre, undated, free on request).

- *Moving on Towards Independence: Second Report on Transition Services for Disabled Young People.* Social Services Inspectorate (London: DoH, 1997; free on request from Department of Health Publications, Wetherby).

Figure 7.1 Information sources on the transition to adulthood

There are a number of reports and guides which may prove useful to young people, their families and practitioners who want to be better informed about good practice, service users' rights and the duties of the various agencies at this time of transition (Figure 7.1).

We have recommended these particular sources of information because they are free or inexpensive and because they reflect a number of key trends in current work on transition. A great deal of this work stresses the duties and responsibilities of service providers as well as what service users should have a right to expect by way of good practice. There is also the issue that those practitioners involved will need to go beyond merely enabling young people and their families to find their way through the existing service maze, difficult though that may be in itself. What already exists in a given area may simply not meet the young person's needs and provide them with very restricted opportunities. If the young people and their families are to have a decent quality of life, they will require a thorough assessment of their needs. As part of this, they may benefit from the chance to develop their ideas about what would really be in their interests and therefore what their aspirations might be. They may need information about options they are unaware of and which do not yet exist in their area. As we have seen, many young people and their families will have led lives fraught with difficulty and they may need time and a variety of appropriate supports if they are to develop confidence that better and realistic alternatives are possible in the future. It also needs to be recognised that young people and their parents may need separate and different forms of information, support, advocacy and representation.

Despite the lives of many having been inextricably bound together, they may each require a distinctive service if they are to explore their different needs and rights. For example, young people who are lacking in self-esteem and have had only limited social networks may benefit from the opportunity to build their confidence within a peer group of other disabled young people and explore the nature of the personal, sexual and social relationships that they would like to develop. They may also welcome a variety of other interventions that enable them to extend their personal development, exercise choice and become aware of some of their rights. Some mothers who have never been able to go out to work because of the caring responsibilities they have had to carry may welcome the chance to look at how positive future provision for their sons or daughters might enable them to have a wider range of choices.

Service provision and planning for transition to adult life

A range of agencies have formal duties in respect of transitional planning and there is a clear expectation that they should work together to secure the best outcome. It is a requirement that a transitional plan should be produced for every young person who has a statement of special educational needs and that the process should be initiated by the local education authority at the first annual review after their fourteenth birthday. This would seem to indicate official recognition that successful transition to adulthood takes time and careful preparation. It is also recognised that it requires co-ordinated effort, planning and service delivery by key agencies with different responsibilities. The legal duties placed on the various parties involved will be specified in the legal commentary that makes up the second half of this chapter. In this section, we shall focus on what young people and those close to them ought to be able to expect in the way of good practice in transitional planning.

The first and perhaps most obvious issue is that disabled young people and their families should be able to expect that those involved do not simply go through the motions. The process of transitional planning should be undertaken in a manner which is meaningful to the young people and their parents and carried out in the spirit as well as to the letter of the law. The perspectives of both the young person and the parents should be central and they should be regarded as partners with the professionals. This may mean using innovative ways of consulting with young people and those close to them. Formal procedures may prove important for all concerned and may safeguard rights, but some young people and their families may feel at a disadvantage and have difficulty representing issues that are important to them.

Second, there needs to be a well-developed local policy to which all relevant agencies are committed. The local education authority is obliged to invite the social services department and the careers service to the first annual review after the young person's fourteenth birthday. If these agencies merely record this notification and do not take any active steps until a later date, the planning process is likely to be flawed from the start. Within such a local policy, there should be agreements about what young people and their families have the right to expect from different agencies and what will happen at every stage. It would be advantageous if, by inter-agency agreement, individual practitioners were designated to take lead responsibility for co-ordinating the work to be undertaken and for acting as the key worker or point of contact for the young person and the parents. This does not preclude the parents or young person having access to independent advocates or advisors.

It is also important to recognise that the responsibilities of the agencies concerned are not limited only by their duties in relation to the transitional planning process. This process may bring to light current unmet needs for services which it is the duty of an agency to address. For example, if the local education authority notifies the social services department that a young person who is disabled has now reached their fourteenth birthday, it may trigger an immediate assessment of need for community care services as well as planning for the future.

In summary, good practice demands that everything about the process should be geared towards enabling young people to have choices that are comparable to those made by people in their age group in the general population as they progress towards adulthood. This requires a careful review of experience to date, the current and future needs of the young person and their family and services which will have to be put in place to meet these needs. More specifically in relation to services, the transitional planning process will need to explore:

- future plans in education
- careers and employment
- health care
- community care services
- housing, accommodation and supported living schemes.

Future plans in education

As well as reviewing what the school curriculum aims specifically to offer the young person so that they may best be prepared personally and academically for adult life, consideration will also need to be given to whether it is in their interests to continue at school beyond the age of 16.

Some young people will, for example, follow an academic curriculum which leads them to stay at school until they are 18 and take GCSEs and A-levels. Some may progress to higher education. Others who are also set to follow CGSE and A-level courses may prefer to leave school at 16 and complete this part of their education either in a local standard college of further education or at one of the specialist colleges. These colleges may also be an option for those not following this type of academic curriculum. For some disabled young people who have been deemed to have special educational needs, there will also be the option of continuing in school until they are 19.

Many schools are likely to offer young people and their parents advice about what further and higher educational opportunities are available, and indeed the responsibility is likely to fall most clearly on the school in the case of those young people who do not have a statement of special educational needs. Nevertheless, it has always been specifically the responsibility of the Careers Service to provide information about further education and this role will be taken over by the new Connexions service due to be phased in from 2001. Parents and young people should expect to be given a range of information about the available options and this should be integrated into the transitional planning process.

While any additional learning support or equipment required by disabled students to meet their educational needs is the responsibility of local education authorities (for students in higher education) or the Further Education Funding Council (for students in further education), the responsibility for funding and providing personal assistance and care support in an educational setting may lie with social services departments. The distinction between these areas of responsibility can sometimes prove problematic for students who wish to attend a residential college or course. This makes early planning essential so that funding responsibilities can be negotiated in good time.

Careers and employment

The Careers Service has had a range of responsibilities in addition to advice and information on further education. Its officers are currently expected to make a comprehensive contribution to the transitional planning process so that all career options, including employment, further education and vocational training are addressed. It is common for some careers officers to specialise in providing services and advice to disabled young people. Where appropriate, the Careers Service has been expected to make links with the Employment Service, which has the role of assisting disabled people to obtain and retain jobs. The majority of disabled people are assisted through mainstream jobcentre services but more specialised help is provided by disability employment advisors. These are also mainly based in jobcentres. Their role is to assist disabled people into training or work, arrange employment assessment and rehabilitation and provide information and support which enables them to take advantage of various employment programmes.

The Careers Service in its present form is due to be replaced. Following the publication of the White Paper *Learning to Succeed* (DfEE 1999) and the report *Connexions: the best start in life for every young person* (DfEE 2000), it is proposed at the time of writing that a new Connexions service be phased in from the year 2001. The service will have responsibility for supporting and guiding all young people aged 13 to 19 as they progress towards adulthood, further and higher education, training and employment. Its staff, personal advisors, will consequently have an advisory role in relation to disabled young people within this age group as well as to those aged 20 to 25 who have been assessed under the terms of the Learning and Skills Bill.

As we have already suggested, despite a greater focus recently on the employment rights of disabled people, entry into paid work is by no means easy for many. For this as well as more positive reasons, day services provided or purchased by social services departments may prove to be important for many young people. There has been substantial criticism of the segregated and limiting nature of some day services, particularly perhaps those for people with learning disabilities (Morris 1999b). Recent years have seen raised expectations and a great deal of innovation in this area of provision as a result, in part at least, of the work of the National Development Team. There has been an increased emphasis on the importance of putting together more individualised, flexible programmes designed to enable young people to acquire skills, knowledge and contacts which can enhance their quality of life and prove useful for independent living. As part of this, they may be assisted to access mainstream leisure, educational and other facilities (Morris 1999b; Social Services Inspectorate 1995a, 1995b, 1997). While these trends are apparent, there is considerable variation in the type, quality and availability of day services from one authority to another.

Health care

As we have seen, disabled young people may be in danger of having unmet health-care needs when they are no longer eligible for children's services. This makes the involvement of the health service in transitional planning extremely important. Young people and their parents need the opportunity to review with professionals the continuing health-care needs and come to an agreement about how these should be met. They should be given information about how the necessary services will be delivered and what will be the key points of contact within the health service.

Community care services

Local authorities have a duty to assess disabled young people's needs for community care services provided under s.2 of the Chronically Sick and Disabled Persons Act 1970. As we have already seen in earlier chapters, a wide range of services is covered which can enable the young person to live more independently and to approach a quality of life comparable to that of others in the general population. The day services of the types already described, practical and personal assistance and support in the home, assistance with travel, access to leisure, holidays and recreation, home adaptations and equipment and the provision of meals can all be made available to aid the young person's chances of living more autonomously. These can be made available within the young adult's own accommodation or at the family home if that is where he or she is still living. We should not assume that no measure of independent living can be achieved by young people who do not live separately from their families of origin. As we discussed in Chapter 3, for those living with their parents, a range of interventions, including mutually beneficial short-term breaks, can be used to help create a lifestyle which is more in keeping with the older age group (Flynne *et al.* 1998).

Earlier, we discussed the provision of support workers and personal assistants to enable children and young people to have access to a wider range of ordinary experiences without always having to rely on their parents or other family members. As young people progress towards adulthood, it becomes even more important to consider such options. Even though the young person's care needs may have been met to date by family members, consideration can be given to whether it is now more appropriate to introduce support and assistance provided by someone else. This may be organised or provided either by the local authority or by the young person and his or her family themselves but with local authority funding. Disabled young people are eligible to apply for funding from the Independent Living Fund from the age of 16 and local authorities can also make direct payments to them from the same age.

The option to have either direct personal care services or the money to buy and control them offers young people and their families scope for improving their lives and increasing the autonomy of everyone concerned. Those who have experience of receiving and providing personal assistance testify to the importance of clear and sensitive agreements, preparation and planning, as well as the piloting and readjustment of arrangements so that a service is reliable and appropriate. Now that there are greater numbers of disabled young people and adults using personal assistants, more source materials are available so that practitioners and service users new to this form of provision can learn from the experience of others (Hasler *et al.* 1999). What is needed is likely to change over time but the transitional planning process, if used positively, can provide the opportunity for young people and their families gradually to find out what services aid the progress to adulthood.

Housing, accommodation and supported living schemes

Research has consistently pointed to the limited housing and accommodation options available to disabled children and adults and those close to them (e.g. Harker and King 1999; Morris 1999b; Oldman and Beresford 1998). It is clear that the quantity and range of accommodation combined with appropriate support services do not match the potential need. The private rented market, the sector that many non-disabled young people rely on to provide their first independent home, often has little that is suitable for their disabled peers. Consequently, young disabled adults may find themselves having to stay with their families of origin for longer than they would otherwise choose or accepting options that they or their families do not regard as suitable. For example, while residential units may be regarded as a positive choice for some people, there are circumstances when this provision can almost be taken as a foregone conclusion without other forms of accommodation and support having been considered. Morris (1999b) suggests that for young people with high support needs leaving residential school, long-term nursing home care is frequently assumed to be the inevitable next stage. Similarly, having a flat of their own may sometimes be ruled out for young people with learning disabilities even though this could be viable given the provision of appropriate community care services.

In view of the fact that accommodation and housing difficulties are well known, it is crucial that as a young person approaches adulthood steps are taken to look at what their needs are and to work towards meeting them in a planned way. This may require co-operation between social services, housing departments and independent providers. Some specialised housing and accommodation schemes have support services incorporated in them. In others, personal assistance and community care support packages are provided entirely separately by the social services department according to the needs of the tenant. For some young adults, there is no need for a specialist scheme though they may need accommodation to be adapted and some community care services provided to enable them to live more independently.

The idea that young disabled people can live independently of their parents may be unfamiliar to both the young person and his or her parents. Again, they may require a great deal of information and discussion about the way different approaches might meet their particular needs. They may need to build confidence that a suitable arrangement can be created, modified and made to work.

Because suitable arrangements do not come about easily, there is often a strong feeling that choices have to be certain and mistakes cannot be made. While this caution is understandable in the circumstances, we have to remind ourselves that we would not regard it as unusual for non-disabled young adults to try something and find that they want to change their minds. A lot of us do not find our preferred living arrangements first time round and only sort out what works by at least a little trial and error.

LEGAL COMMENTARY

Introduction

As we have stressed throughout, disabled children have to negotiate a series of transitions. On each occasion encounters take place with new procedures, new personnel and new administrative cultures.

While the transition into adulthood is a major episode for any adolescent, for disabled young people it can represent a period characterised by acute anxiety and profound difficulties. At this stage many of the key support agencies change; with the gradual (or abrupt withdrawal) of assistance from the education department and children's services, and consequent need to engage in fresh dialogue with adult care services and possibly the further and higher education funding councils (and the new learning and skills councils).

Statutory provisions exist which endeavour to ensure that there is a smooth handover of responsibility from the education department responsible for the special education provision to the social services department responsible for the continuing community care needs of the disabled person.

It is essential therefore that new (or revived) contacts are forged with the new agencies, most obviously social services, although housing and the benefits agency will often have a crucial role. However, since the goal will be for the disabled person to live as normal and independent a life as possible, crucial relationships may also involve the employment and careers services and the further and higher education funding councils.

The statutory provisions that anticipate 'transitional planning' operate on the basis that if social services involvement is not already substantial, the education department will take the initiative to involve the other relevant agencies. If for any reason, however, this does not occur (or the initiative lacks the necessary vigour), early letters expressing concern/making direct contact with the other agencies, should be sent.[1] We consider the relevant legal issues under the following headings:

- education and training responsibilities
- social services responsibilities
- NHS responsibilities
- Independent Living Fund eligibility
- housing responsibilities
- mental incapacity and parental wills/trusts.

Local Education Authority responsibilities

Ss. 5 and 6 Disabled Persons (Services, Consultation and Representation) Act 1986 require education authorities to consult social services authorities to establish whether a child over the age of 14 who has been 'statemented' under Part IV Education Act 1996 is likely to require support from the social services department when s/he leaves school. This duty is reinforced by the Education (Special Educational Needs) Regulations 1994 SI No. 1047, which require the contribution of social services departments and others to the transitional plan (see below).

Once the child has reached the age of 14, the annual reviews of his/her special educational needs statement should involve all agencies who will play a major role during the post-school years. The object of this joint activity is to ensure the transfer of all relevant information in order that the disabled child receives any necessary specialist help or support during his or her continuing education and vocational or occupational training after leaving school (para. 6.43

Code of Practice). In order to achieve this objective, the LEA must convene a review meeting and prepare a transitional plan.

The review meeting

The LEA obligations for review meetings which occur after the child has reached the age of 14 are spelt out in para. 6.44 of the Code of Practice (full copy in Appendix 4 p.252). Invitations to the meeting should be sent to:

- the child's parents
- relevant members of staff (of the child's school)
- any persons specified by the head teacher
- social services
- careers service
- anyone else the LEA considers appropriate.

It is clearly essential that social services and careers personnel are properly briefed prior to the meeting so that they can make a positive input to the meeting and the transitional plan. Their particular roles are amplified below.

The Code of Practice stresses the importance of ensuring that the young person's views are fully taken into account. At para. 6.59 it notes that 'some young people may wish to express these views through a trusted professional, family, independent advocate or adviser, the named person or through an officer of the authority'.

Transitional plan

One of the products of every annual review after the child reaches 14 will be a transitional plan which draws together 'information from a range of individuals within and beyond the school in order to plan coherently for the young person's transition to adult life' (para. 6.45 of the Code of Practice). In producing this report the LEA should consult with (although not necessarily invite to the review meetings) any other relevant professionals such as 'educational psychologists, therapists or occupational psychologists'.

The plan should, among other things, allocate responsibility for different aspects of development to specific agencies and professionals. The key issues which the plan must address are detailed in para. 6.47 of the Code of Practice (full copy in Appendix 4). In relation to the future needs of the young person, it requires the identification of various key factors, including:

- which new professionals need to become involved (such as occupational psychologists, a rehabilitation medicine specialist, occupational and other therapies

- any special health or welfare needs that will require attention by the health or social services authorities

- the need for any technological aids (including training in their use, etc.)

- any further education needs and how they are to be arranged.

Careers service responsibilities

The important role played by careers services in enabling disabled young people to maximise their opportunities for education, training and employment are highlighted by a number of circulars. Thus Circular 99/02 issued by the further education funding councils (see below) provides a detailed overview of the services' responsibilities,[2] stating among other things:

> 22. There is no age or time restriction in respect of people with disabilities, including learning difficulties. They remain part of the client group of the careers service until they are settled in their career intention.

Likewise, the Code of Practice on special educational needs stresses the important role of the careers service in contributing towards the disabled young person's transitional plan. There should however be every expectation that the service's contribution will be equally positive in cases where no statement of special educational needs has been prepared for the disabled young person. In this context, however, the Code of Practice advises as follows:

> 6.53. The careers service must be invited to the first annual review following the young person's 14th birthday, and should also be invited to all subsequent annual reviews. Vocational guidance should be presented in the wider context of information on further education and training courses and should take fully into account the wishes and feelings of the young person concerned. The careers officer with specialist responsibilities should provide continuing oversight of, and information on, the young person's choice of provision, and assist the LEA and school in securing such provision and providing advice, counselling and support as appropriate. In some circumstances careers officers may also wish to involve occupational psychologists, who can contribute to the development of a vocational profile of a young person for whom future planning is giving cause for concern. Schools may in particular welcome guidance on curriculum development in independence, social or other skills, and ways of involving young people themselves in assessment and in strategies to address any behavioural or other

problems which may otherwise adversely affect their further education or future employment.

The careers service should ensure that all disabled young people are made aware of the special schemes that may assist them in obtaining employment, although the young person or his/her parents may make direct contact with the disability service team of the jobcentre if they so choose.

It is proposed that the careers service will become absorbed into a new integrated agency known as the Connexions Service.[3] The service is designed to provide 'universal access' to careers education and guidance for all young people and will be phased in from April 2001. As part of this new programme the Family Fund Trust has published guidance for young disabled people and their parents/carers on learning and work choices post-16. The publication *After 16 – What's New?* is available free to young disabled people and their parents/carers, or direct from the internet (see Appendix 9 for contact details).

Special employment assistance for disabled people

Where because of a disability a person faces complex employment problems, they may be referred to the disability employment adviser who is an employee of the employment services jobcentre working in the disability service team. It is the responsibility of such advisers to provide assistance (and access various schemes) in order to enable the disabled person to obtain employment. There are numerous schemes available including: supported employment; work preparation; Access to Work scheme.

SUPPORTED EMPLOYMENT

This scheme provides for people with severe physical and/or intellectual impairments who without assistance would be unable to maintain employment in the open market. Support provided can include specific placements as well as employment in local authority or voluntary sector workshops, etc.

WORK PREPARATION

This scheme is directed at preparing disabled people for employment by concentrating on specific employment related needs which result from the impairment and which would otherwise prevent the person from entering employment or vocational training. The scheme includes the possibility of paying to the disabled person an employment rehabilitation allowance.

ACCESS TO WORK SCHEME

The Access to Work programme can, among other things, provide funding to cover the extra costs necessary because of disability, including the cost of:

- employing a communicator for people who are deaf or have a hearing impairment
- a part-time reader for someone with impaired vision
- support workers for practical help either at work or getting to work
- special equipment or adaptations to equipment to suit individual needs
- alterations to premises or to the working environment so that an employee with disabilities can work there
- help with travel to work costs such as adaptations to a car, or taxi fares (if public transport cannot be used).

The financial support available depends upon the length of time the disabled person has been employed, but for people about to start work the full cost of the support is available.

Disability Discrimination Act 1995 and employment

The Disability Discrimination Act 1995 makes unlawful 'unjustified discrimination' against a disabled people in relation to many matters, including in the field of employment. The protection of the Act however only applies to all employers with more than 14 employees.

The Act's protection covers job applicants as well as existing employees and requires employers to take reasonable steps to change the working environment to reduce the discrimination experienced by disabled employees. The provisions of the Act are relatively complex, and are considered in outline in Appendix 6.

Further and higher education provision[4]

LEAs are responsible for the provision of a child's education until the age of 16. After this age, responsibilities vary depending upon the course chosen. The situation has many permutations, but the main options are as follows:

1. Once a child has reached the age of 16 s/he may chose to remain in LEA funded full-time secondary education, which normally comes to an end at the age of 18.[5] In this respect, LEAs are specifically obliged to have regard to the requirements of people with learning difficulties who are over the age of 16 (s.15(5)(b) Education Act 1996).

2.   Alternatively s/he may leave secondary school at the age of 16 and commence further education or training at (for instance) a further education college.

3.   Alternatively s/he may enter further education or training at the age of 19 after the end of his or her secondary schooling.

4.   At the age of 19 s/he may enter higher education by going to a university.

Further education

The Code of Practice on special educational needs requires schools to foster links with local further education colleges with a view to 'easing the move for both the young person and staff at the further education college'. It notes that 'link provision with colleges can be of particular benefit to a young person with special educational needs by providing opportunities for integration, extending the curriculum and offering an induction into the adult environment of further education' (para. 6.58).[6]

At the time of writing, the principal Act governing the provision of further and higher education is the Further and Higher Education Act 1992. It places responsibility for the provision of further education in England upon the Further Education Funding Council for England and in Wales on the Further Education Funding Council for Wales, both of which operate helpful websites [www.fefc.ac.uk/] [www.wfc.ac.uk]. Athough the English and Welsh Councils are separate entities with slightly differing policies, in the summary below they are referred to as the 'FEF Councils'.

Learning Skills Council

As a result of the Learning Skills Act 2000 the responsibility for further education provision will be transferred to two Learning and Skills Councils: the Learning and Skills Council for England and the National Council For Education And Training For Wales. The new scheme will be phased in from April 2001, when the present FEF councils will be wound up.

The arrangements for post-16 education of people with learning difficulties under the 2000 Act are modelled on the present arrangements. At the time of writing, guidance on the detail of the new scheme is still awaited; accordingly the present scheme is outlined (and where appropriate the new statutory provisions highlighted in footnotes). The main provisions in the 2000 Act of relevance to disabled children can however be summarised thus:

1. The Learning and Skills Council will, by virtue of s.13 of the 2000 Act, be required to pay particular regard to the needs of people with learning difficulties and, in particular, to the needs disclosed by a s.140 assessment.

2. Under s.140 the DfEE Welsh Assembly must, when deciding how to discharge their obligations to persons with learning difficulties aged under the age of 19, obtain a specialist assessment if:

   • the pupil already has a statement of special educational needs (under s.324 Education Act 1996)

   • the pupil is likely to leave school to continue with post-16 education or training or enter higher education.

3. The DfEE Welsh Assembly has a discretion to obtain such an assessment for other disabled young people who have learning difficulties but do not have special educational needs statements.

4. The Explanatory Memorandum to the Act states that the Education (Special Educational Needs) Regulations 1994 (which set out the procedures for carrying out transitional reviews of pupils with statements of special educational needs) will be amended to enable the Secretary of State's representative to participate in these reviews and to assist in the identification of these young people.

Further Education Funding Council support

The 1992 Act assumes that most disabled children will receive their further education in ordinary further education colleges (i.e. an equivalent of the assumption under the Education Act 1996 that children will receive their education in mainstream schooling). The duty on LEAs in this respect is reinforced by a general duty[7] to secure adequate further education facilities for (among others) adults who have learning difficulties. However, the 1992 Act, like the 1996 Act, makes special provision for people with learning disabilities:

• requiring the FEF councils to 'have regard to the requirements of persons with learning difficulties' (s.4(2))[8]

• where a FEF council is satisfied that the facilities available in local further colleges (or universities) are not adequate for a person aged between 16 and 25 who has learning difficulties, then it must secure the necessary provision for him/her outside those sectors, if it is in his best interests so to do (s.4(3).

In such situations, if the FEF council is also satisfied that such provision cannot be secured unless boarding accommodation is also provided, then it must additionally secure the provision of that accommodation (s.4(4)).[9]

Avoidance of disproportionate expenditure

The duties owed by the FEF councils are subject to the proviso that they must 'make the best use of [their] resources and, in particular...avoid provision which might give rise to disproportionate expenditure' (ss.2(5), 3(4)).[10]

During the passage of the legislation through Parliament, the government explained the intention behind this provision. It was stated that 'the reference to disproportionate expenditure is intended to exclude expenditure which is out of proportion to the need being met, not to rule out provision which is necessarily expensive, such as the provision for students with disabilities'.[11] This distinction was further clarified:

> It would be...nonsense to rule out expensive provision where it is needed for students with learning difficulties, and the Bill does not seek to do so. What the Bill requires is that a council should not build an expensive engineering laboratory for a handful of students when there is another laboratory just down the road. But if the provision is proportionate to the need, even if it be expensive, this clause would not rule it out. There is no threat here to students with disabilities.[12]

Out-of-sector placements

Where it is considered that the facilities available in local further colleges are not adequate for the disabled person, the LEA must carry out an assessment to ascertain whether there is a need for an 'out-of-sector placement'. This generally occurs in response to a parental request or one made by the student. The relevant papers are then forwarded to the FEF council which decides whether to agree to fund the placement. The application procedures have been agreed between the FEF councils and LEAs and are regularly reviewed. The most recent agreement is contained in FEF Council Circular 99/02, (B98/05 in Wales where the process is slightly different) which can be downloaded from the internet.[13] In outline, the procedure is as follows:

1.   The LEA will, of its own volition, or at the request of the student or parent, carry out a 'thorough assessment' of the student's special educational needs. This will have many elements, but LEAs must ensure that:

- the student and his/her parents are fully informed of all the post-16 education and training choices available (including full involvement of the careers service in this respect)

- the student and his/her parents are fully involved in the assessment process

- appropriate advice is obtained from a range of relevant professionals (i.e. educational psychologists, specialist careers officers and other specialist professionals with expert knowledge who have worked with the student during their earlier education)

- all possible alternatives to the out-of-sector placement are investigated (including the possibility of the special educational needs provision being provided locally).

2. In addition to the assessment, the FEF Council requires the LEA to furnish it with:

- any statement of special educational needs it has prepared

- a copy of the transition plan

- a report from the student's current or most recent school

- details of any other support facilities the student requires (including travel assistance)

- details of the extent to which health and social services are willing to contribute to the cost of provision

- a copy of the assessment from the specialist college proposed, together with confirmation that the student has visited the college, and as to whether the student/parents/social services/health authority agree to the recommendation.

3. The LEA submit the relevant documentation and make a specific recommendation to the FEF Council which:

- states what it considers the student's special educational needs to be

- names the course and the specialist college that it considers appropriate (plus an alternative college if this is feasible).

4. The FEF Council then makes a decision. Where it does not agree to secure the recommended provision it will give reasons, and explain how representations can be made to seek a review of the decision.

5. The review procedure is currently detailed in para. 58 of Circular 1999/02, although the FEF Council intends to revise the procedure shortly. In essence, if after receiving further representations the FEF Council confirms its original decision, the student/parents have the

option of requesting an 'independent appeals panel' which has the power to commission additional expert advice where it considers this necessary.

Independent living and communication skills courses

In addition to their specific duty to fund out-of-sector placements, FEF councils have a general obligation to ensure that courses are provided for people with learning difficulties which prepare them for entry into further and higher education.

The duty is spelt out in s.3(1) and Schedule 2(j) of the 1992 Act which requires FEF councils to fund both full-time[14] and part-time courses[15] which teach 'independent living and communication skills to persons having learning difficulties, which prepares them for entry' into certain other specified courses. These are listed in paragraphs (d)–(h) of Schedule 2 of the Act:

(d)   a course which prepares students for entry to another course falling within paragraphs (a) to (c) above[16]

(e)   a course for basic literacy in English

(f)   a course to improve the knowledge of English of those for whom English is not the language spoken at home

(g)   a course to teach the basic principles of mathematics

(h)   in relation to Wales, a course for proficiency or literacy in Welsh.

The FEF council for England has in Circular 96/01, detailed the criteria by which courses of this nature will be funded. However, if there is no reasonable likelihood that an applicant can succeed on such a preparatory course 'to the point where he would be sufficiently prepared to enter' one of the subsequent courses (under paragraphs (d)–(h) of Schedule 2 of the Act) then funding will not be available.[17]

As noted below (see 'educational support services'), social services departments are required, under s.2(1)(c) of the Chronically Sick and Disabled Persons Act 1970, to provide certain non-educational support services for students who live away.

Social services

Most social services authorities divide their services for disabled people into 'adult care' and 'child care' services. While there may be good social work practice reasons for this division (for example, the need of disabled children for a 'childhood' and to share in the common developmental experiences of their peers), there is no significant justification for it at law. Although in general services under the Children Act 1989 cease to be available to disabled children when they reach the age of 18, their entitlement to services under s.2 Chronically Sick and Disabled Persons Act 1970 remains (see p.234). However, many young people and their families (and indeed practitioners) are unaware that disabled children are entitled to services under s.2 of the Chronically Sick and Disabled Persons Act 1970. As they approach transition to adulthood, therefore, they may have to go through the process of finding out about and accessing their entitlements.

There are of course dangers in separating adult and child care services and these often surface when the care responsibilities are being transferred from the child to the adult social work team. As we note above (see p.145) all too often at this stage the quality of the services deteriorates significantly or the child is effectively lost to the system and ceases to receive any continuing care. In this respect the Children Act Guidance notes:[18]

> Although different agencies' statutory responsibilities for children vary by age, authorities may wish to plan around existing team structures to provide support to young people beyond the statutory age of responsibility and to provide support during the transitional period to adulthood. Unless the resources and experience of children's services can be used during the transition to adult life, it is unlikely that young people's special needs will be met. Additionally existing resources and professional expertise will not be used in the most consumer-sensitive and cost-effective way and the skills developed during the school years may be lost in adult life.

As detailed above, the LEAs' obligations under the Disabled Persons (Services, Consultation and Representation) Act 1986 should ensure that social services are fully aware of the needs of the disabled child (who has been statemented) well before his or her educational support comes to an end.

While some social services departments have care workers (or occasionally even teams) with specific responsibility for such transitional planning, problems do occur at this stage – particularly in relation to the transitional arrangements for disabled children who do not have a statement of special educational needs.

As we have repeatedly stressed, social services have a crucial role in ensuring continuity of care and support throughout the disabled child's life and this continues into adult life. If for any reason the social services provision or arrangements are considered to be inadequate, then the appropriate response will generally be for a comprehensive assessment (or reassessment) with a view to the production of a care plan aimed at the promotion of as independent and normal life as possible. We consider the assessment obligations of social services authorities at p.62 above, the provision of community care services at p.152 and 234.

Upon the disabled person reaching the age of 18 the statutory basis changes for a number of the services s/he may be receiving.[19] For instance, if s/he is receiving direct payments in lieu of services under the Children Act 1989 (see p.233), the authority for these payments will cease to be under the 1989 Act and derive from the Community Care (Direct Payments) Act 1996. Likewise if the service received prior to 18 is residential accommodation, after the age of 18 the service will, in general, be made available under s.21 National Assistance Act 1948. This legislative changeover should not, however, in any way affect the services the young person receives.

Educational support services

As noted above (and on p.235) social services departments are required, under s.2(1)(c) of the Chronically Sick and Disabled Persons Act 1970 to provide certain non-educational support services for students who live away. LAC (93)12[20] gives specific guidance on these responsibilities, and in particular stresses that s.2(1)(c) covers funding the personal care requirements of such students so as to enable them to pursue their studies (even if those studies are undertaken outside the local authority's area). The relevant part of the circular states as follows:

9. SSDs have been reminded of their duty under s2(1)(c) of the Chronically Sick and Disabled Persons Act 1970 to make arrangements for assisting a disabled person who is ordinarily resident in their area in taking advantage of educational facilities available to him/her (even where provision is made outside that local authority's area), if they are satisfied that it is necessary in order to meet that person's needs. Such assistance might, in appropriate cases include the funding by the local authority of the personal care required to enable the student in question to pursue his/her studies. It is, of course, for the authority to decide, in each case, what the individual's needs are, and how they are to be met.

10. Disabled students attending higher education courses may be eligible to receive up to three Disabled Students Allowances from the local education authority, as part of their mandatory award. These allowances are for a non-medical helper, major items of special equipment, or minor items such as tapes or braille paper. They are aimed at helping students with costs related to their course, and are not intended to meet other costs arising from their disability which would have to be met irrespective of whether or not they were in a course. For those attending further education courses, similar support may be provided at the discretion of the LEA.

11. There may be occasions where the social services department is asked to consider the provision of additional care support for an individual who will receive a Disabled Students Allowance or discretionary support from the LEA. It will, therefore, be appropriate in some circumstances for the support for an individual's personal care needs to be provided jointly by the SSD and the LEA.

R v Further Education Funding Council & Bradford MBC ex p Parkinson [1996][21] concerned a 20-year-old applicant with severe mental and physical impairments. He was unable to take advantage of a place at a further education college without first being able to communicate to the required standard. He sought to compel the respondents to provide the necessary facilities either under s.41 Education Act 1944[22] or Schedule 2 Higher Education Act 1992. In dismissing the application, Jowitt J observed that although 'purely education facilities' could not be provided under the community care legislation, the applicant might be eligible for services under s.2(1)(c) of the 1970 Act 'as providing assistance to take advantage of education facilities which are available to him'.

NHS responsibilities

The NHS responsibilities for the health-care needs of disabled young people do not change when they attain adulthood, although inevitably the other changes in the young person's life may disrupt contact with the health services. The guidance therefore stresses the 'crucial' role that GPs may play in this transitional period:

> Their contribution to community care through knowledge of the whole family and the local community and their ability to monitor the individual young person's health and well being – as well as the delivery of general medical services – are essential in terms of support to young people living in their local community.[23]

The main focus of recent health and social services guidance is to ensure that insofar as it is possible, young people are not accommodated in hospitals on a long-stay basis.

NHS funded residential and respite care

The care needs of some disabled people are such that they require the provision of substantial (or specialist) nursing care in a residential setting. In relation to such young persons, the guidance stresses that although they 'may spend substantial periods of time receiving care or treatment in an NHS facility, it is against government policy that [they] be placed for long-term residential care in a NHS hospital setting'.[24]

Thus, while the health authority may be responsible for the funding of their care package, the placement should be in 'small homely, locally-based units'.[25] In general these will therefore be specialist independent or private nursing homes (see Chapter 8).

Where a young person has been provided with accommodation by a health body for more than three months, it is under a duty to notify the responsible social services department (i.e. the local authority for the area in which the child lives or was ordinarily resident immediately before being accommodated) of the arrangement.[26]

The Independent Living Fund

A detailed consideration of welfare benefits law is outside the scope of this text. Excellent coverage of this field is given in the *Disability Rights Handbook* (Disability Alliance 2000) which is updated each year. We do however set out below the main rules for funding via the Independent Living Fund.

The original Fund, which was established by the DHSS in 1988, was superseded in 1993 by a new fund, aptly known as the Independent Living (1993) Fund. In order to qualify for a grant from the fund, an applicant must:

- be at least 16 and under 66 years of age
- be receiving the highest rate of the care component of disability living allowance
- be at risk of entering residential care (or currently be in residential care and wish to leave and live independently)
- live alone or with people who cannot fully meet the care needs
- be on income support
- have an income at or around income support levels after care costs are paid
- have savings of less than £8000.

The fund works in partnership with local authorities in that it will only make payments (to a maximum of £375) if the social services department agrees to provide services and/or cash to a minimum value of £200 net a week. The combined value of the local authority and the 1993 Fund provision must not exceed £625 a week; the top-up monies from the fund are paid directly to the user.

Although applications can be made directly to the Fund (see below), in general the social services department should first carry out a full community care assessment and agree to support the application to the fund on the following basis:

1. It will contribute money or services to the value of £200 per week.

2. It is satisfied that the total care package should not exceed £625 per week.

3. The monies from the fund will be used to employ one or more people as care assistants (fund monies cannot be used for other purposes such as equipment, heating bills, home adaptations and transport costs).

4. The applicant is capable of independent living in the community for at least six months.

If an applicant appears to meet all the criteria, the Fund will arrange for an assessment visit to be made. The visit will be carried out jointly by one of the Fund's visiting social workers together with a local authority social worker. Applicants are required to contribute towards the overall cost of the care package:

- all of their severe disability premium and special transitional addition (if these additions to income support are received)
- half of their disability living allowance
- any income above income support level that is not already being used for care.

The contact address and website details for the Independent Living Funds are detailed in Appendix 9.

Housing responsibilities

While a detailed consideration of the entitlement of disabled people to access rented accommodation from the housing authority (either under the housing 'list' process, or via the homelessness provisions of the Housing Act 1996) is outside the scope of this text, we consider briefly two aspects of the duty to accommodate which are of particular relevance to disabled children: homelessness and Children Act housing duties.

Homelessness

The duty to house homeless people is contained in Part VIII of the Housing Act 1996 (ss.175–218). Of particular relevance for disabled children and their families are two aspects of the statutory definition of homelessness. A person is homeless if there is no accommodation which it would be reasonable for him or her to occupy (s.175). In addition, the Act specifies that accommodation can only be regarded as available for a person's occupation if it is available for occupation by him or her together with:

- any other person who normally resides with him or her as a member of his/her family or

- any other person who might be reasonably expected to reside with him or her.

Thus accommodation which is manifestly unsuitable for a disabled child may create a situation of homelessness, requiring action by the housing authority, either to rehouse or to render the property habitable for the child.

Children Act housing duties

Housing may, in limited circumstances, be provided by social services authorities in pursuance of their community care or Children Act responsibilities. Thus in *R v Tower Hamlets LG ex p Bradford* [1997][27] the court ruled that the social services department had fundamentally misunderstood its powers under s.17 Children Act 1989 when confronted with the needs of Mr and Mrs Bradford and their 11-year-old son Simon. It had failed to appreciate (until immediately before the hearing) that they had power under s.17 to provide virtually any service they deemed necessary (including the provision of accommodation for the whole family). The judge stated:

I believe that the reason for the failure (to assess under s.17 Children Act 1989) is that...those responsible for the assessment approached it with a fundamental misunderstanding of their powers in relation to rehousing under the Children Act 1989.

R v Wigan MBC ex p Tammadge [1998],[28] by contrast, concerned the social services department's community care responsibilities. Here the applicant lived with her four children, three of whom had severe learning disabilities. Over a considerable period of time she sought a larger property in order to be able better to provide for their needs. In due course a complaints panel agreed that the family needed a larger property and asked the director of social services to investigate the possibility of one being found. Following the hearing, a social worker visited the applicant on 22 October and made it clear that the social services department accepted the panel's recommendations. Subsequently, on 15 November, a multidisciplinary meeting was convened and it was the view of the officers attending that a larger property was needed; they referred the matter to a meeting of senior officers and councillors. This meeting decided, however, that 'it was not appropriate to commit the authority to the purchase or adaptation of a larger property'.

In quashing that decision, the judge held that by 22 September at the latest Wigan's 'own professionally qualified staff and advisors' had concluded that her need for larger accommodation had been established: 'Once the duty had arisen in this way, it was not lawful of Wigan to refuse to perform that duty because of shortage of or limits upon its financial resources.'

Disabled facilities grants

In addition to their housing provision responsibilities, housing authorities are responsible for administering grants to pay for the provision of disabled facilities in homes. These grants are primarily available to owner-occupiers/tenants for the purpose of:

1. Facilitating a disabled person's access to

   - the dwelling
   - a room usable as the principal family room, or for sleeping in
   - (or the provision of a room for) a WC, bath, shower, etc.

2. Facilitating the preparation of food by the disabled person.

3. Improving/providing a heating system to met the disabled person's needs.

4. Facilitating the disabled person's use of a source of power.

5. Facilitating access and movement around the home to enable the disabled person to care for someone dependent upon them.

6. Making the dwelling safe for the disabled person and others residing with him/her.

The means test for these grants depends upon the financial resources of the disabled person and their partner. If the disabled person is under 18, his or her parent's means are assessed. We set out the main rules for such grants in greater detail below (p.262).

Mental capacity and parental wills/trusts

When young people attain the age of 18, our domestic law treats them as an adult and assumes that they have the ability to make any decision they chose. If however they lack this capacity, a number of problems arise. For instance, they may lack the capacity to make a will, to chose whom they see or do not see, where they live or how they invest their money. As a child some of these problems (for instance, disputes about access or contact arrangements, or about their residence) are capable of resolution by way of an application under the Children Act 1989, but upon attaining 18 these relatively simple procedures are no longer available, and unfortunately there is no simple equivalent procedure for adults. We accordingly outline some of the relevant legal provisions and principles.

Mental capacity

Whether or not an adult has sufficient mental capacity to do a particular act is a legal, not a medical question. The degree of mental capacity required by law varies depending on the nature of the act that is to be undertaken. Thus, for example, a person may have sufficient mental capacity at law to conduct a simple transaction (for instance, handle his or her social security monies), but not sufficient capacity for a complex matter such as buying a house.

If a decision has to be made on behalf of a person who lacks mental capacity and that decision relates to the person's 'property' or 'affairs', then legal mechanisms such as Enduring Powers of Attorney or the Court of Protection are available. Where however the disabled person has always lacked the necessary mental capacity, then the use of an Enduring Powers of Attorney is not possible and the authority of the Court of Protection will generally be required.

The Court Of Protection

The Court of Protection is an Office of the Supreme Court and is now governed by Part VII of the Mental Health Act 1983. The Court has wide powers to 'do or secure the doing of all such things as appear necessary or expedient' concerning persons who lack mental capacity. The Court can however only take action in relation to a person's property and affairs, and only after it has been satisfied (after considering medical evidence) of the necessary mental incapacity. The Court can in particular take action:

- for the maintenance or other benefit of the patient
- for the maintenance or other benefit of the patient's family
- for making provision for other persons or purposes for whom or which the patient might be expected to provide if he were not mentally disordered, or otherwise, for administering the patient's affairs (s.95).

Generally the Court will do this by appointing a 'receiver', although in certain situations this is not necessary, for instance, when the patient's only assets consist of:

- social security benefits

- a pension or similar payment from a government department or local authority
- entitlement under a discretionary trust
- property which does not exceed £5000 in value (in such cases 'short order' can be made avoiding the necessity of a receiver).

Where a receivership order has been made, the incapacitated person is generally referred to as a 'patient' of the Court of Protection. The Court's contact details are given in Appendix 9.

Parental wills/trusts

Many parents face considerable difficulties in deciding how to make financial provision for their disabled child. This is especially so where the extent of a disabled child's impairments are such that s/he will almost certainly have to rely upon means-tested social security benefits during his/her adult life; the parents' concern being that if the child inherits or otherwise receives any substantial sum of money, this will lead to the loss of means-tested benefits until such time as the bulk of the money has been spent.

In some cases parents decide to make no financial provision for the child (for instance, deciding instead to leave the money to another child). Such a will is however vulnerable to be challenged under the Inheritance (Provisions for Family and Dependants) Act 1975 on the ground that provision should have been made for the dependent child.

While a detailed consideration of this issue is beyond the scope of this book,[29] in many cases the solution to the problem involves the making of a will which leaves the disabled child's share on a 'discretionary trust'. The money is then administered by trustees nominated by the parent in his or her will, and the capital value of the trust is ignored for means-tested benefit purposes. While such 'discretionary trust' arrangements appear relatively complex, most solicitors who specialise in probate law should be able to draft a suitable scheme without too much difficulty.

Notes

1   If the child has a special educational needs statement, then the initial letter should be sent to the LEA seeking clarification as to why there has been no planning, and in particular why there has been no 14-plus review (see p.156). If there is no special educational needs statement, then the initial letter should be sent to social services seeking their involvement to prepare care plans which will facilitate a smooth transfers in to adulthood (precedent letters in Appendix 9 can be adapted for these purposes).

2   At Annex A pp.13–15 of the Circular.

3   As a result of the White Paper *Learning to Succeed*, DfEE, June 1999.

4   For legal analysis of the relevant law see FEFC, *Duties and Powers: The Law Governing the Provision of Further Education to Students with Learning Difficulties and/or Disabilities* (HMSO, London, 1996).

5   Unless the child was under 18 when s/he began the course, in which case the age limit is increased to 19 (s.2(2) Education Act 1996).

6   S.140 Learning and Skills Act 2000 requires the Secretary of State to arrange for an assessment of pupils with special educational needs statements during their last year of compulsory schooling if they are leaving school and going on to further or higher education. In addition (under s.140(3)) s/he has the power to arrange for assessments of pupils who lack a special educational needs statement but nevertheless have learning difficulties.

7   S.41 Education Act 1944, as substituted by s.11 Further and Higher Education Act 1992. See also DFE Circular 1/93.

8   S.13 Learning and Skills Act 2000. In addition LEAs are required, by s.528 Education Act 1996 to publish statements concerning the provision facilities for disabled persons in further education.

9   S.13 Learning and Skills Act 2000.

10   S.2(3)(e) Learning and Skills Act 2000.

11   Lord Belstead, *Hansard*, House of Lords 14/1/1992 167. Sections 2(4) & 3(4) Learning and Skills Act 2000 now states that provision 'is not to be considered as giving rise to disproportionate expenditure only because that provision is more expensive than comparable provision'.

12   Lord Cavendish, *Hansard*, House of Lords 9/12/1991 571.

13   The website being [http://194.66.249.219/documents/circulars/index.html]; for the FEFC address, see Appendix 9.

14   For students over 19.

15   For students over 16.

16   Essentially courses designed to prepare students so that they enrol in vocational, GCSE, A level or degree courses.

17   *R v Bradford MBC and the Further Education Funding Council for England ex P Parkinson* [1997] 2 FCR 67.

18   The FEF Council for Wales has adopted a more flexible approach however. Para 16.10, The Children Act 1989: Guidance and Regulations Volume 6 'Children with Disabilities' HMSO (1991).

19   Entitlement to adult services under the Community Care legislation is outside the scope of this book and reference should be made to L. Clements *Community Care And the Law*, 2nd edn (LAG, London, 2000).

20   See paras. 9–11.

21   [1997] 2 FCR 67.

22   Which obliges LEAs to secure adequate further education facilities for (among others) adults who have learning difficulties (see note 8).

23   *The Children Act 1989: Guidance and Regulations, Vol. 6, Children With Disabilities* (HMSO, London, 1991), para. 16.11.

24   *The Children Act 1989: Guidance and Regulations, Vol. 6, Children With Disabilities* (HMSO, London, 1991), para. 13.7.

25   Ibid. para. 13.8.

26   S.85 Children Act 1989; in addition it must also inform the social services department of the area in which a young person proposes to live, if s/he has reached 16 and leaves accommodation which has been provided for at least three months.

27   1 CCLR 294.

28   [1998] 1 CCLR 581.

29   For a fuller account of such schemes, see G. Ashton, *Elderly People and the Law* (Butterworths, London, 1995) and 'Making Provision', a guidance booklet obtainable from MIND (see Appendix 9).

CHAPTER 8

Children Who Live Away from Home

Introduction

In earlier chapters, we have mainly been concerned with disabled children who are brought up by their families of origin and who live at home for the majority of the time. We turn now to those who spend a significant proportion of their childhoods elsewhere. We shall focus primarily on children who have substantial experience of living in communal or residential settings of some sort, though we also refer briefly to substitute family care.

It is only in relatively recent times that those disabled children who live away from home have begun to have any significant presence on the major policy and research agendas. For a very long time, the experiences of other children living away from their families have come under scrutiny. A large body of research as well as official reports have investigated a range of issues relevant to their circumstances and to policy and practice seen to affect their life chances and well-being, including:

- factors which trigger family breakdown and make it likely for children to need to be 'looked after' by the local authority (e.g. Bebbington and Miles 1989; DoH 1991; Owen 1992)

- practice which enables or inhibits the maintenance of appropriate contact between separated children and their families (e.g. Marsh and Treseliotis 1993; Masson, Harrison and Pavlovic 1999; Milham et al. 1986; Quinton et al. 1997)

- the patterns of the 'care careers' of separated children (e.g. Barn 1993; Bebbington and Miles 1989; Bullock, Little and Milham 1993; Milham *et al.* 1986; Rowe and Lambert 1973)

- the abuse, protection and well-being of children in residential settings (e.g. Utting 1997; Warner 1992;)

- placements and other arrangements which offer the most positive and stable upbringing for those who cannot be with their birth families (Berridge 1996; Berridge and Brodie 1998; Jackson and Thomas 1999; Parker *et al.* 1991; Sellick and Thoburn 1996; Thoburn 1990, 1994)

- the ways in which children's experience may be differentiated according, for example, to their social status and ethnic origin (e.g. Bebbington and Miles 1989; Jackson and Thomas 1999)

- young people leaving the care system (e.g. Biehal *et al.* 1995; Broad 1994; Stein 1997)

- the perspectives of children and young people on their own experience of public care (e.g. Coventry Who Cares 1984; Page and Clarke 1977; Voice for the Child in Care 1998; Who Cares? Trust 1993).

The level of this research activity should not of course be taken to indicate that the situation of non-disabled children living away from their families is without its problems. There has long been professional, academic and public recognition that the care system and residential schooling have not invariably served children's interests too well. The 1990s saw a particularly heightened sense of concern as a result of continuing revelations of unsatisfactory standards and sexual, physical and emotional abuse of children in some children's homes and residential schools in the post-war period (Utting 1991, 1997). A number of reports and policy initiatives have given attention to ways of improving the care offered to looked after children (DoH 1998; Utting 1997; Warner 1992). There have also been other more general trends in service development and delivery that have relevance to the situations of children in public care. Partly as a result of professional and public concern about abuse and therefore standards of care, and partly as a response to a more consumerist approach to the provision of public services, the 1990s saw increasing attempts systematically to define and improve quality in social care, including residential provision for a range of service user groups (Kelly and Warr 1992; Residential Forum 1996).

Sadly, however, until the mid-1990s, disabled children were frequently notable by their absence from many of the major policy, practice and research debates about the experience of children living away from their families. Disabled children had only a shadowy presence on the agenda of key concerns which had long since preoccupied researchers, practitioners and policy makers. In the early 1990s, however, significant findings became available on the patterns of care of disabled children living in communal establishments (Loughran, Parker and Gordon 1992). Loughran *et al.*'s reanalysis of the OPCS data of the 1980s high-lighted important trends in the care of disabled children living away from home as well as the significant limitations of the information available about such children. At about the same time, important work began to emerge on the abuse experienced by some disabled children including some in residential settings (Marchant and Cross 1993; Marchant and Page 1992; Westcott 1991, 1993). By the mid-1990s, it was becoming clear that a more comprehensive reassessment was needed in relation to the experiences, quality of life and standards of care for disabled children who spend substantial periods of time living away from their families (Ball 1998; Morris 1995, 1998a, 1998b; Russell 1995).

Limitations of the available information

Describing and making sense of the experience of disabled children who live away from home is no simple task. In Kahan's preface to the report *Positive Choices: Services for Disabled Children Living Away from Home* (Russell 1995), she observed just how little is known about the use of residential provision for disabled children: 'We do not even have reliable statistics of how many children and young people are cared for in local authority provision, voluntary organisations and private sector establishments' (Russell 1995, p.vi). Others too have contributed to mounting concern about the implications of the fragmented and unsatisfactory nature of the available information about disabled children's care careers and experience away from home:

> One of the major barriers to meeting the needs of disabled children who are living away from their families is the hidden nature of their experiences: we don't know enough about who they are, where they are, what their life feels like to them. (Morris 1995, p.89)

In summary, the children concerned can be found in a range of different settings. Some may be placed in non-educational residential establishments in local authority, voluntary and private sectors. In addition, there are those who spend the majority of their year, and in some cases their childhoods, away at residential school. There is also a group of children who spend long periods of time in hospitals or other health service establishments. Some children are placed with foster parents for significant periods. Some appear to use family-based and resi-dential short-term break provision not as one part of a community-based child and family support service, but rather as an element of a substantial package of provision primarily based away from home.

The difficulty of building up a reliable picture of the experiences and lifecourses of such children is related to three main issues. First, the total pool of reliable national and locally held data on disabled children generally is very limited. Gordon *et al.* (2000) argue that there is a serious lack of up-to-date demographic data on disabled children: to a large degree they are rendered invisible in government statistics. Second, the data specifically on disabled children living away from their families is also limited and in some respects confusing. Third, as we have already suggested, the population of disabled children has frequently been excluded from the frame when important research questions were being posed about children separated from their families. As a result, the pool of research on disabled children living away from home is smaller and less developed than that on non-disabled, separated children.

Consequently, we have been heavily reliant on the OPCS surveys of the disabled population in Britain, published at the end of the 1980s, as the major source of information on disabled children and their circumstances (Bone and Meltzer 1989; Meltzer, Smyth and Robus 1989; Smyth and Robus 1989). This survey was undeniably of great importance but subsequent work has drawn attention to its limitations in relation to disabled children living away from home and has recast the data to highlight some significant trends that were previously unclear (Gordon *et al.* 2000; Loughran *et al.* 1992; Morris 1995).

Before turning to the OPCS material on the experience of disabled children away from home, it needs to be acknowledged that the definitions of disability used generally within these surveys have not been without their detractors. They have been challenged among other things for adopting what was argued to be an over-medicalised and individualised set of definitions which drew on the International Classification of Impairments, Disabilities and Handicaps (Abberly 1992, 1996). There are also more specific difficulties associated with definitions of disability and impairment used in surveys on disabled children in the public care system. Gordon *et al.* (2000), Loughran *et al.* (1992) and Morris (1995) point out that because of the definitions of disability applied to the children concerned, the findings encompassed large numbers (almost 50 per cent of the total) who had behavioural problems alone and no physical, sensory or intellectual impairment. In addition, Gordon *et al.* (2000) argue that the threshold for inclusion of behavioural and emotional difficulties was set at a fairly low level. While no one would wish to detract from the needs of those children and young people with behavioural and emotional difficulties however defined, it is important to be circumspect about the nature and size of the population revealed by the survey. Gordon *et al.* (2000) argue that the decision to include children with a wide range of behavioural and emotional difficulties enlarged the conventional definition of disability and increased the proportion of disabled children found to be in local authority care. Relatedly, Morris (1995) suggests that the undifferentiated nature of the definition may have had the effect of obscuring the particular experience of those living with impairment who would usually be regarded as disabled.

The way that data was collected for the OPCS survey of children in communal establishments may also serve to obscure very significant or even dominant experiences of care away from home. Morris (1995), drawing on the reanalysis by Loughran *et al.* (1992), argues that the data generated by the survey had three major limitations which may lead us to underestimate the extent of institutional living experienced by disabled children. First, the survey did not include young people between the ages of 16 and 19 years. Second, it excluded large numbers of children who spend considerable proportions of their time in residential provision, the most significant of group being those at boarding schools. Despite the fact that many of the latter spend the majority of the year and a significant amount of their childhoods away from home, they were included in the private households survey as if they lived with their families. Third, within the 5 to 15 age group, children who lived in communal establishments but who went home to their families at least once a fortnight were not included. Gordon *et al.* (2000) argue that when the data from the 1991 census is taken into account, it is likely that the OPCS surveys substantially underestimated the numbers of disabled children living in residential care.

Potential sources of information other than the OPCS surveys are also disappointing. The way that local authorities collect data on children who are subject to the provisions of the Children Act 1989 does not allow a clear and detailed picture of the position of disabled children to emerge (Morris 1995). Disabled children's legal status is not always clear when they are living away from home. While some may be in a residential or foster care placement on a long-term basis, their status as 'accommodated' or 'looked after' children is not always clarified and recorded (Morris 1998). Concern has also been expressed about the fact that some disabled children may be spending substantial periods away from home in 'short-term break' or 'respite care' provision without appropriate legal safeguards (Robinson 1996) and without their appearing in Department of Health returns on looked after children. In addition, there can often be confusion among practitioners about the legal status of some children in residential schools and about the duties that local authorities have towards them (Abbott, Morris and Ward 2000). The way that formal data are collected also tends not to allow us to form a clear view of children's likely 'care careers' through the placements and systems where they find themselves. Snapshots of populations in particular establishments do not necessarily give indications of either the well-worn paths that children go down or the triggers that set them off and maintain them on a particular course. Finally, local authority registers of disabled children are still underdeveloped (Ball 1998) and do not at present collect data which would fill identified information gaps (Russell 1995).

We are therefore left with an incomplete picture about the patterns of disabled children's lives and experiences away from home and there is undoubtedly an urgent need for data to fill the information gaps. In the meantime, however, some of the fragments that can be pieced together enable us to identify key issues which warrant further investigation or attention by researchers, policy makers and practitioners.

Piecing together the fragments

As the findings of early investigations and research began to emerge, Morris (1995), perhaps most notably, argued that many disabled children experience patterns of care that simply would not be tolerated for their non-disabled peers:

> We all need to feel outraged that so many children have 'gone missing' from our society, that they are denied the things that we all take for granted and that, as they reach adulthood, so many of them 'disappear' into long-term residential provision. (Morris 1995, p.89)

While it needs to be stressed again that the majority of disabled children live at home with their families of origin, a major issue that has come to the fore is that disabled children appear to have a substantially greater chance of being separated from their families than non-disabled children. Of the population of disabled children (as defined by OPCS), 4 per cent were in the care of local authorities. As Gordon *et al.* (2000) point out, this is a rate some ten times greater than that which prevailed in the child population as a whole. The very least that can be said about this trend is that it warrants more attention and investigation than it has been given hitherto.

Parker's observations on the numbers and placements of disabled children in care, in the report *Disabled Children: Directions for their Future Care* (Ball 1998), are based on a reanalysis of the OPCS data:

> Our best estimate from the data available is that at the time of the surveys some 18,700 of the 327,000 children under 16 estimated to be disabled were in local authority care: that is 5.7 per cent. The comparable rate for the child population (under 18) as a whole, was about 6.0 per 1000, or 0.6 per cent. Children with disabilities, therefore, have a greater likelihood of being 'looked after' than other children. Indeed, they have constituted a significant proportion – about a quarter – of all children in care.

> One of the most surprising findings from our closer scrutiny of the OPCS data was that 86 per cent of children with disabilities living in communal establishments were also in local authority care. However, it must be borne in mind that the majority of disabled children in care were not in such settings. Foster care played an important part. Indeed, 40 per cent of the children so placed fell into

the three clusters characterised by the most severe disabilities – compared with 15 per cent for other children living in private households and 13 per cent for those in communal establishments. Obviously, not only were foster carers making a significant contribution to the care of 'looked after' children with disabilities (our estimate is that a fifth of all children in local authority foster care were disabled according to the OPCS definition) but they were also responsible for many with multiple and severe conditions. (Parker 1998, p.11)

As we have already indicated in summary, in addition to those disabled children who are in residential and foster care, there are those who are often assumed to be living with their families but who are in fact spending large amounts of time, sometimes as much as 48 to 52 weeks per year, away at school. Some of these are quite young children (Abbott *et al.* 2000). Only a small proportion (5 per cent) of disabled children go to boarding school and the likelihood of such a placement being made varies substantially from one authority to another (Abbott *et al.* 2000). Gordon *et al.* (2000) point out, however, that the OPCS private households survey revealed 14,400 children at boarding school, making this the most common form of residential provision and 'out of home' care for disabled children. The great majority (75 per cent) were attending residential special schools. Children with the most severe behavioural and emotional problems are the largest group placed in boarding schools, while children with the most severe and multiple disabilities represent the second highest percentage (Gordon *et al.* 2000).

Despite the fact that many of these children spent considerable periods away from home, there is often a lack of clarity among practitioners and their employing authorities about the children's legal status and therefore, the authorities' duties towards them. This means that, even when appropriate, local authorities do not always fulfil their statutory duties to review their circumstances and plan for their future as 'looked after' children (Abbott *et al.* 2000; Morris 1998b). There are also indications that some children are multiple and substantial users of one or more types of provision such as residential care, residential school or 'short-term' break services (Morris 1995; Robinson 1996).

In addition to children in schools, residential care and substitute family placement, Gordon *et al.* (2000) draw attention to the role of health authorities in making residential provision for disabled children. One in ten children in residential care were placed in such settings and the health sector was looking after a disproportionate number of the most severely disabled children, sometimes for very long periods. Gordon *et al.* also point out that this flies in the face of Children Act guidance which emphasises that such health placements should never be regarded as permanent.

Implications for policy and practice

Even though the available information has its limitations, some issues are apparent which may alert both professionals and service users to some hazards in the system. One way of highlighting these hazards and moving towards improved practice is to keep asking the research and practice questions in relation to disabled children that have already been asked in relation to non-disabled children in the public care system. Some of these are summarised in the introduction to this chapter.

The first of a series of interrelated and overlapping questions which we feel are important to ask has to be about why a significant minority of disabled children spend so much time away from their families and what determines where they are placed. It is important to stress once more how fragmented and insufficient is the available information on these important matters. The lack of evidence about what determines whether children leave home and, if so, whether they go to a placement in school, residential care, family placement or a health setting, should make us cautious about drawing too firm conclusions.

In their discussion of why some children are placed in residential care, Gordon *et al.* (2000) argue that a combination of factors related to the children's disabilities, the social circumstances of their families and their 'care careers' propels children towards this sector. They highlight the fact that two-thirds of these children are subject to compulsory orders of some sort. They also point out that the extent to which children in residential care had multiple disabilities was pronounced, but there is very limited reliable information on what distinguishes those disabled children from others placed in substitute families. No conclusions can be drawn about the extent to which severity of disability acts as a determinant in relation to the type of placement. There are some indications, however, that age may be a determinant, with older children more likely to find themselves in communal establishments rather than foster care.

Some research on residential schooling, together with anecdotal accounts and conventional wisdom (Abbot *et al.* 2000; Morris 1995; Russell 1995), suggests that as children get older, particularly if they have high support needs, some families may simply not be able to continue to provide the type and level of care and assistance that they require. This may be particularly the case if they have other stresses, particular crises or other significant calls on their time and personal resources and if they have been offered little in the way of community care services. In Chapter 3, we have referred to research which indicated that for many families, social and practical problems increased as the disabled child grew older (Beresford 1995). It is crucial to note that children from lone-parent households have a disproportionate chance of being at boarding school. While 19 per cent of disabled children in the 5 to 15 age group were living with a lone parent, such children comprised 27 per cent of those at boarding school (Gordon *et al.* 2000).

It is often suggested that even when the reasons for going away from home are primarily social and familial, some families may find residential schooling a more acceptable option than other provision (Abbott *et al.* 2000; Russell 1995). It has also been argued that in some cases placement in residential school may come about as a result of the fact that suitable educational provision to meet the children's needs may not always be available in their own locality (Abbott *et al.* 2000). As rates of placement in boarding school vary substantially from one local authority to another (Abbott *et al.* 2000), it is not unreasonable to conclude that decisions have at least as much to do with local policy and resources as with children's social and educational needs.

Earlier in this book, we have drawn attention to the frequently limited nature of the child and family support services that are made available to disabled children and those close to them. We have also pointed to the way in which short-term break provision or 'respite care' is often the primary (sometimes only) service on offer. It seems important, therefore, that practitioners as well as researchers investigate further the relationship between stress on families, the lack or availability of flexible community care support and the substantial and sometimes multiple use of provision of various sorts away from home. Relatedly, it is important to consider the educational provision, including flexible packages of learning support, that would enable children to stay in their home authorities rather than to go elsewhere. This is not to assume that a place in boarding school, for example, is always a negative choice, but rather to consider the factors which may make such a placement inevitable by default rather than a positive choice for a child and the family.

We also commented earlier on the differential experience that children and their families have in accessing services. Socio-economic status and ethnic origin are key factors associated with differential access to community-based services which meet needs effectively. We need to know more about the ways in which such factors may affect children's and families' chances of living away from each other. The over-representation of children from lone-parent households in residential education would suggest a possible association between socio-economic status and predisposition to separation that is worthy of investigation by practitioners and others.

A second major question has to be concerned with the ways in which some disabled children become cut off from their families and isolated in provision away from home (Abbott *et al.* 2000; Ball 1998; Knight 1998). Gordon *et al.* (2000) point out that a quarter of those in residential establishments neither received visits from parents nor went home. When these children are taken together with those who only had infrequent visits, around one-third of disabled children in residential care were living in isolation from their parents and other family members. There is precious little information about the circumstances of and planning for those children, including those removed from home compulsorily. Without additional information, it remains difficult to propose what the nature and purpose of contact with their families should be (Gordon *et al.* 2000). Local authorities have clear duties in relation to those children who are subject to the provisions of the Children Act 1989 so that appropriate contact with families and significant others may be agreed, planned for, put into practice and adjusted.

For those in residential school, home may be some considerable distance away and arrangements for keeping in close touch may prove expensive. Even when this is not the case, there may be a variety of personal, familial and organisational circumstances which create barriers and make it difficult for everyone involved to maintain a close and sustaining relationship between the disabled child and the rest of the family. Some disabled adults have offered illuminating retrospective accounts of their experience of becoming dislocated from their families and communities (French 1996; Humphries and Gordon 1992; Smith 1994).

When children are out of contact with their parents, there is growing recognition of the importance of their having consistent contact with or access to a key person from outside the residential setting, whether it is a school or home. This person may be, for example, a children's advocate or an independent visitor (Wynne Oakley and Masson 2000). While the Children Act 1989 requires local authorities to appoint independent visitors for those children who are 'looked after' and have had no contact with their parents for more than 12 months, there can be no assumption that such provision will be made available to the majority of disabled children away from home who fall within this category (Knight 1998). Apart from any other considerations, it is not unlikely that the confusion about the legal status of many such children which we have already highlighted may lead to their being overlooked in this respect. There are indications from research, however, that when disabled children are provided with an independent visitor they find the experience positive. The benefits associated with having a visitor include the chance to do ordinary activities, access to the experience of family life, support at reviews, having someone to monitor the child's welfare and assist with planning for the future (Knight 1998).

A third area of concern is related to the 'care careers' that some children may have when they are away from home. A combination of a selection of the factors which we have already acknowledged (lack of clarity over their legal status and the duties that authorities have towards them, a lack of comprehensive and long-term planning, substantial amounts of time away from their families in one or more placements, isolation, lack of community connections and support) may predispose some children, particularly perhaps those with high support needs, to live in a state of 'drift'. In other words, some children may live for long periods in situations which have significant implications for their present and future well-being without anyone taking an appropriate degree of responsibility for looking at all aspects of their current circumstances as well as the directions of their future lives (Morris 1995). Attention needs to be given to how the most positive alternative choices can be systematically reviewed for those disabled children who cannot be with their families of origin and steps taken to ensure that the most effective and active planning is undertaken with their immediate and longer term future in mind. This should include, for example, considerations related to their transition to adulthood. We have seen in earlier chapters how difficult can be the satisfactory transition from childhood to adulthood and from children's to adult services for those at home with their families. Concern has been raised about the particularly hazardous position of those young people who face such issues away from their families (Morris 1995).

The fourth matter to warrant serious attention has to do with the abuse, protection and well-being of disabled children separated from their families. Work on the physical, sexual and emotional abuse of disabled children which began to emerge in the 1990s (for example, Cross 1992; Kennedy 1992, 1996; Marchant and Page 1992, 1993; Westcott 1993, 1998) points to a number of key concerns which are highly relevant to the focus of this chapter.

First, there has been a growing debate about the fact that in some institutional settings for disabled children the standards of care, routine practices and quality of life offered at particular points or over time may be so poor that they should be regarded as abusive or as an infringement of human rights (Morris 1998c). Second, it has been recognised that individual disabled children may be particularly vulnerable to abuse, whether in residential settings or elsewhere. They are often reliant upon a number of other people for intimate care and other assistance and this may mask abusive or exploitative practices. They may have difficulty in making themselves understood and thus it may prove harder for them to let others know of distressing or abusive experiences without mediation. Their relative isolation from other children and adults and the reduced opportunities they have for unhindered social contact may make it easier for abuse and neglect to be hidden.

It is not difficult to speculate how this general vulnerability can be magnified by some of the factors which have already been discussed in this chapter. There may be potentially very serious hazards for children who are out of touch with their families and for whom there is no key person who knows them intimately, reviews their situation, monitors their well-being and plans for their future. The welfare of the children who have 'gone missing' in the system (Morris 1995), who are in a state of 'drift' and who may have a number of unplanned placement experiences, has to be a cause for concern. Again, these matters highlight the importance of ongoing contact with outside individuals who know the child well, individual planning, monitoring and review for children and the adoption of a comprehensive range of strategies to raise general care standards at the same time as protecting individual children (DoH 1999; Utting 1997).

The fifth set of issues which needs to claim our attention is related to the complexities of deciding what are the placements and other circumstances which offer the most positive and stable upbringing for disabled children who cannot be with their birth families for the majority of the time. Again, because of the fragmented and limited nature of the available information on outcomes, we, like others, can only pose what seem to be key policy and practice questions.

A number of reports have acknowledged and expressed concern about the way that the residential or group care sector has been undervalued and relegated to an option of last resort (Berridge and Brodie 1998; Russell 1995; Utting 1997). The revelations of abuse to which we referred earlier have undoubtedly had a negative effect, but it has also been suggested that financial retrenchment and ideological prejudice have contributed substantially to the destabilisation of a sector which can have a valuable role within a range of care services (Utting 1997). It has been argued that for some children, some of the time, group living should be seen as a positive option. It is also recognised that if disabled children with complex care and support needs are to be offered a safe and enhancing experience in residential settings, there is a need to raise standards, address lowered morale and increase staff training (Argent and Kerrane 1997; Gordon *et al.* 2000; Marchant and Cross 1993; Utting 1998). The case for a more positive role for group care is reported in summary by Russell (1995):

> Part of a range of positive options for disabled children, regarded as a valued and well managed service which is part of – not distant from – mainstream thinking about children's needs but which can also respond to some of the most challenging children and facilitate their return to family and community in due course. Assuming that all children live in families all the time is optimistic but unrealistic. A good residential service should facilitate home life but it has a distinct contribution of its own to make to caring for disabled children in the community. (Russell 1995, p.66)

It is possible to argue a similar perspective in relation to residential education. Earlier, we have called into question the way that it can sometimes be used as a default option and have also challenged some of the arrangements made for children who are placed in this sector. Nevertheless, it is important to acknowledge that some parents and children may regard residential school as a very positive option and may successfully integrate such a placement within a strong network of family and community links. Just as some parents of non-disabled children may believe strongly that some boarding schools offer their children the opportunity to enhance their life chances by receiving what they regard as the best education on offer, some who have disabled sons and daughters may feel that the specialist provision offered by a good residential school of their choice cannot be matched elsewhere. As we have already argued, the necessity to provide a high quality of provision and adequate safeguards for children in such settings is increasingly recognised and of paramount importance (Utting 1997).

Another significant provision for disabled children is family placement or foster care. This may be temporary, permanent or on a 'shared care' basis. From the 1980s onwards, there has been a growth in local authority family placement schemes of various sorts for disabled children (Argent and Kerrane 1997; Stalker 1996). We have already referred in this chapter to Parker's (1998) observations on disabled children in care. He draws attention to the substantial role played by foster care in providing for children living away from their families. Parker and his colleagues estimated that one-fifth of all children in local authority foster care were disabled according to the OPCS definitions, and some of these were children with the most severe and complex conditions.

In drawing attention to the substantial use of foster care for disabled children, Parker (1998) raises the issue of what kind of support these substitute families are being given as they undertake this extremely complex work. He also queries whether the placing of some very disabled children in foster homes might be asking too much of foster carers.

While there exists a substantial and growing body of work on shared care short-term break provision for disabled children (Robinson 1996; Russell 1996), there is more limited research evidence about outcomes in permanent family placement (Phillips 1998; Sellick and Thoburn 1996). In addition, while social workers and others may have been developing schemes and placing disabled children, it has sometimes been argued that there has been only a limited range of practice guides or manuals which might help them with these complex tasks (Argent and Kerrane 1997).

Many foster carers undoubtedly offer a valued service and it is important that they receive sufficient support and resources to enable them to do so. Disabled children together with their foster families need access to the range of community-based services which we have already suggested are essential to the well-being of the children's families of origin. Parker (1998) points out that foster carers are seen as something of a special case in that they tend to do rather better than many other groups of carers of disabled children with respect to the provision of such services. While this may indeed be the case, it should not be taken to mean that support is invariably generous or even adequate to meet need. Argent and Karrane's (1997) helpful guide, *Taking Extra Care*, addresses a range of essential practice issues related to the family placement of disabled children. These include assessment and planning in relation to disabled children who may need alternative family care; recruitment of substitute families; training preparation and support for substitute families; working directly with disabled children before, during and after placement; working with parents.

The final issue which we wish to address in this section, is the way in which the voices of disabled children living away from their families have frequently not been heard. Earlier in this book, we have emphasised that it is essential to consult with disabled children, to take account of their wishes, preferences and aspirations and to do so in an imaginative way that is likely to enable them to participate in planning their lives in the short and longer term. This is no less true for those children away from home as those living with their families. In the 1970s and 1980s the Who Cares movement, the National Association of Young People in Care and the Voice for the Child in Care were formed in response to a recognition that children in public care needed a voice (Coventry Who Cares 1984; Page and Clark 1977). Again, however, it was the voices of non-disabled children that were primarily heard. There can be few more momentous issues in the life of a child than those on which we have touched in this chapter. This makes it of paramount importance for practitioners and significant others in the children's lives to make it a routine and central matter to involve them in day-to-day and longer term decision making. Again, it is important to stress that if children's ability to influence their own lives is not to be restricted, they need to be provided with or enabled to develop the means to communicate (Beecher 1998; Marchant and Martyn 1999; Marchant, Jones and Julyan 1999).

More recently, there have been concerted efforts to offer more disabled children away from home the chance to be consulted and to express their opinions about issues generally and about their own specific situations (Chailey Young People's Group 1998; Minkes *et al.* 1994; Morris 1995, 1998a). This not only offers the children positive opportunities to give commentary on and to shape their own lives, but also offers practitioners and policy makers unique insights into an essential set of perceptions of the world which they have long since denied themselves or been denied.

Concluding remarks

While we have acknowledged that the majority of disabled children live at home for most of their childhoods, it is clear that a significant minority spend substantial periods away from their families. It is likely that this will always be the case and, this being so, we need to consider how to increase the responsiveness and quality of the services made available to them. It is our view that it is largely unhelpful to see the different living situations and placements away from home as discrete entities which bear no relation to each other or to community-based services. We believe that it is useful to consider the importance of developing and sustaining a network of varied service provision which children and their families may access appropriately at different points in their lives. We need to consider the way that good quality residential care or schooling might be seen as less of an all-or-nothing option of last resort and become one choice in a pattern of services which vary over time and in response to different circumstances. If a child's experience is dominated by one particular placement or one form of service provision, it may be that significant needs will be neglected.

LEGAL COMMENTARY
Introduction

Disabled children may live apart from their parents and siblings for a variety of reasons. The period of separation may be short or prolonged; a one-off event or occurring at planned and frequent intervals. The separation may occur in order to facilitate the provision of the child's special educational needs or in order to enable them to have a short break (sometimes referred to as 'respite care'). Sometimes, however, the separation results from the parents being unable (for one reason or another) to provide the necessary care.

The law relating to these arrangements has been framed with the aim of ensuring that children are protected and their development promoted. While actual abuse (physical sexual and financial) is a reality, of concern too is the potential for administrative neglect; of the child becoming isolated or left to 'drift' in the system. Accordingly in the Children Act, in regulations and in binding guidance, procedures exist which spell out what should be provided and who is responsible. These have unfortunately generated various legal terms, which need to be understood.

Terminology
Care orders and secure accommodation orders

Most disabled children who live apart from their families do so with their parents' agreement and without any court order having been obtained. For a few, however, there is an element of compulsion, either because there is a 'care order' in force (under s.31 Children Act 1989), or they are subject to a 'secure accommodation order' (under s.25 Children Act 1989). We do not consider the procedures for the making of such orders in this text, since invariably a lawyer will be instructed on behalf of the parents and child and separate and substantial texts exist on this subject.

Accommodated children

Colloquially, many parents refer to their children being in care when they are not in fact the subject of a care order. In such cases the parent has agreed to the arrangement with the local authority and no formal court order has been made. Under this voluntary arrangement the child is 'accommodated'. This is a service provided by the local authority and the parent may at any time bring the arrangement to an end.

Looked after children

A child is 'looked after by a local authority' if he or she is in their care by reason of a court order or is being accommodated for more than 24 hours by agreement with the parents (or with the child if aged over 16).

Parental responsibility

Parental responsibility is defined by s.3 Children Act as including all the rights, powers, authority and duties of parent in relation to a child and his or her property. The child's parents share parental responsibility if they were married at or after the time of conception,[1] otherwise only the child's mother has it, although the father can also acquire it by agreement or a court order.

A local authority does not acquire parental responsibility for the children it is voluntarily accommodating. Although a care order does give the local authority parental responsibility, this does not extinguish the parental responsibilities of the parent, except to the extent that their actions are incompatible with the care order.

Local authority duties to 'looked after' children

As we have noted above, the Children Act places a general obligation on local authorities to provide an appropriate range and level of services in order to safeguard and promote the welfare of children in need and so far as is consistent with that duty to promote their family life (s.17). This duty is reinforced by s.23(6) which requires local authorities to make arrangements to enable accommodated children to live with a parent or relative and under para. 6 of Schedule 2 to the Act which requires that the services be designed:

- to minimise the effect on disabled children of their disabilities

- to give such children the opportunity to lead lives which are as normal as possible.

The guidance emphasises this point by stressing (among other things):[2]

1. the family home is the natural and most appropriate place for the majority of children; and

2. the family has a unique and special knowledge of a child and can therefore contribute significantly to that child's health and development – albeit often in partnership with a range of service providers.

In order to ensure that disabled children are properly provided for, local authorities must not only provide services themselves, but also actively consider assisting voluntary organisations (and 'others' – such as extended family members and friends) to provide help to the child and his or her family. The help may consist of day and domiciliary services (p.233), guidance and counselling (p.232), respite and other care services.

Duties prior to placement

If, during the assessment process, a local authority anticipates that the child may need to live apart from its family, then it is subject to specific care planning obligations.[3] In every case compliance with these obligations must be on the basis of fully involving the child and the family, clearly formulating objectives and considering all the available options to meet these. The care plan which emerges from this process must detail who is responsible for which service and the timescale in which tasks must be achieved or reassessed.[4] We consider the law and good practice in relation to assessment and care planning on pp.41 and 229.

Local authorities must have particular regard to certain specified matters, namely: healthcare; education; race, culture, religion and linguistic background.

Health care

Local authorities are obliged to take a positive approach to the child's health care and act as 'good parents'.[5] Before any placement there should be medical examination and written health assessment in order to provide a comprehensive health profile and a basis for monitoring the child's development. Children must be registered with a GP and dentist and the child's needs for specialist health-care services fully co-ordinated with the relevant health body. The procedures for obtaining the necessary consents for health-care examinations and treatment are outlined in the guidance.[6]

Education

The guidance stresses that looked after children have the same rights as all children to education, including further and higher education and to other opportunities for development. Authorities must therefore bear in mind the need to provide extra help to compensate for early educational deprivation, the value of peer group relationships made in educational settings, as well as the importance of continuity of education and of taking a long-term view. The aim should be to help all children to achieve their full potential and equip themselves as well as possible for adult life.

Local authorities must notify the local education authority (LEA) of a placement 'in good time' so that arrangements for liaison and co-ordination can be put in place without delay.[7] Specifically however s.28 Children Act provides that where a local authority proposes to place a child in an establishment at which education is provided for children accommodated there, it must consult the relevant LEA[8] before doing so. We consider the general provisions relating to special educational needs assessments on p.127.

Race, culture, religion and linguistic background

Guidance advises[9] that as a guiding principle of good practice (and other things being equal) 'in the great majority of cases, placement with a family of similar ethnic origin and religion is most likely to meet a child's needs as fully as possible'. However it cautions against generalisations in this area, stating that there will be cases where such a placement is not possible or desirable.

The placement plan

Local authorities are required to draw up a placement plan detailing the arrangements for the placement and in particular:[10]

1. the child's identified needs (including needs arising from race, culture, religion or language, special educational or health needs);

2. how those needs might be met;

3. aim of plan and timescale;

4. proposed placement (type and details);

5. other services to be provided to child and or family either by the local authority or other agencies;

6. arrangements for contact and reunification; support in the placement;

7. likely duration of placement in the accommodation;

8.   contingency plan, if placement breaks down;

9.   arrangements for ending the placement (if made under voluntary arrangements);

10.   who is to be responsible for implementing the plan (specific tasks and overall plan);

11.   specific detail of the parents' role in day to day arrangements;

12.   the extent to which the wishes and views of the child, his parents and anyone else with a sufficient interest in the child (including representatives of other agencies) have been obtained and acted upon and the reasons supporting this or explanations of why wishes/views have been discounted;

13.   arrangements for input by parents, the child and others into the ongoing decision-making process;

14.   arrangements for notifying the responsible authority of disagreements or making representations;

15.   arrangements for health care (including consent to examination and treatment);

16.   arrangement for education; and

17.   dates of reviews.

The procedure by which the plan is formulated will follow the typical assessment and care planning process[11] and once the plan has been formulated it must be notified in writing to 'the parents, the child and other carers, representatives of other agencies involved with the child and others with a sufficient interest in the child'.[12]

Placements outside England and Wales

The Children Act (para. 19 Schedule 2) empowers local authorities to make placements for 'looked after' children outside England and Wales, subject to:

- suitable arrangements being made for the reception and welfare of the child in the new country
- the arrangements being in the child's best interests
- the necessary consents being obtained (i.e. generally that of the parents).[13]

Duties during placement

Record keeping

Local authorities must ensure that 'accurate, comprehensive and well organised' records are kept in relation to 'looked after' children since such records are essential for continuity of care as social workers and carers change.[14] The records should carefully record agreements and decisions relating to the plan for the child, the aim of the placement and the child's progress in that placement. The authority must keep two types of record, namely:[15]

1.   A central register which records the identity and whereabouts of every child the local authority has placed.

2.   Personal carer records for each child which contain all information about family history, involvement with the authority and progress which is relevant to the child.

In addition the following material should be kept with the record:[16]

(a)   a copy of the arrangements made for the child (the plan);

(b)   copies of any written reports in the responsible authority's possession concerning the welfare of the child; this will include family history and home study reports, reports made at the request of a court, reports made of visits to the child, his family or his carer, health reports etc;

(c)   copies of all the documents used to seek information, provide information or record views given to the authority in the course of planning and reviewing the child's case and review reports (see also Regulation 10 of the Review of Children's Cases Regulations);

(d)   details of arrangements for contact and contact orders and any other court orders relating to the child.

(e)   details of any arrangements made for another authority, agency or person to act on behalf of a local authority or organisation which placed a child; and

(f)   any contribution the child may wish to make such as written material, photographs, school certificates etc.

Access to such records (and other local authority material) is considered on p.74 above.

Reviews

The care planning process for 'looked after' children is continuous, and in order to ensure that the child's welfare is safeguarded and promoted in the most effective way, it is essential that progress is regularly reviewed. The Children Act Regulations put such reviews on a statutory basis.[17] Local authorities must hold review meetings at specified intervals:

- *First review*: within four weeks of the date on which the child begins to be looked after
- *Second review*: within three months of the first review
- *Subsequent reviews*: at six-monthly intervals thereafter (i.e. within six months of the date of the previous review).

The guidance deals with the good practice that local authorities must adopt in order to ensure an efficient, fair and effective system of reviews occur.[18] In particular it must provide for:

- the full participation of both children and parents in the decision-making process
- a structured, co-ordinated approach to the planning of child care work in individual cases
- a monitoring system for checking the operation of the review process.

Reviews meetings should be chaired by a local authority officer senior to the case worker, have a proper agenda and take place in a setting conducive to the relaxed participation of all those attending, with particular regard being paid to the needs of the child and, as a minimum, reviews should consider:[19]

1.   The child's and the parent's views as to the local authority's care plan.

2.   The extent to which the plan fulfils the authority's duty under the Children Act[20] to safeguard and promote the child's welfare, and in this respect, the following specific issues:

   (a) where the child is in the care of a local authority, whether or not the care order can be discharged or varied to a lesser order;

   (b) whether the placement continues to be appropriate;

   (c) the views of the child's carer;

   (d) whether the plan makes necessary provision for the child's religious persuasion, racial origin and cultural and linguistic background;

(e) where a child is looked after, whether the plan takes account of the duty under section 23(6) to enable the child to live with a parent, other person with parental responsibility, relative, friend; and where the child is in care, a person in whose favour a residence order was in force immediately before the care order was made, or other person with a legitimate interest in the child;

(f) the arrangements made for contact and, where the child is looked after by a local authority with regard to the duty on the local authority in paragraph 15 of Schedule 2 to the Act, to promote and maintain contact between the child and his family;

(g) where a child is looked after, the views of an independent visitor if one has been appointed, and if not whether to appoint one;

(h) whether the plan takes account of any particular needs the child may have, e.g. the child's disability;

(i) the arrangements made for the child's health (including consent to examination or treatment);

(j) the arrangements made for the child's education;

(k) the arrangements, if any, for financial support of the placement;

(l) where the child is provided with accommodation by voluntary agreement, whether or not the arrangements for the involvement of the parents in the child's life are appropriate; whether the social worker needs to encourage greater exercise of the parents' continuing responsibility to the child; whether or not there is still a need for accommodation or whether another sort of service would be more appropriate, or whether, in the case of a local authority there is a need to take care proceedings;

(m) reunification of the child with his parents and family;

(n) where a child has been in an agreed placement (not in care) for some time, whether the existing plan ensures that the child and the carer have an adequate sense of stability. Whether the carer should seek a residence order, for example; and

(o) where appropriate, arrangements for aftercare.

A written report of each review must be prepared and retained with the child's records. A summary of the review should be sent to the child and the parents and 'other appropriate persons'.

Contact

Whereas the procedures for determining 'reasonable' contact for children the subject of a care order are governed by statute,[21] contact arrangements for 'accommodated' children are merely 'a matter for negotiation and agreement' between the local authority, the older child, the parents and others seeking contact.[22] The guidance follows the research evidence by stressing the general importance of contact, particularly in the early days of a placement.

Contact visits can of course cause financial hardship to the visitor and accordingly the Children Act (para. 16, Schedule 2) provides local authorities with power to help with such costs. The guidance reminds authorities that 'the power is not limited to assistance with travelling expenses, but can be used to meet all reasonable costs associated with visiting'.[23]

Independent visitors

As we have noted above, a recurrent theme emerging from the research is the importance of the child's voice being heard. While our domestic law assumes that parents will fulfil this responsibility (and where necessary act as the child's advocate), they are not always able to discharge this role when the child is living away. Accordingly the Children Act[24] makes provision for the appointment of an 'independent visitor' in certain situations, namely where the local authority believe:

- it is in the child's best interests; and either
- it appears that communication between the child and parent has been infrequent; or
- the child has not been visited by a parent during the preceding 12 months.

The guidance states[25] however that in certain circumstances the local authority may decide that an appointment is not in the child's best interests (even though no visits have occurred) if, for example, the child is well settled in a foster placement and has sufficient contacts, friends and – if necessary – opportunities to seek advice.

Independent visitors must be 'independent' and Regulations[26] specifically exclude local authority officers and persons connected with the care home (and their spouses) from being considered. Independent visitors are unpaid although they can be reimbursed for their travel and other out-of-pocket expenses. Their role is to visit, advise and befriend the child[27] and (among other things) to encourage the child to exercise his or her rights and participate in decisions which affect him/her. The guidance explores in some depth the range of roles and skills required, the process for recruitment, training[28] and matching the visitor to the particular needs and personality of the child. It anticipates that the independent visitor will, on occasions, speak on behalf of the child ('as a friend') in order to resolve difficulties or deal with particular issues that have arisen. However, it is not the visitor's role to become involved where more serious complaints arise (for instance, a significant dispute between the child and the local authority or in relation to an allegation of abuse). In such cases the concerns should be raised at an appropriate level within the local authority and it may be that the child additionally be provided with a specialist advocacy service (see p.47 where advocacy as a service is considered).

Duties to children and young people leaving care

S.24 Children Act 1989 obliges local authorities to prepare young people whom they have been 'looking after' for the time when they cease to be 'looked after' and to provide a range of after care advice and assistance services. In relation to young people between the ages of 16 and 21 who cease to be 'looked after', the local authority has the additional power to make a 'leaving care grant' – the purpose of which is to provide help in the following ways: [29]

- by contributing to expenses incurred by the young person in living near the place where s/he is or will be employed, in seeking employment or in receipt of education or training

- by making a grant to enable the young person to meet expenses connected with his education or training.

Local authorities must prepare a 'leaving care plan' for each child and provide the support that a 'good parent might be expected to give', to help with the child's transition into adulthood and independence. In Chapter 7 we consider the general legal duties on the statutory agencies to assist the disabled child in his or her transition into adulthood.

The duty under s.24 will be radically amended when the Children (Leaving Care) Act 2000 comes into effect.

The Children (Leaving Care) Act 2000

The Children (Leaving Care) Act 2000 implements proposals first detailed in the consultation document *Me, Survive, Out There? – New Arrangements for Young People Living in and Leaving Care.*[30] The consultation document set out detailed proposals for improving the life chances of young people living in and leaving local authority care. Essentially the new arrangements give practical effect to the 'Quality Protects' policy (p.40) and endeavour to ensure that local authorities provide the same level of support as children who have not been in care might in general expect from their parents.

The Act is likely to come into effect in October 2001. Its main purpose is to help young people who have been looked after by a local authority to move from care into living independently in as stable a fashion as possible. It achieves this aim by amending key provisions of the Children Act 1989 by placing a duty on local authorities: [31]

- to assess and meet the care and support needs of children in care aged 16 and 17 who have been looked after for 13 weeks, either continuously or in aggregate (but excluding certain respite care periods)
- to assist children and young people who were formerly in care particularly in respect of their employment, education and training needs.

These duties will include obligations:

- to 'keep in touch' with such care leavers, including those aged 18 to 21 and beyond in some cases
- to prepare 'Pathway Plans' which take over from the child's existing care plan and run at least until the age of 21, covering education, training, career plans and support needs; subject to review every six months
- to provide each child with a keyworker, to be known as a 'young person's adviser', who will help to draw up the Pathway Plan and ensure that it develops with the young person's changing needs and is implemented. S/he will be responsible for keeping in touch with the care leaver (until the age of 21) and for ensuring that s/he receives the advice and support to which they are entitled
- to provide the advice and support assessed as required under the Pathway Plan, which may include accommodation and support in kind or in cash; where appropriate the cash may be given regularly and the circumstances need not be exceptional
- the provision of 'vacation support' for care leavers in higher education (e.g. vacation accommodation where needed)
- to provide assistance with employment, such as the costs associated with employment
- to provide help with the costs of education and training support (extending beyond the age of 21 if necessary)

- to provide 'general assistance' to young people aged 18 or over, who when 16–17 were in care, which may include assistance in kind or, exceptionally, in cash.

The Act provides a unified structure for financial support of eligible young people by transferring to local authorities the funds that were previously paid to such care leavers under the income support, housing benefit or income-based job-seekers allowance schemes. Local authorities must use this money to support care leavers (aged 16–17) who, in turn, cease to be entitled to these means-tested benefits from 'eligible' and 'relevant' children.

It is however intended that Regulations will provide for exceptions to the removal of benefits rule, particularly in relation to disabled children who will have rights under the new regime and retain their right to certain benefits.

Specific accommodation arrangements

Whether a child is provided with accommodation as a short-term break or long term – in a foster home placement or residential care – the local authority should ensure not only that it is suitable for his or her needs,[32] but also that it minimises the effects of the his/her disability.[33] Every effort should be taken to place children as close to their family home as is practicable, so as to maintain family links.

Care Standards Act 2000

At the time of writing the duties in relation to looked after children are to be found in the Children Act 1989 and the regulations made thereto. These provisions, in due course, will be repealed by the Care Standards Act 2000, when this Act comes into force. The Act regulatory framework extends not only to children's residential homes, but also to local authority fostering and adoption services, as well as to the welfare arrangements in all boarding schools and further education colleges which accommodate children. It is unlikely that the Act will be brought into force until April 2001 and accordingly the Children Act regulatory scheme is outlined below.

Short-term breaks (respite care)

Short-term breaks should be provided as part of an overall care plan. They should be flexible and local authorities should avoid seeing respite care merely as a crisis service, but instead strive to make it:[34]

A local service, where the child can continue to attend school as if still living at home;

Good quality child care in which parents have confidence and which ensures that the child is treated first as a child and then for any disability which may require special provision;

Planned availability. Research into different models of respite care has clearly indicated the importance of parents (and older child) choosing patterns of use and being able to use a service flexibly;

A service which meets the needs of all children. Concern has been expressed about the lack of respite care for children with complex needs. The service should be available to children living with long-term foster carers or adoptive parents;

Care which is compatible with the child's family background and culture, racial origin, religious persuasion and language;

Age-appropriate care – so that young children and adolescents are given relevant care and occupation; and

An integrated programme of family support which sees planned respite care as part of a wider range of professional support services to meet family needs. Escalating use of respite care may indicate a need for other family support services.

While the guidance reminds authorities of the NHS's continuing obligation to provide respite care for children who have substantial medical, paramedical and nursing needs, it stresses that such care should not be provided in long stay mental handicap hospitals but in 'small homely, locally-based units'.[35]

S.7 Carers and Disabled Children Act 2000 (which is likely to come into force in April 2001) provides for regulations to be issued which will enable a local authority (among other things) to issue vouchers to the parents of disabled children; the vouchers being redeemable at various agreed providers of respite care.

Fostering

Local authority arranged foster placements are governed by the Foster Placement (Children) Regulations 1991.[36] The guidance encourages local authorities actively to consider involving people with disabilities as foster parents or as contributors to training programmes. Continuity in education should be a high priority in making any placement and in particular the need for foster parents to become involved (as appropriate) in such programmes as paired reading, speech and physiotherapy and independence training exercises.[37]

One of the benefits of a foster placement is that it can enable the child to live in his or her local community. However, as the guidance notes, ordinary homes may be neither automatically assessable or suitable for children with disabilities. Accordingly local authorities are required to make every effort to ensure that the accommodation is suitable by (if necessary) providing appropriate equipment and adaptations to make sure that the child's living environment is as barrier free as possible.[38] The guidance continues:

> 12.10. It is essential that children with disabilities (who may have incontinence or special personal care needs) should have privacy in bathroom and bedroom and that they should not be excluded from the main areas of the home such as living rooms and kitchen (and the social activities which take place in these areas) because of access difficulties. In many instances access problems can be resolved through the use of relatively simple and cheap modifications such as the use of moveable ramps and other aids. It is quite unacceptable for a child to be placed in a setting where he or she is more restricted than would have been the case in the natural home or in a residential setting. Similarly accommodation may be suitable in itself, but the child will be severely limited in his or her use of it if the carers lack confidence in the management of a child with, for example, a severe visual handicap or if the child concerned is hyperactive. SSDs should additionally ensure that the accommodation is safe for the child in question and that access (and egress) can be easily accomplished in the case of fire. If a child is hyperactive or for some other reason is liable to be at risk if playing outside the house, the safety of any garden gates and fences should also be assessed. It would be inappropriate for a child with a disability to have to be confined unnecessarily to particular rooms because of problems of safety relating to the physical environment of the placement.

Residential care

S.53 Children Act 1989 provides that every local authority is under a duty to make arrangements to ensure that community homes are available for the care and accommodation of (among others) disabled children looked after by them. The Act also creates a statutory framework for the registration and inspection of children's homes.[39] This regulatory regime for such homes is complex (there are, for instance, five different types of home in which a child may be accommodated)[40] and its analysis is beyond the scope of this text. In addition, at the time of writing these arrangements are (as noted above) in the process of reform via the Care Standards Bill 2000.

Homes which accommodate disabled children must provide the necessary equipment, facilities and adaptations[41] and although this is of great importance the guidance advises that the aim should be to integrate the disabled child in every aspect of life in the home, not merely the physical aspects.[42]

Children accommodated by the NHS or an education authority

Because of the nature or degree of their disabilities, some children will inevitably spend prolonged periods of time in an NHS facility. The guidance however emphasises that 'it is against government policy that such children should be placed for long-term residential care in an NHS hospital setting'[43] and that the 'use of NHS facilities should reflect a child's need for assessment, treatment or other services which cannot' be provided by social services. Remaining in such a facility cannot however 'constitute a permanent placement'. Even in those 'rare circumstances where it is necessary for children and young people to receive specialist medical care and treatment which can only be provided in a hospital setting (for example, children with terminal or life-threatening conditions), the NHS should aim to provide this care in 'small homely, locally-based units'.

Notification duties

If a child is provided with accommodation by the NHS or LEA for more than three months on a consecutive basis or the intention is that this will happen, the health authority, NHS trust or LEA must notify the 'responsible social services department'.[44] On being notified, the authority must 'take all reasonably practicable steps to enable them to decide whether the child's welfare is adequately safeguarded and promoted while he stays in the accommodation and to decide whether it is necessary to exercise any of their functions under the Act'.[45]

Educational/social services placements

In relation to such placements, the guidance notes[46] that:

Some children with disabilities and special needs attend independent or non-maintained residential special schools – some on a 52 weeks a year basis. The use of a residential school, after careful joint assessment by the LEA, the SSD and the relevant DHA may represent an important resource for the development of a particular child. Residential school placements should be made with a clear understanding of the nature and objective of the placement. Close links with the SSD in question will ensure that there is clear and coherent planning for the school holidays, the maintenance of family and community links and future arrangements for the child when leaving school. Placements in a residential school should never be made by SSDs without consultation with their LEA.

Notes

1   S.2(1) Children Act 1989.
2   *The Children Act 1989: Guidance and Regulations, Vol. 6, Children with Disabilities* (HMSO, London, 1991), para. 6.1.
3   The Arrangements for Placement of Children (General) Regulations 1991, Regs 3, 4, 5 and *The Children Act 1989: Guidance and Regulations, Vol. 4, Residential Care* (HMSO, London, 1991), Chap. 2.
4   Ibid., para. 2.20.
5   The Arrangements for Placement of Children (General) Regulations 1991, Regs 6 & 7 and *The Children Act 1989: Guidance and Regulations, Vol. 4, Residential Care* (HMSO, London, 1991), paras. 2.23 et seq.
6   Ibid., para. 2.30 et seq.
7   *The Children Act 1989: Guidance and Regulations, Vol. 4, Residential Care* (HMSO, London 1991), paras. 2.34 et seq.
8   The LEA within whose area the local authority falls, or if there is a special educational needs statement, the LEA which maintains that statement; ibid., para. 2.39.
9   Ibid., para. 2.40.
10   Ibid., at para. 2.62.
11   See pp.41 and 62 above; and ibid. paras. 2.43–2.67.
12   Ibid., para. 2.70.
13   Ibid., para. 2.77.
14   Ibid., para. 2.78.
15   The Arrangements for Placement of Children (General) Regulations 1991, Regs 8 & 10.
16   *The Children Act 1989: Guidance and Regulations, Vol. 4, Residential Care* (HMSO, London, 1991), para. 2.81.
17   Review of Children's Cares Regulations 1991, SI 895 as amended by Children Short Term Placement (Miscellaneous Provisions) Regulations 1995. The reviews do not apply to series of short-term break (respite) placements, provided that they all occur with the same carer at the same establishment and are individually shorter than 4 weeks and the total period in any one year does not exceed 120 days; Regulation 11.
18   *The Children Act 1989: Guidance and Regulations, Vol. 4, Residential Care* (HSMO, London, 1991), paras. 3.8–3.25.
19   Ibid., paras. 3.10–3.120 and The Review of Children's Cares Regulations 1991, Schedule 2.
20   Ss.22(3), 61(1) or 64(1).
21   S.34 The Children Act 1989 and The Contact with Children Regulations 1991, No.891.
22   *The Children Act 1989: Guidance and Regulations, Vol. 4, Residential Care* (HMSO, London, 1991), para. 4.7.
23   Ibid., para. 4.23.
24   Para. 17, Schedule 2.
25   *The Children Act 1989: Guidance and Regulations, Vol. 4, Residential Care* (HMSO, London, 1991), para. 6.11.
26   Definition of Independent Visitors (Children) Regulations 1991, No. 892.
27   Para. 17(2) Schedule 2 Children Act 1989.
28   *The Children Act 1989: Guidance and Regulations, Vol. 4, Residential Care* (HMSO, London, 1991), paras 6.12–6.46.
29   S.24(2) Children Act 1989 and *The Children Act 1989: Guidance and Regulations, Vol. 4, Residential Care* at para. 7.10
30   30 LASSL (99) 15, Department of Health, London.
31   The responsible local authority is the one who last looked after the child, even if the child has since moved into the area of another authority.
32   S.23(8) Children Act 1989.
33   Ibid., para. 6 Schedule 2.

34   *The Children Act 1989: Guidance and Regulations, Vol. 6, Children with Disabilities* (HMSO, London,
     1991), para. 11.11; and see also Vol. 4, para. 2.37 which advises that even during short-term
     placements opportunities to develop and pursue leisure activities should be encouraged.

35   *The Children Act 1989: Guidance and Regulations, Vol. 6, Children with Disabilities* (HMSO, London,
     1991), para. 11.12.

36   SI No. 910 and general guidance for all children (whether or not disabled children) contained in
     The Children Act 1989: Guidance and Regulations, Vol. 4, Residential Care (HMSO, London, 1991),
     Chap. 4.

37   *Vol. 6*, op. cit., para. 12.4.

38   Ibid., para. 12.9.

39   Children Act 1989 Parts VI, VII, VIII; Children's Homes Regulations 1991, No. 1506 and *Vol. 4
     Guidance*, op. cit.

40

     1   *A local authority children's home:* a community home provided by the local authority.

     2.   *A controlled community home:* a community home provided by a voluntary (non-profit
          making) organisation in collaboration with the local authority, with the local authority
          taking primary responsibility for the management, equipment and maintenance of the
          home.

     3.   *An assisted community home:* a community home provided by a voluntary (non-profit
          making) organisation in collaboration with the local authority, with the voluntary
          organisation taking primary responsibility for the management, equipment and
          maintenance of the home.

     4.   *A voluntary home:* a home provided by a voluntary (non-profit making) organisation
          alone.

     5.   *A registered children's home:* a home provided by a private organisation for profit.

41   *The Children Act 1989: Guidance and Regulations, Vol. 4, Residential Care* (HSMO, London, 1991),
     para. 1.78.

42   Ibid., para. 1.81.

43   *The Children Act 1989: Guidance and Regulations, Vol. 6, Children with Disabilities* (HMSO, London,
     1991), para. 13.7.

44   S.85 Children Act 1989; defined as the social services authority for the area in which the child
     lives or was ordinarily resident immediately before being accommodated or (if there is no such
     authority) the authority in whose area the accommodation for the child is being provided.

45   Ibid., para. 13.9.

46   Ibid., para. 13.13.

PART II

Resource Materials

References

Abberley, P. (1992) 'Counting us out: a discussion of the OPCS surveys.' *Disability, Handicap and Society 7*, 2, 139–155.

Abberley, P. (1996) 'Disabled by numbers.' In R. Levitas and W. Guy (eds) *Interpreting Official Statistics.* London: Routledge.

Abbott, D., Morris, J. and Ward, L. (2000) *Disabled Children and Residential Schools: A Survey of Local Authority Policy and Practice.* Bristol: Norah Fry Research Centre, University of Bristol.

Abbott, P. and Sapsford, R. (1992) 'Leaving it to mum: "community care" for mentally handicapped children.' In P. Abbott and R. Sapsford (eds) *Research into Practice: A Reader for Nurses and the Caring Professions.* Buckingham: Open University Press.

Ahmad, W. (2000) *Ethnicity, Disability and Chronic Illness.* Buckingham: Open University Press.

Ahmad, W. and Atkin, K. (1996) 'Ethnicity and caring for a disabled child: the case of sickle cell or thalassaemia.' *British Journal of Social Work 26*, 755–775.

Aldgate, J., Bradley, M. and Hawley, D. (1995) *Report to the Department of Health on the Use of Short-Term Accommodation in the Prevention of Long-term Family Breakdown.* London: HMSO.

Anderson, H. (1995) *Disabled People and the Labour Market.* Birmingham: West Midlands Low Pay Unit.

Appleton, P. and Minchom, P. (1991) 'Models of parent partnership and child development centres.' *Child: Care, Health and Development 17*, 27–38.

Appleton, P., Boll, V., Everett, J., Kelly, A., Meredith, K. and Payne, T. (1997) 'Beyond child development centres: care coordination for children with disabilities.' *Child: Care, Health and Development 23*, 1, 29–40.

Argent, H. and Kerrane, A. (1997) *Taking Extra Care: Respite, Shared and Permanent Care for Children with Disabilities.* London: BAAF.

Aries, P. (1973) *Centuries of Childhood.* Harmondsworth: Penguin.

Association of Metropolitan Authorities (1994) *Special Child: Special Needs. Services for Children with Disabilities.* London: Association of Metropolitan Authorities.

Atkin, K. (1992) 'Similarities and differences between informal carers.' In J. Twigg (ed) *Carers: Research and Practice.* London: HMSO.

Atkinson, N. and Crawforth, M. (1995) *All in the Family: Siblings and Disability.* London: NCH Action for Children.

Audit Commission (1992) *Getting in on the Act.* London: HMSO.

Audit Commission (1994) *Seen But Not Heard: Coordinating Community Child Health and Social Services for Children In Need.* London: HMSO.

Baldwin, S. (1985) *The Costs of Caring, Families with Disabled Children.* London: Routledge and Kegan Paul.

Baldwin, S. and Carlisle, J. (1994) *Social Support for Disabled Children and their Families: A Review of Literature.* Edinburgh: HMSO.

Baldwin, S. and Glendinning, C. (1982) 'Children with disabilities and their families.' In A. Walker and P. Townsend (eds) *Disability in Britain: A Manifesto of Rights.* Oxford: Martin Robertson.

Baldwin, S. and Glendinning, C. (1983) 'Employment, women and their disabled children.' In J. Finch and D. Groves (eds) *A Labour of Love: Women, Work and Caring.* London: Routledge and Kegan Paul.

Ball, M. (1998) *Disabled Children: Directions for Their Future Care.* London: Department of Health (in association with Social Services Inspectorate and the Council for Disabled Children).

Ballard, K., Bray, A., Shelton, E. and Clarkson, J. (1997) 'Children with disabilities and the education system: the experience of fifteen fathers.' *International Journal of Disability, Development and Education, 44,* 3, 229–241.

Bamford, C., Qureshi, H., Nicholas, E. and Vernon, A. (1999) *Outcomes of Social Care for Disabled People and Carers.* York: Social Policy Research Unit, University of York.

Barn, R. (1993) *Black Children in the Public Care System.* London: Batsford.

Barnardo's Policy Development Unit (1996) *Transition into Adulthood.* Barkingside: Barnardo's.

Barnes, C. (1991) *Disabled People in Britain and Discrimination.* London: Hurst/University of Calgary Press, in association with the British Council of Organisations of Disabled People.

Barnes, C. and Mercer, G. (eds) (1996) *Exploring the Divide: Illness and Disability.* Leeds: Disability Press.

Barton, L. (1986) 'The politics of special educational needs.' *Disability, Handicap and Society 1,* 3, 273–290.

Baxter, C., Kamaljit, P., Ward, L. and Nadirshaw, Z. (1990) *Double Discrimination: Issues and Services for People with Learning Difficulties from Black and Ethnic Minority Communities.* London: King's Fund Centre.

Bebbington, A. and Miles, J. (1989) 'The background of children who enter local authority care.' *British Journal of Social Work 19,* 5, 349–368.

Beecher, W. (1998) *Having a Say! Disabled Children and Effective Partnership, Section 2: Practice Initiatives and Selected Annotated References.* London: Council for Disabled Children.

Begum, N. (1992) *Something to be Proud of: The Lives of Asian Disabled People and Carers in Waltham Forest.* London: Waltham Forest Race Relations Unit and Disability Unit.

Begum, N., Hill, M. and Stevens, A. (1994) *Reflections: The Views of Black Disabled People on their Lives and Community Care.* London: CCETSW.

Beresford, B. (1994) *Positively Parents: Caring for a Severely Disabled Child.* York: Social Policy Research Unit/HMSO.

Beresford, B. (1995) *Expert Opinions: A National Survey of Parents Caring for a Severely Disabled Child.* Bristol: Policy Press.

Beresford, B. (1997) *Personal Accounts: Involving Disabled Children in Research.* London: HMSO.

Beresford, B., Sloper, P., Baldwin, S. and Newman, T. (1996) *What Works in Services for Families with a Disabled Child?* Barkingside: Barnardo's.

Berridge, D. (1996) *Fostercare: A Research Review.* London: HMSO.

Berridge, D. and Brodie, I. (1998) *Children's Homes Revisited.* London: Jessica Kingsley Publishers.

Bertoud, R., Lakey, J. and McKay, S. (1993) *The Economic Problems of Disabled People.* London: Policy Studies Institute.

Biehal, N., Clayden, J., Stein, M. and Wade, J. (1995) *Moving On: Young People and Leaving Care Schemes.* London: HMSO.

Blackburn, C. (1991) *Poverty and Health: Working with Families.* Buckingham: Open University Press.

Bone, M. and Meltzer, H. (1989) *The Prevalence of Disability among Children.* OPCS Surveys of Disability in Great Britain, Report 3. London: HMSO.

Booth, T. (1999) 'Inclusion and exclusion policy in England: who controls the agenda?' In F. Armstrong, D. Armstrong and L. Barton (eds) *Inclusive Education: Policy, Contexts and Comparative Perspectives.* London: Fulton.

Booth, T. and Potts, P. (eds) (1983) *Integrating Special Education.* Oxford: Blackwell.

Booth, T. and Swann, W. (1987) *Including Pupils with Disabilities.* Milton Keynes: Open University Press.

Booth, T., Swann, W., Masterson, M. and Potts, P. (eds) (1992) *Curricula for Diversity in Education.* London: Routledge in association with the Open University.

Broad, B. (1994) *Young People Leaving Care: Life After The Children Act 1989.* London: Jessica Kingsley Publishers.

Bullock, R., Little, M. and Milham, S. (1993) *Going Home: The Return of Children Separated from their Families.* Aldershot: Avebury.

Burkhart, L. (1993) *Total Communication in the Early Childhood Classroom.* Elderburg: Burkhart.

Butt, J. and Mirza, K. (1996) *Social Care and Black Communities.* London: HMSO.

Cameron, R. (1997) 'Early interventions for young children with developmental delay: the Portage approach.' *Child: Care, Health and Development 23,* 1, 11–27.

Cameron, C. and Statham, J. (1997) 'Sponsored places: the use of independent day-care services to support children in need.' *British Journal of Social Work 27*, 85–100.

Cavet, J. (1998) 'Leisure and friendship.' In C. Robinson and K. Stalker (eds) *Growing Up With Disability*. London: Jessica Kingsley Publishers.

Chailey Young People's Group with Sue Virgo (1998) 'Group advocacy in a residential setting.' In C. Robinson and K. Stalker (eds) *Growing Up With Disability*. London: Jessica Kingsley Publishers.

Chamba, R., Ahmad, W., Hirst, M., Lawton, D. and Beresford, B. (1999) *On the Edge: Minority Ethnic Families Caring for a Severely Disabled Child*. Bristol: Policy Press.

Corbett, J. and Barton, L. (1992) *A Struggle for Choice: Students with Special Needs in Transition to Adulthood*. London: Routledge.

Court Report (1976) *Fit for the Future: The Report of the Committee on Child Health Services*. Cmnd 6684. London: HMSO.

Coventry Who Cares (1984) *Barbara's Case Conference*. Coventry: CRIS.

Cross, M. (1992) 'Abusive practices and disempowerment of children with physical impairments.' *Child Abuse Review 1*, 3, 194–197.

Crow, L. (1996) 'Including all of our lives.' In J. Morris (ed) *Encounters with Strangers: Feminism and Disability*. London: Women's Press.

Cunningham, C. (1983) 'Early support and intervention: the HARC infant project.' In P. Mittler and H. McConachie (eds) *Parents, Professionals and Mentally Handicapped People: Approaches to Partnership*. London: Croom Helm.

Cunningham, C. (1994) 'Telling parents their child has a disability.' In P. Mittler and H. Mittler (eds) *Innovations in Family Support for People with Learning Disabilities*. Chorley: Lisieux Hall.

Cunningham, C., Morgan, P. and McGucken, R. (1984) 'Down's syndrome: Is dissatisfaction with disclosure of diagnosis inevitable?' *Developmental Medicine and Child Neurology 26*, 33–39.

Dalrymple, J. and Burke, B. (1995) *Anti-oppressive Practice: Social Care and the Law*. Buckingham: Open University Press.

Dearden, C. and Becker, S. (1998) *Young Carers in the UK*. London: Carers National Association in association with Young Carers Research Group.

Department for Education and Employment (DfEE) (1994) *The Code of Practice on the Identification and Assessment of Special Educational Needs*. London: HMSO.

Department for Education and Employment (DfEE) (1997) *Making Connections: A Guide for Agencies Helping Young People with Disabilities Make the Transition from School to Adulthood*. London: The Stationery Office.

Department for Education and Employment (DfEE) (1998) *Excellence for All Children, Meeting Special Educational Needs*. London: The Stationery Office.

Department for Education and Employment (DfEE) (1999) *Learning to Succeed*. London: The Stationery Office.

Department for Education and Employment (DfEE) (2000) *Connexions: The Best Start in Life for Every Young Person*. London: The Stationery Office.

Department of Health (DoH) (1991) *Patterns and Outcomes in Child Placement: Messages from Current Research and their Implications*. London: HMSO.

Department of Health (DoH) (1998) *Quality Protects*. London: The Stationery Office.

Department of Health (DoH) (1999) *Working Together to Safeguard Children: A Guide to Inter-agency Working to Safeguard and Promote the Welfare of Children*. London: The Stationery Office.

Department of Health (DoH) (2000a) *Assessing Children in Need and their Families: Practice Guidance*. London: The Stationery Office.

Department of Health (DoH) (2000b) *Quality Protects: Disabled Children Numbers Categories and Families*. London: Department of Health.

Department of Health (DoH), Department for Education and Employment (DfEE) and Home Office (2000) *Framework for Assessing Children in Need and their Families*. London: The Stationery Office.

Disability Alliance (2000) *The Disability Rights Handbook*. London: Disability Alliance Educational and Research Association.

Dobson, B. and Middleton, S. (1998) *Paying to Care: The Cost of Childhood Disability*. York: Joseph Rowntree Foundation/York Publishing Services.

Dyson, S. (1987) *Mental Handicap: Dilemmas of Parent–Professional Relations*. London: Croom Helm.

Dyson, S. (1992) 'Blood relations: educational implications of sickle-cell anaemia and thalassaemia.' In T. Booth, W. Swann, M. Masterson and P. Potts (eds) *Curricula for Diversity in Education*. London: Routledge in association with the Open University.

Dyson, S. (1998) '"Race", ethnicity and haemoglobin disorders.' *Social Science and Medicine, 47*,1, 121–131.

Family Focus (1984) *Swimming Against the Tide: Working for Integration in Education*. Coventry: CRIS.

Ferguson, T. and Kerr, A. (1960) *Handicapped Youth*. Oxford: Oxford University Press.

Flynn, M. and Hirst, M. (1992) *This Year, Next Year, Sometime…? Learning Disability and Adulthood*. London and York: National Development Team and Social Policy Research Unit.

Flynn, M., Cotterill, L., Hayes, L. and Sloper, T. (1998) 'Innovation in supporting adults with learning disabilities.' In C. Robinson and K. Stalker (eds) *Growing Up With Disability*. London: Jessica Kingsley Publishers.

French, S. (1996) 'Out of sight, out of mind: the experience and effects of "special" residential school.' In J. Morris (ed) *Encounters with Strangers: Feminism and Disability*. London: Women's Press.

Glendinning, C. (1983) *Unshared Care: Parents and Their Disabled Children*. London: Routledge and Kegan Paul.

Glendinning, C. (1986) *A Single Door: Social Work with the Families of Disabled Children*. London: Routledge and Kegan Paul.

Goodey, C. (1991) *Living in the Real World: Families Speak about Down's Syndrome*. London: Twenty-One Press.

Gooding, C. (1994) *Disabling Laws, Enabling Acts: Disability Rights in Britain and America.* London: Pluto Press.

Gordon, D., Parker, R. and Loughran F. with Heslop, P. (2000) *Disabled Children in Britain. A Re-analysis of the OPCS Disability Surveys.* London: The Stationery Office.

Gough, D., Li, L. and Wroblewska, A. (1993) *Services for Children with a Motor Impairment and their Families in Scotland.* Glasgow: Public Health Research Unit, University of Glasgow.

Graham, H. (1985) 'Providers, negotiators and mediators: women as the hidden carers.' In E. Lewin and V. Olesen (eds) *Women, Health and Healing Towards a New Perspective.* New York: Tavistock.

Graham, H. (1993) *Hardship and Health in Women's Lives.* Brighton: Harvester Wheatsheaf.

Green, J.M. and Murton, F. E. (1996) 'Diagnosis of Duchenne muscular dystrophy: parents' experiences and satisfaction.' *Child: Care, Health and Development 22,* 113–128.

Gregory, S. (1991) 'Challenging motherhood: mothers and their deaf children.' A. Phoenix, A. Woollett and E. Lloyd (eds) *Motherhood, Meanings and Practices.* London: Sage.

Hall, D. (1997) 'Child development teams: are they fulfilling their purpose?' *Child: Care, Health and Development 23,* 1, 87–99.

Harker, M. and King, N. (1999) *An Ordinary Home: Housing and Support for People with Learning Disabilities.* London: IDEA.

Hasler, F., Campbell, J. and Zarb, G. (1999) *Direct Routes to Independence: A Guide to Local Authority Implementation of Direct Payments.* London: PSI/NCIL.

Haylock, C., Johnson, A. and Harpin, V. (1993) 'Parents' views of community care for children with motor disabilities.' *Child: Care, Health and Development 19,* 209–220.

Hevey, D. (1992) *The Creatures Time Forgot.* London: Routledge.

Hirst, M. (1987) 'Careers of young people with disabilities between ages 15 and 21.' *Disability, Handicap and Society 2,* 61–74.

Hirst, M. and Baldwin, S. (1994) *Unequal Opportunities.* London: HMSO.

Hirst, M., Parker, G. and Cozens, A. (1991) 'Disabled young people.' In M. Oliver (ed) *Social Work: Disabled People and Disabling Environments.* London: Jessica Kingsley Publishers.

Hubert, J. (1993) 'At home and alone: families and young adults with challenging behaviour.' In J. Bornat, C. Pereira, D. Pilgrim and F. Williams (eds) *Community Care: A Reader.* Basingstoke: Macmillan in association with the Open University.

Humphries, S. and Gordon, P. (1992) *Out of Sight: The Experience of Disability 1900–1950.* Plymouth: Northcote House Publishers.

Jackson, S. and Thomas, N. (1999) *On the Move Again.* Barkingside: Barnardo's.

Jigsaw Partnerships (1994) *Strategies for Change. Youthwork with Young Disabled People.* Lancashire: Jigsaw Partnerships and Lancashire County Council Youth and Community Service.

Kagan, C., Lewis, S. and Heaton, P. (1998) *Caring to Work: Accounts of Working Parents of Disabled Children.* London: Family Policy Studies Centre.

Kelly, D. and Warr, B. (1992) *Quality Counts. Achieving Quality in Social Care Services.* London: Whiting and Birch.

Kennedy, M. (1992) 'Not the only way to communicate: a challenge to the voice in child protection work.' *Child Abuse Review 1,* 169–177.

Kennedy, M. (1996) 'The sexual abuse of disabled children.' In J. Morris (ed) *Encounters with Strangers: Feminism and and Disability.* London: The Women's Press.

Kestenbaum, A. (1998) *Work, Rest and Pay: The Deal for Personal Assistance Users.* York: York Publishing Services.

Knight, A. (1998) *Valued or Forgotten? Independent Visitors and Disabled Young People.* London: National Children's Bureau.

Lawton, D. (1989) 'Very young children and the Family Fund.' *Children and Society 3,* 3, 212–225.

Lawton, D. (1998) *Complex Numbers: Families with more than One Disabled Child.* York: Social Policy Research Unit, University of York.

Leighton Project with Simon Grant and Daisy Cole (1998) 'Young people's aspirations.' In C. Robinson and K. Stalker (eds) *Growing up With Disability.* London: Jessica Kingsley Publishers.

Lewis, A. (1995) *Children's Understanding of Disability.* London: Routledge.

Lonsdale, S. (1990) *Women and Disability.* Basingstoke: Macmillan.

Loughran, F., Parker, R. and Gordon, D. (1992) *Children with Disabilities in Communal Establishments: A Further Analysis and Interpretation of the Office of Population Censuses and Surveys Investigation.* Bristol: University of Bristol.

MacHeath, C. (1992) 'Maresa.' In J. Morris (ed) *Alone Together: Voices of Single Mothers.* London: Women's Press.

McConachie, H. (1997) 'The organisation of child disability services.' *Child: Care, Health and Development 23,* 1, 3–9.

McConachie, H., Smyth, D. and Bax, M. (1997) 'Services for children with disabilities in European Countries.' *Developmental Medicine and Child Neurology 39,* supplement 75.

Marchant, R. and Cross, M. (1993) 'Places of safety: institutions, disabled children and abuse.' In *ABCD Reader.* London: NSPCC.

Marchant, R. and Martyn, M. (1999) *Make it Happen: Communication Handbook.* Brighton: Triangle.

Marchant, R. and Page, M. (1992) 'Bridging the gap: investigating the abuse of children with multiple disabilities.' *Child Abuse Review 1,* 179–183.

Marchant, R., Jones, M. and Julyan, A. (1999) *Listening on all Channels: Consulting with Disabled Children.* Brighton: Triangle.

Marsh, P. and Treseliotis, J. (eds) (1993) *Prevention and Reunification in Child Care.* London: Batsford.

Masson, J., Harrison, C. and Pavlovic, A. (1999) *Lost Parents.* Aldershot: Avebury.

Meltzer, H., Smyth, M. and Robus, N. (1989) *Disabled Children: Services, Transport and Education.* OPCS Surveys of Disability in Great Britain, Report 6. London: HMSO.

Middleton, L. (1999) *Disabled Children: Challenging Social Exclusion.* Oxford: Blackwell.

Milham, S., Bullock, R., Hosie, K. and Haak, M. (1986) *Children Lost in Care: The Family Contacts of Children in Care.* Aldershot: Gower.

Minkes, J., Robinson, C. and Weston, C. (1994) 'Consulting the child: interviews with children using residential respite services.' *Disability and Society 9*, 1, 561–571.

Mittler, P. and McConachie, H. (eds) (1983) *Parents, Professionals and Mentally Handicapped People.* London: Croom Helm.

Morgan, D. (1996) *Family Connections.* Cambridge: Polity Press.

Morris, J. (1991) *Pride Against Prejudice.* London: Women's Press.

Morris, J. (1993) *Independent Lives: Community Care and Disabled People.* Basingstoke: Macmillan.

Morris, J. (1995) *Gone Missing? A Research and Policy Review of Disabled Children Living Away from their Families.* London: Who Cares? Trust.

Morris, J. (1998a) *Still Missing? Vol. 1, The Experiences of Disabled Children Living Away from their Families.* London: Who Cares? Trust.

Morris, J. (1998b) *Still Missing? Vol. 2, Disabled Children and the Children Act.* London: Who Cares? Trust.

Morris, J. (1998c) *Accessing Human Rights: Disabled Children and The Children Act.* Barkingside: Barnardo's.

Morris, J. (1998d) *Don't Leave Us Out: Involving Children and Young People with Communication Impairments.* York: York Publishing Services.

Morris, J. (1999a) *Move On Up: Supporting Disabled Children in the Transition to Adulthood.* Barkingside: Barnardo's.

Morris, J. (1999b) *Hurtling into the Void. Transition to Adulthood for Young Disabled People with 'Complex Health and Support Needs.'* Brighton: Pavilion Publishing.

Moss, P. and Penn, H. (1996) *Transforming Nursery Education.* London: Paul Chapman.

Mukherjee, S., Beresford, B. and Sloper, P. (1999) *Unlocking Keyworking: An Analysis and Evaluation of Keyworker Services for Families with Disabled Children.* Bristol: Policy Press/Community Care.

Murray, P. and Penman, J. (1996) *Let Our Children Be.* Sheffield: Parents with Attitude.

National Association of Citizens Advice Bureaux (NACAB) (1994) *Unequal Opportunities: CAB evidence on Discrimination in Employment.* London: National Association of Citizens Advice Bureaux.

Newton, D. (1995) *Inclusion in the Early Years. A Report on the Work of a Partnership between Save the Children and Birmingham Social Services.* Birmingham: Birmingham City Council Social Services Department/Save the Children.

Noyes, J. (1999) *'Voices and Choices': Young people who Use Assisted Ventilation: Their Health and Social Care and Education.* London: The Stationery Office.

Office of Population, Censuses and Surveys (OPCS) (1991) *General Household Survey 1989.* London: HMSO.

Oldman, C. and Beresford, B. (1998) *Homes Unfit for Children: Housing Disabled Children and their Families.* Bristol: Policy Press.

Oliver, M. (1996) *Understanding Disability.* London: Macmillan.

Owen, M. (1992) *Social Justice and Children in Care.* Aldershot: Avebury.

Page, R. and Clark, G. (eds) (1977) *Who Cares? Young People in Care Speak Out.* London: National Children's Bureau.

Parker, R. (1998) 'Counting with care, a re-analysis of OPCS data.' In M. Ball *Disabled Children: Directions for their Future Care.* London: Department of Health (in association with the Social Services Inspectorate and the Council for Disabled Children).

Parker, R., Ward, H., Jackson, S., Aldgate, J. and Wedge, P. (eds) (1991) *Looking After Children: Assessing Outcomes in Child Care.* London: HMSO.

Phillips, R. (1998) 'Disabled children in permanent substitute families.' In C. Robinson and K. Stalker (eds) *Growing Up With Disability.* London: Jessica Kingsley Publishers.

Philp, M. and Duckworth, D. (1982) *Children with Disabilities and their Families: A Review of the Literature.* Windsor: NFER-Nelson.

Powell, M. and Perkins, E. (1984) 'Asian families with a pre-school handicapped child – a study.' *Mental Handicap 12,* 50–52.

Priestley, M. (1998) 'Childhood disability and disabled childhoods: agendas for research.' *Childhood 5,* 2, 207–223.

Pugh, G. (ed) (1992) *Contemporary Issues in the Early Years.* London: Paul Chapman.

Pumpian, I. (1996) 'Foreword.' In D. Sands and M. Wehmeyer (eds) *Self-Determination Across the Lifespan. Independence and Choice for People with Disabilities.* Baltimore: Paul Brookes.

Quine, L. (1993) 'Working with parents: the management of sleep disturbance in children with learning disabilities.' In C. Kiernan (ed) *Research into Practice? Implications of Research on the Challenging Behaviour of People with Learning Disability.* Clevedon: BILD.

Quine, L. and Pahl, J. (1986) 'First diagnosis of severe mental handicap: characteristics of unsatisfactory encounters between doctors and parents.' *Social Science and Medicine 22,* 53–62.

Quinton, D., Rushton, A., Dance, C. and Mayes, D. (1997) 'Contact between children placed away from home and their birth parents: research, issues and evidence.' *Clinical Child Psychology and Psychiatry 2,* 3, 393–413.

Read, J. (1991) 'There was never really any choice: the experience of mothers of disabled children in the United Kingdom.' *Women's Studies International Forum 14,* 6, 561–571.

Read, J. (1996) *A Different Outlook: Services Users' Perspectives on Conductive Education.* Birmingham: Foundation for Conductive Education.

Read, J. (1998) 'Conductive education and the politics of disablement.' *Disability and Society 13,* 2, 279–293.

Read, J. (2000) *Disability, Society and the Family: Listening to Mothers.* Buckingham: Open University Press.

Read, J. and Clements, L. (1999) 'Research, the law and good practice in relation to disabled children: an approach to staff development in a local authority.' *Local Governance 25,* 2, 87–95.

Reisser, R. (1992) 'Internalised oppression, how it seems to me.' In T. Booth, W. Swann, M. Masterson and P. Potts (eds) *Policies for Diversity in Education.* London: Routledge in association with the Open University.

Reisser, R. and Mason, M. (1992) *Disability Equality in the Classroom*. London: Disability Equality in Education.

Residential Forum (1996) *Creating a Home from Home. A Guide to Standards*. London: Residential Forum/National Institute for Social Work.

Riddell, S. (1998) 'The dynamic of transition to adulthood.' In C. Robinson and K. Stalker (eds) *Growing Up With Disability*. London: Jessica Kingsley Publishers.

Robinson, C. (1996) 'Breaks for disabled children.' In K. Stalker (ed) *Developments in Short-term Care. Breaks and Opportunities*. London: Jessica Kingsley Publishers.

Robinson, C. and Jackson, P. (1999) *Children's Hospices: A Lifeline for Families?* London: National Children's Bureau.

Robinson, C. and Stalker, K. (1993) *Out of Touch: non-users of respite care services*. Bristol: Norah Fry Research Centre.

Rowe, J. and Lambert, L. (1973) *Children Who Wait: A Study of Children Needing Substitute Families*. London: Association of British Adoption Agencies.

Russell, P. (1988) 'Community approaches to serving children and their families.' In D. Towell (ed) *An Ordinary Life in Practice*. London: King Edward's Hospital Fund for London.

Russell, P. (1991) 'Working with children with physical disabilities and their families – the social work role.' In M. Oliver (ed) *Social Work Disabled People and Disabling Environments*. London: Jessica Kingsley Publishers.

Russell, P. (1995) *Positive Choices: Services for Disabled Children Living Away from Home*. London: Council for Disabled Children.

Russell, P. (1996) 'Short-term care: parental perspectives.' In K. Stalker (ed) *Developments in Short-Term Care*. London: Jessica Kingsley Publishers.

Russell, P. (1998) *Having A Say: Disabled Children and Effective Partnership in Decision Making, Section 1: The Report*. London: Council For Disabled Children.

Scope (1996) *Right from the Start*. London: Scope.

SCOVO (1989a) *Parents Deserve Better*. Cardiff: SCOVO.

SCOVO (1989b) *Practical Steps to Better Practice. Better Early Counselling in Wales*. Cardiff: SCOVO.

Sebba, J. and Sachdev, D. (1997) *What Works in Inclusive Education?* Barkingside: Barnardo's.

Sellick, C. and Thoburn, J. (1996) *What Works in Family Placement?* Barkingside: Barnardo's.

Shah, R. (1992) *The Silent Minority: Children with Disabilities in Asian Families*. London: National Children's Bureau.

Shah, R. (1997) 'Services for Asian families and children with disabilities.' *Child: Care, Health and Development 23*, 1, 41–46.

Shaw, L. (1998) 'Children's experiences of school.' In C. Robinson and K. Stalker (eds) *Growing Up With Disability*. London: Jessica Kingsley Publishers.

Shaw, M., Dorling, D., Gordon, D. and Davey Smith, G. (1999) *The Widening Gap: Health Inequalities and Policy in Britain*. Bristol: Policy Press.

Sheik, S. (1986) 'An Asian mothers' self-help group.' In S. Ahmed, J. Cheetham and J. Small (eds) *Social Work with Black Children and their Families*. London: Batsford.

Simons, K. (1998) *Home, Work and Exclusion: The Social Policy Implications of Supported Living and Employment for People with Learning Disabilities*. York: York Publishing Services.

Sloper, P. and Turner, S. (1992) 'Service needs of families of children with severe physical disability.' *Child: Care Health and Development 18*, 259–282.

Sloper, P., Knussen, C. Turner, S. and Cunningham, C. (1991) 'Factors related to stress and satisfaction with life in families of children with Down's syndrome.' *Journal of Child Psychology and Psychiatry 32*, 655–676.

Sloper, P. and Turner, S. (1993) 'Determinants of parental satisfaction with disclosure of disability.' *Developmental Medicine and Child Neurology 35*, 816–825.

Sloper, P., Turner, S., Knussen, C. and Cunningham, C. (1990) 'Social life of school children with Down's syndrome.' *Child: Care, Health and Development 16*, 235–251.

Smith, A. (1994) 'A damaging experience: black disabled children and educational and social services provision.' In N. Begum, M. Hill and A. Stevens (eds) *Reflections: Views of Black Disabled People on their Lives and Community Care*. London: CCETSW.

Smyth, M. and Robus, N. (1989) *The Financial Circumstances of Families with Disabled Children Living in Private Households*. OPCS Surveys of Disability in Great Britain, Report 5. London: HMSO.

Social Services Inspectorate (1994) *Services to Disabled Children and their Families: Report of the National Inspection of Services to Disabled Children and their Families*. London: Department of Health.

Social Services Inspectorate (1995a) *Growing Up and Moving On: Report of an SSI Project on Transition Services for Disabled Young People*. London: Department of Health.

Social Services Inspectorate (1995b) *Opportunities or Knocks: National Inspection of Recreation and Leisure in Day Services for People with Learning Disabilities*. London: Department of Health.

Social Services Inspectorate (1997) *Moving on Towards Independence: Second Report on Transition Services for Disabled Young People*. London: Department of Health.

Social Services Inspectorate (1998) *Removing Barriers for Disabled Children: Inspection of Services to Disabled Children and Their Families*. London: Department of Health.

Spastics Society (1992) *A Hard Act to Follow*. London: Spastics Society.

Stalker, K. (1991) *Share the Care: An Evaluation of Family Based Respite Care Service*. London: Jessica Kingsley Publishers.

Stalker, K. (1996) 'Principles, policy and practice in short-term care.' In K. Stalker (ed) *Developments in Short-term Care. Breaks and Opportunities*. London: Jessica Kingsley Publishers.

Stallard, B. and Lenton, S. (1992) 'How satisfied are parents of pre-school children who have special needs with the services they have received?' *Child: Care, Health and Development 18*, 197–205.

Statham, J. (1996) *Young Children in Wales: An Evaluation of the Implementation of The Children Act 1989 on Day Care Services*. London: Thomas Coram Research Institute.

Statham, J. and Read, J. (1998) 'The pre-school years.' In C. Robinson and K. Stalker (eds) *Growing up With Disability.* London: Jessica Kingsley Publishers.

Stein, M. (1997) *What Works in Leaving Care?* Barkingside: Barnardo's.

Strong, P. (1979) *The Ceremonial Order of the Clinic, Doctors and Medical Bureaucracies.* London: Routledge and Kegan Paul.

Swann, W. (1987) 'Statements of intent: an assessment of reality.' In T. Booth and W. Swann (1987) *Including Pupils with Disabilities.* Milton Keynes: Open University Press.

Thoburn, J. (1990) *Success and Failure in Permanent Family Placement.* Aldershot: Gower Avebury.

Thoburn, J. (1994) *Child Placement: Principles and Practice.* Aldershot: Arena.

Thomas, C. (1999) *Female Forms. Experiencing and Understanding Disability.* Buckingham: Open University Press.

Thompson, N. (1993) *Anti-discriminatory Practice.* London: Macmillan.

Thompson, G., Ward, K. and Wishard, J. (1995) 'The transition to adulthood for children with Down's Syndrome.' *Disability and Society 10,* 325–340.

Thornton, P., Sainsbury, R. and Barnes, H. (1997) *Helping Disabled People to Work: A Cross-National Study of Social Security and Employment Provisions. A Report for the Social Security Advisory Committee.* London: The Stationery Office.

Townsley, R. and Robinson, C. (2000) *Food for Thought.* Bristol: Norah Fry Research Centre, University of Bristol.

Tozer, R. (1999) *At the Double: Supporting Families with Two or More Disabled Children.* London: National Children's Bureau.

Traustadottir, R. (1991) 'Mothers who care: gender, disability and family life.' *Journal of Family Issues 12,* 2, 211–228.

Twigg, J. and Atkin, K. (1994) *Carers Perceived Policy and Practice in Informal Care.* Buckingham: Open University Press.

Utting, W. (1991) *Children in the Public Care.* London: HMSO.

Utting, W. (1997) *People Like Us: The Report of the Review of the Safeguards for Children Living Away from Home.* London: The Stationery Office.

Voice for the Child in Care (1998) *Shout to be Heard: Stories from Young People in Care about Getting Heard and Using Advocates.* London: Voice for the Child in Care.

Walker, A. (1982) *Unqualified and Underemployed. Handicapped Young People in the Labour Market.* London: Macmillan.

Ward, L. (1997) *Seen and Heard: Involving Disabled Children and Young People in Research and Development Projects.* York: Joseph Rowntree Foundation.

Warner, N. (1992) *Choosing with Care.* London: HMSO.

Warnock Committee (1978) *The Report of the Committee of Enquiry into the Education of Handicapped Children and Young People.* Cmnd 7212. London: HMSO.

Westcott, H. (1991) *Institutional Abuse of Children – From Research to Policy: A Review.* London: NSPCC.

Westcott, H. (1993) *Abuse of Children and Adults with Disabilities.* London: NSPCC.

Westcott, H (1998) 'Disabled children and child protection.' In C. Robinson and K. Stalker (eds) *Growing Up With Disability*. London: Jessica Kingsley Publishers.

Who Cares? Trust (1993) *Not Just A Name*. London: National Consumer Council.

Williams, E. (1992) 'One hundred thousand families to support.' *Search 13*, September.

Williams, F. (1993) 'Women and community.' In J. Bornat, C. Pereira, D. Pilgrim and F. Williams (eds) *Community Care: A Reader*. Basingstoke: Macmillan.

Williams, G. (1996) 'Representing disabilities: some questions of phenomenology and politics.' In C. Barnes and G. Mercer (eds) *Exploring the Divide: Illness and Disability*. Leeds: Disability Press.

Wishart, J., MacLeod, H. and Rowan, C. (1993) '"Parent" evaluations of pre-school services for children with Down's syndrome in two Scottish regions.' *Child: Care, Health and Development 19*, 1–23.

Wynne Oakley, M. and Masson, J. (2000) *Official Friends and Friendly Officials*. London: NSPCC.

Yerbury, M. (1997) 'Issues in multidisciplinary teamwork for children with disabilities.' *Child: Care, Health and Development 23*, 1, 77–86.

Younghusband, E., Birchall, D., Davie, R. and Kellmer Pringle M. (1970) *Living with Handicap*. London: National Children's Bureau.

Local authority complaints materials

Local authorities must have fair and efficient complaints procedures. Although the law clearly defines the shape and content of the complaints system social services departments must operate, this is not the case in relation to complaints about other departments such as housing or education. Accordingly we outline the social services procedures first and then consider the requirements for other departments.

Although complaints concerning community care and other social services functions are governed by different regulations to those which relate to services under the Children Act 1989,[1] the two systems are very similar and accordingly are considered 'as one' below. Guidance concerning general complaints procedures has been issued as *The Right To Complain* (1991)[2] and in relation to complaints under the Children Act 1989, *The Children Act 1989: Guidance and Regulations, Volume 3, Family Placements* paras. 10.33 et seq.[3]

Who can complain?

Complaints may be made by anyone for whom the authority has a power or duty to provide a service as well as by the parents of the disabled child.

The structure of the complaints system

Social services departments must appoint an officer who is responsible for co-ordinating all aspects of the complaints procedures and in practice all social services complaints procedures have three distinct stages:

- the informal or problem-solving stage
- the formal or registration stage
- the review stage.

The Children Act guidance[4] stresses that 'every effort should be made to work with local disability groups to ensure that the procedures are accessible, useable and effective when dealing with issues relating to disabilities'.

The informal or problem-solving stage

Direction 5(1) states that where a local authority receives representations from any complainant, it must attempt to resolve the matter informally. At this stage there is no requirement that the complaint be in writing (policy guidance, para. 6.17). *The Right to Complain*[5] explains:

> Normal good practice should sort out, to the user's satisfaction, the queries and grumbles which are part of a social work department's daily workload. Stage 1 then alerts the relevant worker, supervisor or manager to the fact that there is a more fundamental problem, as perceived by the user or her or his representative. It gives users the right to decide whether or not to pursue the issue and ensures that it is taken seriously and not dismissed by busy staff. The fact, however, that this stage is not 'formal' does not mean that it is 'casual'.[6]

The first stage of the complaints process is simply an opportunity for the local authority to attempt 'problem-solving, conciliation and negotiation'. It is not subject to any statutory timescale, although in practice many authorities specify in their local procedures maximum periods for this phase (often in the region of one to four weeks).

Local authorities should provide complainants with a simple explanation as to how the complaints process works and the relevant timescales. The provision of a leaflet with this information does not obviate the need to advise complainants (in correspondence at the appropriate times) of their rights at subsequent stages (i.e. of the right to seek a panel hearing if dissatisfied with the outcome of the formal stage).

Local authorities will need to ensure that advocacy assistance is available to disabled children and their parents, in appropriate cases. In particular the guidance notes[7] that 'many children and young people with sensory or learning disabilities will have more complex communication needs that can be met by the provision of an interpreter'.

The formal stage

This stage involves the formal registration of the complaint. A complainant is entitled to go straight to this stage (omitting the informal stage) if s/he so wishes.

At the formal stage, complaints should be put in writing. A precedent complaints letter is to be found in Appendix 8. *The Right to Complain* (para. 4.10) explains:

> Many people will need support and advice from someone they trust either from within or outside the department. Some people will need help in writing and sometimes formulating a complaint. Those who give help in writing down the complaint must ensure that it fully reflects what the complainant wishes to say and ask the complainant to sign it.

The mere fact that a complaint has progressed to the formal stage does not absolve the authority from its duty to try and resolve the problem.[8]

Social services departments must consider the complaint and then formulate a response within 28 days of its receipt. If for any reason it is not possible to comply with the 28-day period, the authority must (within that period) explain to the complainant why this is so and when the response will be given. In any event, the response must be forthcoming within three months.

Authorities may, if the need arises, appoint an independent person[9] at this stage to oversee the investigation. If the complaint concerns services under the Children Act 1989, they must appoint such an independent person.[10] When such an independent person is appointed his/her role is, as stated, to 'oversee the investigation'. This means that s/he may accompany the local authority complaints investigator and also interview complainants separately. Generally independent persons file separate reports to those filed by the local authority investigator.

On occasions the investigation may need to call upon specialist outsiders:

> In some instances complaints may relate to inappropriate services for children with disabilities, for example where there are poor access facilities, unsuitable furnishings or equipment or where children are unnecessarily excluded from the full range of activities appropriate to their ages, interests and general ability. In these instances expert advice on the particular disability should be identified e.g. from within the SSD, from a [health authority] or from a voluntary organisation and the SSD's existing arrangements for placement reassessed to avoid similar difficulties in the future.[11]

At the conclusion of its investigation, the local authority must notify the complainant in writing of the result of its investigation. If the complaint has been made by a parent or carer on behalf of a disabled child, then notification must also be sent to the child (unless the authority considers that s/he is not able to understand). Complainants should generally be given the opportunity of commenting upon a draft of the investigators' report[12] (particularly in relation to any contra-allegations that may have been made)[13] prior to the final report being produced.

The review stage

The disabled child or his/her parents/carers may (if dissatisfied), within 28 days of receiving the decision, request that the complaint be referred to a panel for review. Such a request must be made in writing. In such cases the local authority is required to convene a panel hearing within 28 days of receipt of the request. The panel comprises three persons, an independent chairperson plus two wing members, one of whom is generally a social services officer and the other a local authority councillor.

Panel hearings

Panel hearings are held in private and conducted as informally as possible. The panel hearing must follow the rules of natural justice, although the chairperson is entitled to set reasonable time limits on the oral submissions to be made by the parties, provided these are used as 'guidelines rather than guillotines'.[14]

The local government ombudsman has made a number of criticisms about the conduct of panel hearings, including:

- a failure to ensure that key witnesses attended the panel hearing[15]

- the panel interviewing witnesses at an adjourned hearing, in the absence of the complainant[16]

- the failure of the local authority to ensure that the panel had clerical assistance: 'the job entrusted to Panels is complex and stressful enough and they need adequate administrative support to be able to perform efficiently and effectively'[17]

- the introduction of new material by the local authority, at the hearing[18]

- the need for independent advocates to assist complainants when the complaint is serious or particularly distressing (for instance, involving bereavement)[19]

- the presence of a senior social services officer throughout a panel hearing as this may have 'inhibited junior staff from saying all they felt to be pertinent'[20]

- the interviewing of several members of staff, at different levels of seniority, simultaneously.[21]

Within 24 hours of the review hearing, the panel must reach a decision in writing and forward its recommendations (and reasons) to the local authority and the complainant (i.e. the disabled child or his/her parents/carers). The local authority then has 28 days to decide what action should be taken.

While a local authority is not bound to accept a panel's recommendation, it will in practice have to have extremely cogent reasons for deciding differently.

Sedley J held in *R v Islington LBC ex p Rixon*[22] 'a failure to comply with a review panel's recommendations is not by itself a breach of law; but the greater the departure, the greater the need for cogent articulated reasons if the court is not to infer that the panel's recommendations have been overlooked'.

Local authority complaints not covered by the specific social services rules

Education complaints

With the exception of complaints concerning the national curriculum,[23] there is no statutory complaints process for parental/student disputes with the LEA or school governors.

In 1989 the Department of Education issued guidance on the need for complaints procedures (Circular 1/89) and as a consequence most local authorities have adopted a model complaints code formulated jointly by the Associations of Metropolitan and County Councils. This involves a phased response, commencing at the first stage with local resolution via teacher and parent, followed by formal complaint to the governors and thence to the LEA. The LEA stage provides for a 'designated officer' to investigate and for the results of the investigation to be considered by a panel of three LEA members.

Although LEAs are obliged to provide parents/students with information concerning their complaints process, the 'model' procedure is far from perfect. It contains no time limits for the completion of each stage and the final LEA stage has no 'independent' element. Accordingly, where disputes arise it is generally prudent to stress in the initial letter of complaint that:

- the investigation (at each stage) must occur with expedition
- the investigation must be impartial
- the parent/student must have the opportunity of responding to any contra-allegations made by the school/LEA
- throughout the parent/student must be kept fully informed, particularly if any delay occurs (in which case an explanation for this must be provided)
- given the absence of clear statutory guidance on the process, it is expected that the investigation will comply with the good practice guidance issued by the ombudsman.

Other local authority complaints

Although, as noted, local authority complaints which concern non-social services matters are not governed by strict statutory procedures, the ombudsman has nevertheless emphasised that equally clear local procedures must also be in place to deal with such complaints. Thus in a complaint against Nottingham County Council she noted that, although the complainant was not a qualifying individual, it was nevertheless important that her 'complaints were still given full and proper consideration in a way which equated to the standard of service a complaint would have received under the council's formal complaints procedure'.[24]

The local ombudsman in pursuance of this policy has issued guidance to local authorities on how such complaints procedures should be operated;[25] in essence adopting many of the principles present in the social services statutory procedures.

Notes

1   The former are regulated by the Local Authority Social Services (Complaints Procedure) Order 1990 (which applies to persons aged 18 or over) and the latter by the Representations Procedure (Children) Regulations 1991.

2   (1991) Department of Health, London.

3   *Children Act 1989 Guidance Vol.3, Family Placements* (HMSO, London, 1991).

4   *Children Act 1989: Guidance and Regulations, Vol. 6, Children With Disabilities* (HMSO, London, 1991), para. 14.4.

5   Para. 4.3.

6   Ibid., para. 4.2–3.

7   *Children Act 1989: Guidance and Regulations, Vol. 6, Children With Disabilities* (HMSO, London, 1991), para. 14.7.

8   Local Government Ombudsman Complaint against Liverpool (1999) 98/C/3591.

9   *The Right to Complain*, para. 4.12.

10   See Representations Procedure (Children) Regulations 1991 SI No. 894 regs 5 and 6 and *The Children Act 1989: Guidance and Regulations, Vol. 3*, Family Placements (HMSO, London, 1991), paras. 10.33 et seq.

11   *Children Act 1989: Guidance and Regulations, Vol. 6, Children With Disabilities* (London, HMSO, 1991), para. 14.8.

12   Local Government Ombudsman Complaint No. 97/C/4618 against Cheshire (1999).

13   Local Government Ombudsman Report No. 98/C/1294 against Calderdale MBC.

14   Ibid.

15   Local Government Ombudsman Complaint No. 97/B/2441 against Hampshire (1999).

16   Ibid.

17   Ibid.

18   Local Government Ombudsman Complaint No. 96/B/4438 against Devon (1998); although it will amount to serious maladministration for the local authority to suggest that evidence put forward by a complainant at a panel hearing is 'new material' when it is not, Local Government Ombudsman Complaint No. 97/C/1614 against Bury MBC (1999).

19   Local Government Ombudsman Complaint No. 97/C/4618 against Cheshire (1999).

20   Ibid.

21   Ibid.

22   *The Times* 17 April 1996. QBD. (1996) 1 CCLR 119.

23   Curriculum/information disputes are subject to the provisions of s.409 Education Act 1996 (and if the local resolution of such a complaint fails, provision exists for them to be made directly to the Secretary of State under ss.496–7 of the 1996 Act).

24   Report No. 94/C/2959 against Nottingham City Council, 28 November 1994. See also Local Government Ombudsman Complaint No. 97/C/1614 against Bury MBC (1999), where the Ombusdsman accepted that part of the complaint lay outside the statutory complaints process but

nevertheless warranted investigation, and commented, 'It is hard to identify any aspect of the Council's handling of Mr Redfern's complaints which was in the proper manner or in full accordance with the statutory complaints procedure and/or the Council's own written complaints procedure.'

25   Good Practice 1: 'Devising a Complaints System'. Local Government Ombudsman, February 1992.

Social services materials

The social services assessment and care planning obligations

Assessments under the Children Act 1989[1]

While there is no specific duty to assess under the Children Act 1989 equivalent to that found in NHS and Community Care Act 1990 (considered below), nevertheless there is a power to assess (which is strongly reinforced by guidance). In most cases disabled children will be entitled to a community care assessment under the NHS and Community Care Act 1990 and also by other authorities (such as the education department under the Special Educational Needs provisions). In order to avoid duplications, the Children Act provides that these various assessments can be combined,[2] stating that local authorities may, at the same time as assessing under the Children Act 1989, also carry out an assessment under:

• the Chronically Sick and Disabled Persons Act 1970
• Part IV of the Education Act 1996
• the Disabled Persons (SCR) Act 1986
• any other enactment.

In discharging these various functions, social services departments must be sensitive to the needs and requirements of ethnic minority families, and in particular ensure that assessments take into account individual circumstances and are not based on a stereotypical view of what may be required.[3]

The Children Act 1989 Guidance and Regulations: Vol. 2, Family Support amplifies what is required in such assessments:

2.7 Good practice requires that the assessment of need should be undertaken in an open way and should involve those caring for the child, the child and other significant persons. Families with a child in need, whether the need results from family difficulties or the child's circumstances, have the right to receive sympathetic support and sensitive intervention in their family's life.

2.8 In making an assessment, the local authority should take account of the particular needs of the child – that is in relation to health, development, disability, education, religious persuasion, racial origin, cultural and linguistic background, the degree (if any) to which these needs are being met by existing services to the family or the child and which agencies' services are best suited to the child's needs.

The Children Act guidance specifically concerned with disabled children (vol. 6) provides further detail, as follows:

5.1. SSDs will need to develop clear assessment procedures for children in need within agreed criteria which take account of the child's and family's needs and preferences, racial and ethnic origins, their culture, religion and any special needs relating to the circumstances of individual families.

5.2. In many cases children with disabilities will need continuing services throughout their lives. It will therefore be particularly important that for these children the assessment process takes a longer perspective than is usual or necessary for children without disabilities, who will usually cease to have a need for services after reaching adulthood.

5.3. The requirements of children with disabilities may need to be met from a number of sources. In conducting assessments and managing the care provided, SSDs will need to ensure that all necessary expertise is marshalled and that all those providing services are involved from both within and beyond the SSD. The outcome of assessment should be a holistic and realistic picture of the individual and family being assessed, which takes into account their strengths and capacities as well as any difficulties and which acknowledges the need to make provision appropriate to the family's cultural background and their expressed views and preferences.

Assessment under the Community Care Legislation[4]

While the Children Act 1989 requires local authorities to make general provision for the needs of disabled children, certain community care statutes are more specific in their requirement that help be provided; the most important of these statutes being the Chronically Sick and Disabled Persons Act 1970[5] (considered below). Except in cases of emergency, local authorities cannot provide services under this statute, unless they have first carried out a community care assessment under s.47 NHS and Community Care Act 1990.

The law does not require the local authority to carry out a separate community care assessment to that under the Children Act. Good practice dictates that these assessments be combined to ensure that a comprehensive picture is obtained, not only of the needs of the disabled child and his/her family, but also of the services which may be provided to meet those needs.

Care planning[6]

Government guidance[7] has characterised the community care assessment process as comprising three distinct processes:

1.   Assessment of the users' circumstances.

2.   Preparation of a care package.

3.   Implementation and monitoring.

Assessment of the users' circumstances

What is required at this stage is that the social services department, in an open-minded, 'unblinkered' way, gathers as much information as necessary in order to establish what are the reasonable needs of the disabled child or his/her carers.

Preparation of a care package

Having accumulated information about the disabled person, the social worker then decides which of the various 'needs' are sufficiently substantial to warrant the provision of assistance or services. In relation to these, the obligation is to design a 'care package' in agreement with the users' carers and relevant agencies to meet these identified needs.[8]

If the decision is that services need not be provided, then the authority must give a clear explanation as to the reasons for this (so that the disabled person or carer can invoke the complaints process if necessary (see p.222 for an outline of the complaints procedures).

Implementation and monitoring

The social services department then makes arrangements to ensure that the necessary services are available and monitors the 'care plan'; reviews its effectiveness (both for users and carers) and makes any necessary revision of service provision.

Thus the assessment may reveal that the disabled child has many needs: for instance, help getting up in the morning; help in the bathroom; help dressing and feeding; help being moved from place to place within the house; a need for social interaction with his or her peer group; a need for short breaks from the home (sometimes called respite care), and so on. The local authority then has to decide which of these needs are necessary to meet, and to spell out in the 'care plan' how this is to occur. The care plan may, for instance, state that in general the parents provide the necessary help first thing in the morning (getting up, dressing, feeding and in the bathroom). It will then list which other needs are to be met by the parents and other family carers (provided they are 'willing and able') and those needs which will be met by outside carers, for instance, a placement at a day centre, provision of a cooked meal during the day, home help, respite care, etc. (in each case specifying precisely who is to do what and when and where, etc.).

The plan will also specify other relevant matters, such as the provision of special equipment (i.e. a hoist, a wheelchair, etc.) or adaptations to the home, as well as the date of the next review.[9]

Community care assessments are about constructing a service designed to meet the disabled person's needs rather than trying to force him or her into an existing service. This aim is expressed in the following terms by the official guidance:[10]

> It is easy to slip out of thinking 'what does this person need?' into 'what have we got that he/she could have?' The focus on need is most clearly achieved where practitioners responsible for assessment do not also carry responsibility for the delivery or management of services arising from that assessment (at para. 22 of the guide's summary).[11]

Services for disabled children

Services for disabled children under the Children Act 1989 [12]

As we note on p.63 above, once the 'needs' of a disabled child have been identified then s.17 Children Act 1989 specifies that the social services department must ensure that a range of support services is available in order to safeguard and promote his or her welfare. The basic aim of such services is 'to promote the upbringing of such children by their families'.

The services that can be provided under the Children Act are almost unlimited, including, by s.17(6), the giving of 'assistance in kind or, in exceptional circumstances, in cash'.

Schedule 2 Part I of the Act deals further with the provision of services for children in need. It gives an illustration of the type of services which may be provided, but it is clear that this list is not exhaustive:

(a) advice, guidance and counselling;

(b) occupational, social, cultural, or recreational activities;

(c) home help (which may include laundry facilities);

(d) facilities for, or assistance with, travelling to and from home for the purpose of taking advantage of any other service provided under this Act or of any similar service;

(e) assistance to enable the child concerned and his family to have a holiday.

As a result of an amendment to the 1989 Act (by the Carers and Disabled Children Act 2000) social services are also specifically entitled to make the following services available:

- instead of providing services for a disabled child, to make to the parent carer (or a disabled child aged 16–17) a direct payment in lieu of those services to enable the parent to arrange for the provision of those services rather than rely on direct service provision from the local authorities (section 17A Children Act);

- in similar fashion, section 17B provides for regulations to be made which will enable local authorities to issue to parent carers vouchers which enable them to arrange for someone to care for their disabled child while they take a short break from their caring responsibilities.

The guidance to the Children Act (para. 2.11, *Volume 2: Family Support*) summarises the breadth of powers available to social services authorities in such cases:

This general duty is supported by other specific duties and powers such as the facilitation of 'the provision by others, including in particular voluntary organisations of services' (section 17(5) and Schedule 2). These provisions encourage SSDs to provide day and domiciliary services, guidance and counselling, respite care and a range of other services as a means of supporting children in need (including children with disabilities) within their families. The Act recognises that sometimes a child can only be helped by providing services for other members of his family (section 17(3)) 'if it [the service] is provided with a view to safeguarding or promoting the child's welfare'. ... The SSD may make such arrangements as they see fit for any person to provide services and support 'may include giving assistance in kind, or in exceptional circumstances in cash' (section 17(6)). However, where it is the SSD's view that a child's welfare is adequately provided for and no unmet need exists, they need not act.

The duties owed to disabled children are underwritten by a requirement (in para. 6 of Part 1 of Schedule 2 to the Act) that authorities provide services designed to minimise the effect on disabled children within their area of their disabilities and to give such children the opportunity to lead lives which are as normal as possible.

Respite/short-break care[13]

Respite or 'short-break' care is, as we have noted above, a highly valued service by carers and (where the service provides appropriate stimulation and support) by disabled children.

While we have considered (p.167) the obligations of the NHS to provide such a service, the duty will more commonly be that of the social services department. In order to obtain the social services support for such a service there must first be an assessment which concludes that respite care should be provided as part of the care plan.

If the assessment fails to determine that respite care is required (or if there is a dispute as to the amount or quality of that care), then the assessment could be challenged through the complaints process (see Appendix 2).

As we have noted above once the local authority has assessed the service as being required, it must make it available and cannot use financial resource constraints as a reason for not providing the service. If it seeks to use this reason, then again the complaints process should be invoked.

Even if the local authority constraint concerns the lack of suitable facilities (rather than financial resources), that alone is not itself a satisfactory reason for failing to provide the care. In such cases the local authority must make urgent and determined efforts to find a suitable provider. This may involve searching outside its area, discussing with voluntary and private sector providers the possibility of creating a purpose-made service or the local authority itself (possibly in conjunction with the health authority or primary care trust) providing the service via a new 'in-house' initiative. In short, the local authority must take the matter seriously and, by purposefully pursuing a systematic search, demonstrate that the assessed need will be met as soon as is reasonably practicable.

Services under the Community Care legislation[14]

Services for disabled children are available not only under the Children Act 1989, but also under s.2 Chronically Sick and Disabled Persons Act 1970.[15] In addition, and to very limited degree, services are also available under Schedule 8 NHS Act 1977 (in relation to laundry assistance, which is considered at the end of this section).

Services under s.2 Chronically Sick and Disabled Persons Act 1970 [16]

The interplay between this Act and the Children Act 1989 was considered in *R v Bexley LBC ex p. B* [1995],[17] a case which concerned the provision of care services for a severely disabled boy of ten. The council argued that his home care services were being provided under the Children Act 1989 rather than under the 1970 Act. The Court did not agree, stating:

The relationship between the Children Act 1989 and the Chronically Sick and Disabled Persons Act 1970 is an uneasy one... Authorities are, however, under an obligation to make provision under the Chronically Sick and Disabled Persons Act 1970 whenever they are satisfied that the relevant conditions have been met ... In the present case...it seems to me that the respondents were satisfied that it was necessary to provide practical assistance for him in the house in order to meet his needs. [The social worker] clearly decided that to expect his mother to go on meeting those needs without further help would be to the applicant's disadvantage. He had a need for full time care of a quality which one person could not be expected to continue to provide in the way the applicant's mother was then providing it. The only conclusion which a reasonable Authority could reach in that situation was that it was under a duty pursuant to section 2(1) of the Chronically Sick and Disabled Persons Act 1970 to provide practical assistance in his home. The respondents, in so far as they considered that they were simply exercising their general duties pursuant to the Children Act 1989 were wrong, and in breach of their duty under the Chronically Sick and Disabled Persons Act 1970.

Once a social services authority has carried out an assessment of the needs of a disabled person and decided that the provision of services under s.2 is necessary in order to meet that person's needs, then the authority is under an absolute duty to provide that service. The services detailed in s.2 are:

1. *Practical assistance in the home*: this includes services primarily concerned with the maintenance of the home (i.e. house cleaning, ironing, decorating, etc.) and those concerned with the personal care of the disabled person (i.e. help with getting out of and into bed, dressing, cooking, laundry etc.).[18] While a rigid policy of not providing the former services under s.2 would amount to a breach of statutory duty, it is the case that personal care will generally be of higher priority in any system of eligibility criteria.

2. *The provision of a wireless, TV, library, etc.*: the service described consists of the social services authority actually providing (or helping with the acquisition of) equipment to satisfy a recreational need; it clearly includes such an item as a personal computer, hi-fi system, etc.

3. *Provision of recreational / educational facilities*: this covers two separate services:

   - recreational facilities – included within this provision are traditional day centres as well as such recreational activities as outings and so on
   - educational facilities – the educational service required in this case may be either home based or otherwise and may include funding of the personal care requirements of students so as to enable them to

pursue their studies (even if those studies are undertaken outside the local authority's area).[19]

4.   *Travel and other assistance:* this will cover the provision of travel to and from a day centre or other recreational activity.

5.   *Home adaptations/ disabled facilities:* social services departments are obliged to provide assistance to enable necessary adaptations to be carried out in the disabled child's home and to provide any 'additional facilities designed to secure his greater safety, comfort or convenience'. Grant assistance (known as 'disabled facilities grants') may also be available to cover the cost of significant home adaptations (see p.262):

- adaptations – home adaptations may concern such matters as stair lifts, ground floor extensions, doorway widening, ramps, wheel chair accessible showers and so on. Where such work is required the local authority will arrange for a detailed assessment to be carried out (frequently by an Occupational Therapist), the test being whether the works are necessary in order to meet the needs of the disabled child (by securing his or her greater safety, comfort or convenience). If the work is needed, then an application can be made for grant assistance, by way of a 'disabled facilities grant'.

- additional facilities – social services departments are obliged to provide disabled children with those 'additional facilities' which are needed in order to secure the child's greater safety, comfort or convenience. This includes all manner of fittings and gadgets such as handrails, alarm systems, hoists, movable baths, adapted switches and handles, and so on. Guidance[20] on the nature of this duty states:

Equipment which can be installed and removed with little or no structural modification to the dwelling should usually be considered the responsibility of the [social services] authority. However, items such as stair lifts and through-floor lifts, which are designed to facilitate access into or around the dwelling would, in the view of the Secretaries of State, be eligible for disabled facilities grant. With items such as electric hoists, it is suggested that any structural modification of the property – such as strengthened joists or modified lintels – could be grant aidable under the disabled facilities grant, but that the hoisting equipment itself should be the responsibility of the [social services] authority. [Social services] authorities can, under s17 of the HASSASSA Act, charge for the provision of equipment. If the [social services] authority choose to make only a revenue charge (for example to cover maintenance), or not to charge at all, they would retain ownership of the equipment, and be able if they so wished to re-use it in another property if no longer required by the original recipient. [Social services] authorities are encouraged to make maximum use of their opportunities to recover and re-use equipment such as stairlifts, and to foster local arrangements for direct provision of such equipment where this can be done effectively and economically.

6.   *Holidays*: the 1970 Act requires local authorities to assist disabled children to take holidays (where the authority consider this necessary). This duty is in addition to the power enjoyed by social services departments under the Children Act (noted above) although strictly speaking the duty under the 1970 Act only extends to the disabled child and any carer essential to enable the holiday to take place,[21] whereas under the Children Act the local authority power enables a holiday to be provided for the whole family.

7.   *Meals*: the duty under the 1970 Act to provide disabled children with meals (when considered necessary by the social services department) covers the provision of meals within their own homes as well as at day centres, etc.

8.   *Telephone and ancillary equipment*: although reference in the Act to the provision of a telephone and other ancilliary equipment may in general be of more relevance to the needs of disabled adults, the duty extends to other equipment such as amplifiers/inductive couples for personal hearing aids and visual transmission machines such as minicom, fax and possibly modems for computer e-mail transmission, etc.

Laundry assistance under Schedule 8 NHS Act 1977

Schedule 8 of the 1977 Act enables social services authorities to provide a laundry service for households where such help is required owing to the presence of (among others) a person who is 'handicapped as a result of having suffered from illness or by congenital deformity'. There is an overlap here with the power of the health services (in limited situations) to provide laundry assistance (see p.100).

Social Services' responsibilities towards carers

The Carers (Recognition and Services) Act 1995

The 1995 Act provides recognition for carers by requiring the social services department (if so requested) to carry out a separate assessment of the carer when it is assessing the disabled child's needs. The carer can be of any age (i.e. adult or child) and there may of course be more than one carer in any particular household.

In order to qualify for such an assessment the carer must be providing (or intending to provide) a substantial amount of care on a regular basis.[22] The guidance accepts that the Act essentially entitles all parents of disabled children to a Carers Act assessment when their child is also being assessed,[23] since they all provide 'substantial and regular care'. This will also be the case, in general, even if the disabled child is living away from home, provided the parents have regular contact, since that contact will be of substantial importance to the child and be 'regular'.[24] Separate guidance has in any event indicated that the word 'substantial' should be given a wide interpretation which fully takes into account individual circumstances.[25]

All such 'regular and substantial' carers (including sibling carers) are entitled to such an assessment, provided they make a formal request. The guidance however requires social workers to 'inform any carer who appears eligible under this Act of their right to request an assessment'.[26]

The Act entitles qualifying carers to an assessment of their ability to provide and continue to provide care. A typical example might be an assessment which disclosed that the parent was still having to carry the disabled child manually when moving him or her around the home. Because the child had grown, this was now posing a risk of back-strain on the parent, which would impair the 'ability to continue to provide care'.[27] Likewise, if a non-disabled sibling was going through a difficult period this might result in the parent being 'unable to provide care'.

If as a consequence of such an assessment it transpires that the carer is no longer able (or willing)[28] to provide the same level of care, then the authority will have to decide whether to change the service user's care plan by increasing the services provided by another agency or agencies to compensate.

Young carers

The Carers (Recognition and Services) Act 1995 applies to all carers irrespective of their age. Carers who are under the age of 18 are generally referred to as 'young carers'. They are eligible, in addition to the benefits detailed above, to services in their own right.

There is no legislation which specifically refers to young carers. Guidance concerning young carers has however been issued by the Social Services Inspectorate (CI(95)12). The guidance adopts a definition of a 'young carer' as 'a child or young person who is carrying out significant caring tasks and assuming a level of responsibility for another person, which would usually be taken by an adult'. Such duties as are owed to young carers by a social services authority are primarily contained in the Children Act 1989 and in the guidance issued by the Department of Health (*Volume 2: Family Support; Volume 6: Children with Disabilities*).

As we have noted (p.232) s.17(1) Children Act 1989 places a general duty on social services authorities to safeguard and promote the welfare of children within their area who are 'in need', and empowers authorities to provide almost unlimited services towards this goal.

In relation to young carers, one is not in general concerned with 'disabled children' and accordingly it is necessary to establish that the child is 'in need' either because of the risk of harm or impaired development. Because of the prevalent resource shortages within social services authorities, the criteria for obtaining services or funding under s.17 have become increasingly severe. In a number of authorities, the position was reached that they were only considering a non-disabled child to be in need if his or her name was on the child protection register. Such a high threshold for accessing services effectively ruled young carers out; the fear of social services child protection powers being a major reason why many young carers and their families avoid making contact with such authorities (para. 17 practice guidance to Carers Act LAC (96)7).

In order to improve the help available to young carers it was necessary for such restrictive definitions of 'in need' to be curtailed. This has been achieved by the SSI issuing specific guidance on young carers as a chief inspector's 'guidance letter' (28 April 1995). Annex A at para. 1.1 refers to (among other things) research which it states: 'has demonstrated that many young people carry out a level of caring responsibilities which prevents them from enjoying normal social opportunities and from achieving full school attendance. Many young carers with significant caring responsibilities should therefore be seen as children in need'.

The key issue therefore is whether the young carer's caring responsibilities are 'significant'. In this respect the practice guidance LAC (96)7 points out (at para.15.2) that young carers should not be expected to carry out 'inappropriate' levels of caring (i.e. age inappropriate). If the young carer's caring responsibilities are significant, then s/he will be eligible for an assessment and possibly services under the Children Act 1989. S/he will, in addition almost certainly be entitled to a carer's assessment (if the care provided is 'regular and substantial'). Obviously in such cases only one combined assessment will be carried out although there will inevitably be policy and practice differences as to whether a children's team or adult care social worker actually does the assessment.

The Children Act 1989 assessment procedures and service provision arrangements for young carers are the same as for any other child (and are detailed above). S.17(1)(b) emphasises that a principal purpose for the provision of services to children in need is to promote the upbringing of such children by their families.

The Carers and Disabled Children Act 2000

The 2000 Act adds to the rights enjoyed by carers. It entitles them:

- to an assessment, even if the disabled person for whom they care refuses to have an assessment carried out of their own care needs

- to receive directly from social services any service which helps them care for the disabled person

- to receive direct payments, in lieu of the provision of services which they have been assessed as needing. The Act also entitles 16- and 17-year-old disabled children to receive direct payments for services that meet their own assessed needs.

- to receive vouchers redeemable for respite or 'short-term breaks' care.

Social services are permitted to charge carers for any services they receive under the 2000 Act.

The power of social services department to charge for services

As noted above, social services are empowered to charge for the services they provide under the Children Act 1989 although, as noted below, it is doubtful whether there is any power to charge for services provided to a disabled child under the Chronically Sick and Disabled Persons Act 1970.

Charging for non-accommodation services under the Children Act

S.29(1) deals with charging for non-accommodation services and empowers the authority to recover 'such charge as they consider appropriate'. This is subject to the following restrictions:

- that no person can be charged while in receipt of income support, working families tax credit or disabled person's tax credit

- that where the authority is satisfied that a person's means are insufficient for it to be reasonably practicable for him or her to pay the charge, the authority cannot require him or her to pay more than s/he can reasonably be expected to pay.

S.29(4) specifies who can be charged, namely the parents, unless the young person is aged 16 or older, in which case the child him/herself.[29]

Charging for accommodation services under the Children Act

Schedule 2 Part III Children Act 1989 empowers (but does not oblige) local authorities to charge for the cost of accommodating children. The rules are the same as for non-accommodation services, save only that (in addition):

- the local authority cannot charge a sum greater than 'they would normally be prepared to pay if they had placed a similar child with local authority foster parents'

- provision is made for the local authority to serve what is known as a 'contribution notice' which they are able to enforce through the magistrates court if necessary; which court can also arbitrate on any dispute as to the reasonableness of such a notice.

Charging for services under the Chronically Sick and Disabled Persons Act 1970

It is doubtful if social services departments can charge for any services provided under s.2 of the 1970 Act, and in general few attempt to do so.[30] The reasons why charges for 1970 Act services for disabled children are unlikely to be lawful are complex. It stems from the difficult relationship between s.2 of this Act and s.29 of the National Assistance Act 1948.

While there is no statutory authority to charge for services under s.2, in *R v Powys County Council ex p Hambidge* [1998][31] the Court of Appeal held that services under s.2 (in relation to adults) are actually provided 'in exercise of functions under s.29' of the 1948 Act. Since there is power to charge for services provided under s.29, the court reasoned that this also extended to s.2 services. However, s.29 of the 1948 Act only applies to services for people aged 18 or over, and so it is likely that there is no authority to charge for services provided under s.2 to disabled children.

Authorities cannot seek to circumvent this problem by alleging that services are being provided under the Children Act rather than the 1970 Act (where they could be provided under either) since in *R v Bexley LBC ex p B* [1995][32] the court held that most domiciliary services provided to disabled children are provided under the 1970 Act and not the 1989 Act.

Notes

1   end note text
2   Para.3 of Schedule 2.
3   *The Children Act 1989: Guidance and Regulations, Vol. 6, Children with Disabilities* (HMSO, London, 1991), para. 6.4.
4   See p.62 above.
5   Although other community care statutes also provide for services to be made available for disabled children, including para. 3 Schedule 8, NHS Act 1977 and in certain situations under s.117 Mental Health Act 1983.
6   See p.62 above.
7   *The Children Act 1989: Guidance and Regulations, Vol 6, Children with Disabilities* (HMSO, London, 1991), para. 5.7.
8   The guidance contains the following additional comments at this point, namely ' within the care resources available including help from willing and able carers'. While the care plan will record input from carers, it is not correct to suggest (as this section does) that the services provided to meet an assessed need are constrained by the local authority's 'available resources'.
9   For a detailed account of the requirements of a community care assessment and care plan, see L. Clements *Community Care and the Law*, 2nd edn (LAG, London, 2000).

10   Care Management and Assessment – A Practitioners' Guide (HMSO, London, 1991), para. 3.1.

11   In *R v Islington LBC ex p Rixon* [1996], *The Times* 17 April; 1 CCLR 119 Sedley J put it thus: 'The practice guidance…counsels against trimming the assessment of need to fit the available provision.'

12   See p.62.

13   See p.102.

14   See p.64.

15   By virtue of s.28A Chronically Sick and Disabled Persons Act 1970.

16   See p.64.

17   (1995) 3 CCLR 15

18   Disabled children are also entitled to such services under para. 3 of Schedule 8 NHS Act 1977 which requires/enables social services departments to provide 'on such a scale as is adequate for the needs of their area…home help for households where such help is required owing to the presence of a person who is suffering from illness, lying-in…handicapped as a result of having suffered from illness or by congenital deformity' and 'the provisions of laundry facilities'. If the need is health related, then laundry services can also be provided by the NHS.

19   Circular LAC(93)12; see also p.166.

20   Para. 19 circular LAC (90)7.

21   *R v North Yorkshire County Council ex p Hargreaves (No 2)*, 1 CCLR 331.

22   People who provide the care as a result of a contract of employment or as a volunteer placed by a voluntary organisation are excluded.

23   See para. 18.1, Carers (Recognition and Services) Act 1995 Practice Guidance.

24   'Regular' should be distinguished from 'frequent'; it merely connotes an event which recurs or is repeated at fixed times or uniform intervals.

25   LAC (93)10 Appendix 4, para. 8.

26   LAC (96)7, para. 20.

27   See p.134 where the manual handling regulations are considered.

28   Para. 9.8 of the practice guidance accompanying the Act states that social workers should not 'assume a willingness by the carer to continue, or continue to provide the same level of support'.

29   Unless the service is actually being provided for a member of the child's family, in which case it is that member who is charged.

30   For detailed consideration of this issue, see L. Clements *Community Care and the Law*, 2nd edn (LAG, London, 2000), para 8.116.

31   1 CCLR 458.

32   Current Law 1995, 3225.

Education Materials

Code of Practice on the Identification and Assessment of Special Educational Needs

The Principles and Procedures that underlie the code are stated as follows.

1.2 The Fundamental Principles of the Code

1. The needs of all pupils who may have special educational needs either throughout, or at any time during, their school careers must be addressed; the Code recognises that there is a continuum of needs and a continuum of provision, which may be made in a wide variety of different forms.

2. Children with special educational needs require the greatest possible access to a broad and balanced education, including the National Curriculum.

3. The needs of most pupils will be met in the mainstream, and without a statutory assessment or statement of special educational needs. Children with special educational needs, including children with statements of special educational needs, should, where appropriate and taking into account the wishes of their parents, be educated alongside their peers in mainstream schools.

4. Even before he or she reaches compulsory school age a child may have special educational needs requiring the intervention of the LEA as well as the health services.

5. The knowledge, views and experience of parents are vital. Effective assessment and provision will be secured where there is the greatest possible degree of partnership between parents and their children and schools, LEAs and other agencies.

1.3 The practices and procedures essential in pursuit of these principles

1. All children with special educational needs should be identified and assessed as early as possible and as quickly as is consistent with thoroughness.

2. Provision for all children with special educational needs should be made by the most appropriate agency. In most cases this will be the child's mainstream school, working in partnership with the child's parents: no statutory assessment will be necessary.

3. Where needed, LEAs must make assessments and statements in accordance with the prescribed time limits; must write clear and thorough statements, setting out the child's educational and non-educational needs, the objectives to be secured, the provision to be made and the arrangements for monitoring and review; and ensure the annual review of the special educational provision arranged for the child and the updating and monitoring of educational targets.

4. Special educational provision will be most effective when those responsible take into account the ascertainable wishes of the child concerned, considered in the light of his or her age and understanding.

5. There must be close co-operation between all the agencies concerned and a multidisciplinary approach to the resolution of issues.

The Code of Practice: guidance on the preliminary stages

Notice of a proposal to make a statutory assessment

3.9 LEA will then consider whether to issue, under section [323(1)] a notice to the parents that the LEA propose to make an assessment.

Before making an assessment, the LEA must write to the child's parents to explain their proposal. The LEA must also inform the parents of the procedure to be followed in making an assessment; of the name of the officer of the authority from whom further information may be

obtained; and of their right to make representations and submit written evidence within a given time limit, which must not be less than twenty-nine days [section 323].

3.10   When issuing such a notice, the LEA must:

i.   tell parents of their right to make representations and submit written evidence. The LEA must set a time limit, which must not be less than 29 days. The LEA should encourage parents to make representations and to submit evidence, pointing out the importance of their contribution. When parents make representations orally, the LEA should agree a written summary with the parents. The LEA may invite parents to indicate formally if they do not wish to make or add to representations, in order that the LEA can then immediately consider whether a statutory assessment is necessary

ii.   tell parents the name of an officer of the LEA who liaises with the parents over all the arrangements relating to statutory assessment and the making of a statement. This person is often known as the Named LEA Officer[1]

iii.   set out clearly for parents the procedures that they will follow during statutory assessment and the possible subsequent drawing up of a statement. The LEA should also explain the precise timing of each of the various stages within the overall six-month time limit; indicate ways in which parents can assist the LEA in meeting the time limits; and explain the exceptions to the time limits.

3.11   LEAs should also:

i.   give parents information about sources of independent advice, such as local or national voluntary organisations and any local support group or parent partnership scheme, which may be able to help them consider what they feel about their child's needs and the type of provision they would prefer

ii.   tell parents about the role of the Named Person.[2] This is someone who is preferably independent of the LEA and who can give the parents information and advice about their child's special educational needs, supporting them in their discussions with the LEA. The LEA should explain the difference between the Named Person and the Named LEA Officer. If the LEA do eventually make a statement, they must, at that stage, write to the parents, confirming the identity of the Named Person – see paragraphs 4: 70–4: 73. But there can be advantage in the LEA and the parents considering the identity of the Named Person at the start of the assessment process. The Named Person, who may be from a parents' group or a voluntary organisation, can then attend meetings, help parents express their views effectively, and thereby encourage parental participation at all stages. The LEA might inform parents that a local parent partnership scheme or a voluntary organisation can help them choose their Named Person

iii. ask the parents whether they would like the LEA to consult anyone in addition to those whom the LEA must approach for educational, medical, psychological and social services advice, should the LEA decide to proceed with the statutory assessment. The LEA should list those whom they must consult. The LEA should tell parents that they may also present any private advice or opinions which they have obtained and that this advice will be taken into account

iv. give parents information about the full range of provision available in maintained mainstream and special schools within the LEA. The information should be available at the earliest possible stage so that parents have every opportunity to consider their child's future placement and arrange visits to particular schools. Thus, by the time they submit representations to the LEA or express a preference for a particular school, they can do so from an informed point of view. It will be in the LEA's best interests to facilitate this process wherever possible, but they should be careful not to preempt the parents' preference or any representations they may later make.

3.12 Assessment can be stressful for parents. The value of early information and support to parents cannot be over-emphasised. The better informed and the better supported parents are, the better they are able to contribute as partners to the assessment of their child. The less well informed and the less well supported they are, the more likely they are to be anxious and defensive and the greater is the potential for confrontation.

3.13 LEAs should present information to parents in a manner that is not intimidating and which encourages participation and open discussion. All the above information should, if possible, be available in the first language of the child's parents and LEAs may wish to consider taped or video-taped versions of the information for parents who may find the information more accessible in that form.

3.14 LEAs may wish to consider whether the letter informing the parents of the LEA's proposal to assess should be personally delivered, for example by an education welfare officer. Personal delivery, along with the information about assessment, can provide parents with an additional opportunity to ask any questions and seek further advice. At this stage, the LEA should also seek parents' consent to any medical examination and psychological assessment of their child during the making of a statutory assessment. This will save time if the LEA decide that they must make an assessment.

3.15 If the school and the parents have been working closely with each other, this will not be the first the parents know of the possibility of a statutory assessment. There should be only a very small number of instances in which a sudden change in the child's circumstances, for example resulting from an accident or a sudden acceleration of a degenerative condition, or if the child had just moved into the area, might mean that the letter announcing the LEA's proposal to assess was unexpected. Even in such extreme instances, the LEA should attempt to inform parents first, in a familiar setting, of the intention to make an assessment.

Notification to other agencies of a proposal to assess

3.16 When informing parents of the proposal to assess, the LEA must copy the proposal to:

- **the local authority's social services department**
- **the district health authority**
- **the head teacher of the child's school. (Regulation 5(1))**

The LEA should address the copy of the proposal to the designated officers of the social services department and [health authority] and should also copy the proposal to their own educational psychology service and any other relevant agencies, such as the education welfare service, who might he asked for advice should the assessment proceed. LEAs are not at this point asking these agencies to provide advice, but alerting them to the possibility of a request for advice in the near future. Such notice will give the health service and other agencies the opportunity to collate records and consult others who might be involved in providing advice. Early action at this stage within the health service and social services departments will in effect serve to extend the time available to those agencies for gathering advice, and thus help them meet the statutory time limits.

A formal request from a parent

3.17 Under section [328 or 329] of the Act, parents may ask the LEA to conduct a statutory assessment. The LEA must comply with such a request, unless they have made a statutory assessment within six months of the date of the request or unless they conclude, upon examining all the available evidence, that a statutory assessment is not necessary.

3.18 If schools, external specialists, including LEA support and educational psychology services, and parents have been working in partnership at stage 3, the parental request for a statutory assessment will often have been discussed between them and should come as no surprise to the LEA. But a parental request for a statutory assessment may reflect dissatisfaction or disagreement with the action taken in the school-based stages. Whatever the background, the LEA must take all parental requests seriously and take action immediately.

An LEA is responsible for a pupil at an independent school if he or she lives in their area and has been placed in that school at the expense of the LEA or the Funding Authority or has been brought to the LEA's attention as having or probably having special educational needs. The LEA must identify any such children who require statements. [Section 321]

3.19 Where a child attends an independent school, a parental request for an assessment may be the first that an LEA hear about that child. The procedure they follow and the factors they consider in deciding whether to make an assessment should be the same, regardless of the type of school the child attends: the LEA will wish to investigate evidence provided by the child's school and parents as to his or her learning difficulties and evidence about action taken by the school to meet those difficulties. LEAs may find it helpful to inform independent schools in their area of their duty to identify children for whom they are responsible and who require statements of special educational needs; to tell those schools of the procedures they will adopt and of the information they would expect to be given; and to encourage those schools to give the LEA early notification of any child who may require a statutory assessment.

3.20 When a child is referred by a parental request for a statutory assessment, the LEA should not issue a notice that they propose to make an assessment under [section 323(1)]. But the LEA should immediately contact the parents in order to:

- **investigate further the nature of their concern**
- **ascertain the degree of their involvement and agreement with the special educational provision which has been made for their child at school**
- **give them full details of the assessment process and the information set out at paragraphs 3:10 and 3:11 above**.

Where under section 172(2) or 173(1) a parent has asked the LEA to arrange an assessment, the LEA shall give notice in writing to the social services department, the district health authority and the head teacher of the child's school of the fact that the request has been made, and tell them what help the LEA are likely to request if they decide to make an assessment. (Regulation 5(3))

3.21 The LEA must inform the child's head teacher that the parents have made a request for a statutory assessment and should also ask the school for written evidence about the child, in particular, for the school's assessment of the child's learning difficulty and the school's account of the special educational provision that has been made. At the same time, the LEA should notify the educational psychology service and any other bodies which might later be asked for advice, and must notify the designated medical officers of the district health authority and the social services department.

Statement Of Special Educational Needs

PART 1: INTRODUCTION

1.   In accordance with section 324 of the Education Act 1996 ('the Act') and the Education (Special Educational Needs) Regulations 1994 ('the Regulations'), the following statement is made by [*here set out name of authority*] ('the authority') in respect of the child whose name and other particulars are mentioned below

2.   When assessing the child's special educational needs the authority took into consideration in accordance with regulation 10 of the Regulations, the representations, evidence and advice set out in the Appendices to this statement.

Child

Surname	Other names
Home address	
	Sex
	Religion
Date of birth	Home language

Child's parent or person responsible

Surname	Other names
Home address	
	Relationship to child
Telephone no.	

PART 2: SPECIAL EDUCATIONAL NEEDS

[Here set out the child's special educational needs, in terms of the child's learning difficulties which call for special educational provision, as assessed by the authority.]

PART 3: SPECIAL EDUCATIONAL PROVISION

Objectives

[Here specify the objectives which the special educational provision for the child should aim to meet.]

Educational provision to meet needs and objectives

[Here specify the special educational provision which the authority consider appropriate to meet the needs specified in Part 2 and to meet the objectives specified in this Part, and in particular specify –

(a) any appropriate facilities and equipment, staffing arrangements and curriculum,

(b) any appropriate modifications to the application of the National Curriculum,

(c) any appropriate exclusions from the application of the National Curriculum, in detail, and the provision which it is proposed to substitute for any such exclusions in order to maintain a balanced and broadly based curriculum; and

(d) where residential accommodation is appropriate, that fact].

Monitoring

[Here specify the arrangements to be made for –

(a) regularly monitoring progress in meeting the objectives specified in this Part,

(b) establishing targets in furtherance of those objectives,

(c) regularly monitoring the targets referred to in (b),

(d) regularly monitoring the appropriateness of any modifications to the application of the National Curriculum, and

(e) regularly monitoring the appropriateness of any provision substituted for exclusions from the application of the National Curriculum.

Here also specify any special arrangements for reviewing this statement.]

PART 4: PLACEMENT

[Here specify –

(a) the type of school which the authority consider appropriate for the child and the name of the school for which the parent has expressed a preference or, where the authority are required to specify the name of a school, the name of the school which they consider would be appropriate for the child and should be specified, or

(b) the provision for his education otherwise than at a school which the authority consider appropriate.]

PART 5: NON-EDUCATIONAL NEEDS

[Here specify the non-educational needs of the child for which the authority consider provision is appropriate if the child is to properly benefit from the special educational provision specified in Part 3.]

PART 6: NON-EDUCATIONAL PROVISION

[Here specify any non-educational provision which the authority propose to make available or which they are satisfied will be made available by a health authority, a social services authority or some other body, including the arrangements for its provision. Also specify the objectives of the provision, and the arrangements for monitoring progress in meeting those objectives.]

Appendix A: Parental Representations

Appendix B: Parental Evidence

Appendix C: Advice from the Child's Parent

Appendix D: Educational Advice

Appendix E: Medical Advice

Appendix F: Psychological Advice

Appendix G: Advice from the Social Services Authority

Appendix H: Other Advice Obtained by the Authority

Special Educational Needs: Transitional Plan[3]
Para. 6.46 of the Code of Practice

The Transitional Plan should address the following questions:

The School

- What are the young person's curriculum needs during transition? How can the curriculum help the young person to play his or her role in the community; make use of leisure and recreational facilities; assume new roles in the family; develop new educational and vocational skills?

The Professionals

- How can they develop close working relationships with colleagues in other agencies to ensure effective and coherent plans for the young person in transition?

- Which new professionals need to be involved in planning for transition, for example occupational psychologists; a rehabilitation medicine specialist; occupational and other therapists?

- Does the young person have any special health or welfare needs which will require planning and support from health and social services now or in the future?

- Are assessment arrangements for transition clear, relevant and shared between all agencies concerned?

- How can information best be transferred from children's to adult services to ensure a smooth transitional arrangement?

- Where a young person requires a particular technological aid, do the arrangements for transition include appropriate training and arrangements for securing technological support?

- Is education after the age of 16 appropriate, and if so, at school or at a college of further education?

The Family

- What do parents expect of their son's or daughter's adult life?

- What can they contribute in terms of helping their child develop personal and social skills, an adult life-style and acquire new skills?

- Will parents experience new care needs and require practical help in terms of aids, adaptations or general support during these years?

The Young Person

- What information do young people need in order to make informed choices?

- What local arrangements exist to provide advocacy and advice if required?

- How can young people be encouraged to contribute to their own Transition Plan and make positive decisions about the future?

- If young people are living away from home or attending a residential school outside their own LEA, are there special issues relating to the location of services when they leave school which should be discussed in planning?

- What are the young person's hopes and aspirations for the future, and how can these be met?

Notes

1   The person from the LEA who liaises with the parents over all the arrangements relating to statutory assessments and the making of a statement. LEAs are required to inform parents of the identity of the Named Person when they issue a notice of a proposal to make a statutory assessment of a child.

2   The person whom the LEA must identify when sending the parents a final version of a statement. The Code states (at p.128) that the Named Person should usually be identified in co-operation with the parents and must be someone who can give the parents information and advice about their child's special educational needs. He or she may be appointed at the start of the assessment process and can then attend meetings with parents and encourage parental participation throughout that process. The Named Person 'should normally be independent of the LEA and may be someone from a voluntary organisation or parent partnership scheme'.

3   Specific and further guidance on transitional planning has now been issued as 'A Guide to Transition Planning for Secondary and Special Schools' DfEE (1999).

NHS Complaints Materials

NHS complaints

Complaints against NHS bodies, such as health authorities, trusts and GPs are governed by statute,[1] and there are many parallels between the NHS and social services procedures, the most significant difference being that the NHS system has only two stages – and the complainant has no automatic entitlement to progress from the first to the second stage.

Complaints may be made by existing or former users of NHS trust services. People may complain on behalf of existing or former users where the trust (usually through its complaints manager), or the convenor at the independent review stage, accepts them as a suitable representative. In relation to GPs, the complainants may be existing or former patients, or people who have received services from that GP.

A complaint should be made within six months of the event giving rise to it (or of the patient becoming aware of that event). There is, however, a discretion to extend the time limit where it would be unreasonable in the circumstances of a particular case for the complaint to have been made earlier and where it is still possible to investigate the facts of the case.

The guidance advises that this power to vary the time limit should be used with flexibility and sensitivity.

Stage 1

The legislation requires every GP's practice, NHS trust or health authority to appoint a 'complaints manager' who is responsible for ensuring complaints are responded to.

During the first stage of the complaints procedure the complaints manager must provide the 'fullest possible opportunity for investigation and resolution of the complaint, as quickly as is sensible in the circumstances, aiming to satisfy the patient, while being scrupulously fair to staff'.

The entire Stage 1 process may be conducted orally. The guidance states, however, that where the complainant is dissatisfied with the oral response, or that s/he wishes to take the matter further, then:

> It is recommended that Local Resolution be best rounded off with a letter to the complainant. Any letter concluding the Local Resolution stage (whether signed by the chief executive because it is a written complaint, or by some other appropriate person) should indicate the right of the complainant to seek an Independent Review of the complaint, or any aspect of the response to it with which the complainant remains dissatisfied, and that the complainant has twenty-eight days from the date of the letter to make such a request.

Stage 2: the independent review panel

Any request for an independent review panel hearing (whether made orally or in writing) must be passed to the 'convenor' within 28 days. The convenor is a non-executive director of the trust or health authority and his or her function is to consider (and determine) requests that complaints be referred to the independent review panel. The convenor must acknowledge receipt in writing, and then: 'before deciding whether to convene a panel, the convenor must obtain a signed statement signed by the complainant setting out their remaining grievances and why they are dissatisfied with the outcome of Local Resolution'.

Before deciding whether to convene the panel the convenor must:

- decide whether all opportunities for satisfying the complaint at Stage 1 have been explored and fully exhausted

- consult with one of the independent lay chairmen (ideally not the one who will actually chair the panel) in order to obtain an 'external independent view', although ultimately the decision to recommend the convening of a panel is the convenor's alone

- take appropriate clinical advice (if any question of clinical judgment is involved in the complaint). Detailed guidance is given on this aspect of complaints and from whom such advice should be sought.

The complainant must be informed in writing of the convenor's decision and reasons must be given if s/he decides to advise that a panel should not be set up. In such cases the complainant must be advised of the right to complain to the ombudsman.

The panel

If a panel is convened it will comprise three members:

- an independent chairman
- the convenor, and
- either

(a) in the case of a trust panel, a health authority representative
(b) in the case of a health authority, another independent person.

If the convenor considers the complaint to be a clinical complaint, then the panel will be advised by at least two independent clinical assessors.

The panel should be convened within four weeks of the convenor's decision to convene, and it should complete its work within 12 weeks. Its process should be informal, flexible and non-adversarial. No legal representation is permitted, although the complainant may be accompanied by a person of his/her choosing.

A draft of the panel's report should be sent to the relevant parties (to check its accuracy) 14 days before it is formally issued. The report is confidential and should set out the results of the panel's investigations, outlining its conclusions with any appropriate comments or suggestions. Following receipt of the panel's report, the chief executive must write to the complainant informing him or her of any action that is to be taken as a result of the panel's report and of the right of the complainant to take his or her grievance to the ombudsman if s/he remains dissatisfied.

Note

1   Directions to NHS Trusts, Health Authorities and Special Health Authorities for Special Hospitals on Hospital Complaints Procedures 1996; Miscellaneous Directions to Health Authorities for Dealing with Complaints 1996; given under s.17 NHS Act 1977, Schedule 2 para. 6(2)(a) NHS&CCA 1990 and the NHS (Functions of Health Authorities) (Complaints) Regulations 1996 SI No.669.

Disability Discrimination Act 1995 Materials

Employment

Part II of the Disability Discrimination Act 1995 deals with discrimination in the field of employment. Regulations[1] and a Code of Practice[2] have been issued in relation to Part II.

The employment provisions apply to all employers with more than 14 employees. It makes unlawful discrimination against a disabled person in the field of employment; and protects the following:

1. *Prospective employees by subjecting to scrutiny:*

   - the arrangements which the employer makes for the purposes of determining who should be offered employment

   - the terms on which the employer offers the disabled person employment, or

   - refusing to offer, or deliberately not offering the disabled person employment.

2. *Existing employees by subjecting to scrutiny:*[3]

   - the terms of employment offered to a disabled person

   - opportunities for promotion, a transfer, training or receiving any other benefit

   - any refusal to afford (or deliberately not affording) the disabled person any such opportunity

- any dismissal or other detriment to which the disabled person is subjected.

Primary discrimination occurs when:

- for a reason which relates to a disabled person's disability,
- the employer treats him or her less favourably than the employer treats others to whom the reason does not (or would not) apply, and
- the employer cannot show this treatment is justified.

Unlawful discrimination may also occur when:

- an employer fails to make any 'reasonable adjustment' to facilitate the disabled person and
- the employer cannot show that this failure is justified.

Reasonable adjustments

Employers are now under a duty to take reasonable steps to change the working environment to reduce the discrimination experienced by disabled employees. The duty however only arises when the disabled person is placed at a substantial disadvantage.

The Act gives examples[4] of steps that an employer may have to take in relation to a disabled person in order to comply with the duty to make reasonable adjustments:

(a) making adjustments to premises;

(b) allocating some of the disabled person's duties to another person;

(c) transferring him to fill an existing vacancy;

(d) altering his working hours;

(e) assigning him to a different place of work;

(f) allowing him to be absent during working hours for rehabilitation assessment or treatment;

(g) giving him, or arranging for him to be given, treatment;

(h) acquiring or modifying equipment;

(i) modifying instructions or reference manuals;

(j) modifying procedures for testing or assessment;

(k) providing a reader or interpreter;

(l)   providing supervision.

The Act states that in deciding whether it is reasonable for an employer to have to take a particular step in order to make a reasonable adjustment, regard shall be had, in particular to:

- the extent to which taking the step would prevent the effect in question
- the extent to which it is practicable for the employer to take the step
- the financial and other costs which would be incurred by the employer in taking the step and the extent to which it would disrupt any of the employer's activities
- the extent of the employer's financial and other resources
- the availability to the employer of financial or other assistance with respect to taking the step (see p.151 above where details are given of the main assistance schemes).

Justification

Less favourable treatment is justified if, but only if, the reason for it is both:

- material to the circumstances of the particular case and
- substantial.

An employer can only sustain less favourable treatment if the disabled person cannot do the job concerned, and no adjustment, which would enable the employee to do the job, is practicable.

Goods, facilities and services

Part III of the DDA deals with discrimination in the areas of goods, facilities, services and premises. We outline below the key provisions relating to goods, facilities and services; the principles applied in relation to premises are broadly analogous.

It is unlawful for a provider of goods, facilities or services to discriminate against a disabled person[5] in the following ways:

- by refusing to provide, or deliberately not providing a service, goods or facilities
- by failing to take reasonable steps to make adjustments to practices, policies or procedures
- by the manner in which the service, goods or facilities are provided
- by the terms of service, subject to which the service, goods or facilities are provided.

If the provider can show that the treatment was justified, then the action is not unlawful.[6]

Goods

'Goods' are not defined by the Act, but clearly include 'personal and moveable property' including money.

Facilities

'Facilities' are not defined, but it has been suggested that 'facilities' has been included 'to embrace any matter which is obviously neither goods nor services and yet the refusal of which involves the denial of a legitimate right or interest of the individual'.[7]

Services

An illustrative list of examples of services is given by s.19 of the Act:

(a)   access to and use of any place which members of the public are permitted to enter;

(b)   access to and use of means of communication;

(c)   access to and use of information services;

(d)   accommodation in a hotel, boarding house or other similar establishment;

(e)   facilities by way of banking or insurance or for grants, loans, credit or finance;

(f)   facilities for entertainment, recreation or refreshment;

(g)   facilities provided by employment agencies or under section 2 of the Employment Training Act 1973;

(h)   the services of any profession or trade, or any local or other public authority.

It is irrelevant whether the services are provided for money or not, although the provision of services will only come within the Act if they are 'to the public' or 'a section of the public' – thus private clubs may therefore be excluded. 'Services' includes such areas as the health service, the judicial system (except jury service) libraries, restaurants, conference centres, petrol stations, etc.

Exclusions

Education and transport are not 'services' as they are dealt with by the Act under a separate heading. Also excluded are certain youth and community services that are provided by education authorities or voluntary organisations.[8]

Discrimination

A person or organisation discriminates against a disabled person when: [9]

- for a reason which relates to a disabled person's disability, it treats him or her less favourably than it treats (or would treat) others to whom the reason does not (or would not) apply, and

- it cannot show this treatment was justified.

The discrimination can take the form of actually refusing to provide the disabled person with a service, but it can also be less direct. The Act accordingly (at s.19) makes it unlawful for any person or organisation to discriminate against a disabled person:

- in refusing to provide any service it provides (or is prepared to provide) to members of the public

- in the standard of service it provide or the manner in which it is provided

- in the terms on which the service is provided.

Notes

1   Disability Discrimination (Employment) Regulations 1996 SI 1996/1456.
2   Code of Practice for the elimination of discrimination in the field of employment against disabled persons or persons who have a disability (The Stationery Office, London, 1996).
3   S.4(3) provides certain exceptions to these restrictions – primarily in relation to situations where the benefit denied is a benefit which the employer is concerned with providing to the public; this slightly contorted provision exists merely to prevent overlap between the provisions of Part II and Part III DDA.
4   At s.6(3).
5   S.19 DDA 1995.
6   S.20.
7   B. Doyle, *Disability Discrimination* (Jordans, London, 1996), p.104.
8   Regulation 9 Disability Discrimination (Services and Premises) Regulations 1996.
9   Under ss.19, 20, 21, 24.

Disabled facilities grants materials[1]

Disabled facilities grants are paid towards the cost of building works which are necessary in order to meet the needs of a disabled occupant. The housing authority is responsible for the administration and payment of the grant, although the original application may be instigated (and referred to it) by a social services authority after a community care assessment. The maximum mandatory grant is currently £20,000, although local authorities have the discretion to make higher awards.[2] The grant is payable to disabled occupants who are either owner-occupiers or tenants (including housing association, council tenants and certain licensees).

The relevant statutory provision for disabled facilities grants is Part I Housing Grants, Construction and Regeneration Act 1996 upon which detailed guidance has been issued by the Department of the Environment as Circular 17/96. There is considerable overlap between the duties of the housing authority to process these grants, and the duties owed by social services authorities to facilitate such adaptations.

The housing authority is responsible for the administration of the disabled facilities grant, through all stages from initial enquiry (or referral by the social services authority) to post-completion approval. As part of this obligation it must decide whether it is 'reasonable and practicable' to carry out the proposed adaptation works. It must also consult the social services authority in order to obtain its view as to whether the proposed works are 'necessary and appropriate'.

Mandatory grants

This applies to work which is aimed at:

- making the dwelling safe
- facilitating access and provision:
  - the principal family room
  - a room used for sleeping (or providing such a room)
  - a room in which there is a lavatory, a bath or shower and a washbasin (or providing such a room)
- providing a room usable for sleeping
- providing a bathroom
- facilitating preparation and cooking of food
- providing heating, lighting and power.

Discretionary grants

Local authorities have the discretion to award disabled facilities grants for works which make the dwelling suitable for the accommodation, welfare or employment of the disabled occupant in any other respect. The guidance explains what works of this nature might comprise:

Accommodation

This will generally comprise work which is more extensive than strictly necessary for the mandatory grant; for instance, extending or enlarging a dwelling which is already suitable for the disabled occupant in all other respects.

Welfare

Examples of such works might be to provide access to a garden adjacent to a property, or a safe play area for a disabled child, especially if such work is carried out at the same time as work under a mandatory grant.

Employment

This might include adapting a room for the use of a disabled person who is housebound but nevertheless able to work from home.

Eligibility

All owner-occupiers, tenants (both council, housing association and private) and licensees[3] are potentially eligible to apply for disabled facilities grants as are landlords on behalf of disabled tenants.

Eligibility for a disabled facilities grant is dependent upon satisfying a means test. Only the financial circumstances of the disabled occupant[4] and their partner are assessed and not other members of the household. In the case of adaptations for a disabled child, the test takes into account the resources of the parents.

The details of the means test are determined by regulations,[5] are relatively complex and set out in detail in the guidance. In many instances, the calculation adopts housing benefit principles; thus the value of a person's savings is determined in the same way as for housing benefit and a tariff income of £1 per £250 is applied to any capital in excess of £5000 (there is no upper capital limit).

Income is also assessed on basic housing benefit principles and the person's relevant 'applicable amount' is the current housing benefit sum. Where the financial resources do not exceed the relevant applicable amount plus a 'grant premium' of £40, the disabled facilities grant will be the cost of the approved works. Where the financial resources are greater than the applicable amount, a staggered taper is applied to the surplus, designed to produce what the regulations term an 'affordable loan' (regulation 10); the idea being that the contribution made by the applicant constitutes 'an affordable loan that could be raised based on the current standard national rate of interest, over repayment periods of 10 years for owner-occupiers and 5 years for tenants'.

Timescales

The local authority must approve or refuse a grant application within six months of the date of application and the grant must be paid within twelve months following the date of the application.

Notes

1   See p.171 above.
2   The Disabled Facilities Grants and Home Repair Assistance (Maximum Amounts) Order 1996.
3   S.19(5) extends eligibility for a DFG to a range of licensees, for example, secure or introductory tenants who are licensees, agricultural workers, and service employees such as publicans.
4   The disabled occupant may or may not be the applicant.
5   Housing Renewal Grants Regulations 1996.

Precedent Letters

Letter 1: Requesting the initial involvement of social services

Ms Jane Smith
Flat 11, Any Street
Anytown
AnyShire AE15 7LB
Tel: 01234 56789

Director of Social Services[1]
Disabled Children's Section
Anyshire Council
Council Offices
Shire Street
Anytown AE1 0BU

1 February 2001

Dear Director of Social Services

Request for assistance: register of children with disabilities
Richard Smith born 30 October 1999

I would be most grateful if a social worker could contact me at the earliest opportunity in relation to the care needs of my above named son.

Richard was born on 30 October last year and has been diagnosed as having cerebral palsy.

I have not as yet had any formal contact with a social worker from your authority and understand that you are able to provide assistance in relation to a number of matters and particularly concerning:

1. the entry of Richard's name on your register of children with disabilities

2. the assessment of Richard's needs for care services and of myself under the Carers Act 1995 and the Carers and Disabled Children Act 2000

3. the provision of practical help in coping with Richard's needs

4.   advice on what help I can expect from the other relevant agencies, details of voluntary groups in my area who I can also contact and also on the availability of social security benefits.

I am not presently working and am generally available most mornings (until about midday) on the above telephone number.

I look forward to hearing from you at the earliest opportunity.

Yours sincerely

Jane Smith

Letter 2: Expressing concern about failure of hospital discharge planning

The first letter goes to the social services department.

Ms Jane Smith
Flat 11, Any Street
Anytown
AnyShire AE15 7LB
Tel: 01234 56789

The Senior Social Worker
Hospital Social Work Team
Shiretown General Hospital
Shire Street
Anytown AE1 0BU

1 February 2001

Dear Senior Hospital Social Worker

Richard Smith born 30 October 1999
Expression of concern about failure of hospital discharge planning

I write to express my dissatisfaction with the arrangements that were made for Richard's discharge from Shiretown General Hospital. While this is not a formal complaint I do require from you a satisfactory response and an assurance that the continuing problems will be resolved and that there will be no re-occurrence of these difficulties.

I appreciate that some of my dissatisfaction arises because of the hospital's actions and I am accordingly writing to the trust manager in similar terms. However, since I understand that your authority and the trust have an obligation to 'work together', I require a full response from you as well as from the trust. The relevant facts are as follows: [*here set out the facts, e.g.*]

1.   Richard was born on 30 October last year and has been diagnosed as having cerebral palsy.

2.   He was admitted to the Peter Pan ward on 1 September 2000 for a prearranged heart operation and I accompanied him. He was discharged initially on 10 September but readmitted as an emergency on the 12th. His final discharge occurred on 20 September.

My dissatisfaction concerns the following matters:

1.   At no stage did I receive any clear statement as to when Richard was likely to be discharged; indeed the likely time and date varied depending upon who I spoke to.

2.   In my view Richard was prematurely discharged on 10 September; he had lost weight and was having difficulty feeding.

3.   No arrangements were made for me to travel home with Richard on the 10th (or indeed on the 20th) despite my having no access to a car. Eventually my mother, who lives some distance away, had to arrange for a friend to drive me home, for which I paid a contribution to the petrol of £15.00 on each occasion.

3.   On return home, I found that no liaison had occurred with the community nurse or my GP. The nurse left a message on my answerphone sometime before I arrived home on 10th September saying she hoped to drop in after the weekend.

4.   I was left without any means of support and no one had explained to me what I should expect in the way of back-up and health/social care services.

6.   On night of 12 September when Richard had not fed for 24 hours I contacted the GP out of hours who immediately arranged for Richard to be admitted as an emergency

7.   As a result of, etc.

I understand that this state of affairs is contrary to good practice and that Richard and I have a right to expect adequate health and social care support services and for the arrangements that are being made, to be properly co-ordinated and clearly explained to me. There has been a serious failure in relation to both the discharge planning and service provision arrangements for Richard and I therefore look forward to hearing from you as a matter of urgency.

Yours sincerely

Jane Smith

cc. Director of Social Services,
Anyshire Council

A 'mirror' letter (i.e. one in almost identical terms) is then sent to the senior hospital manager but it is copied to the health authority.[2]

Letter 3: Complaint to social services

Ms Jane Smith
Flat 11, Any Street,
Anytown,
AnyShire AE15 7LB
Tel: 01234 56789

Director of Social Services[3]
Disabled Children's Section
Anyshire Council
Council Offices
Shire Street
Anytown AE1 0BU

1 February 2001

Dear Director of Social Services

Formal Complaint:

**Representations Procedure (Children) Regulations 1991
Richard Smith born 30 October 1999**

I ask that you treat this letter as a formal complaint concerning the discharge by your authority of its functions in respect of myself and my son Richard Smith.

I require the complaint to be investigated under the formal process detailed in Part III Children Act 1989. My complaint is:

[Here set out as precisely as possible

(a) what it is that is being complained about

(b) the names of the key social workers who the complaints investigator will need to speak to;

(c) the dates of the relevant acts/omissions;

If possible also enclose copies of any relevant papers.]

What I want to achieve by making this complaint is *[here set out as precisely as possible what you want to be the result of your complaint: i.e. an apology, a changed service provision, an alteration to practice, compensation, etc.]*

I understand that your complaints receiving officer will wish to contact me in order to investigate this complaint. I suggest that this be done by *[here give a telephone contact number and the time/days you are normally available or some other convenient way you can be contacted]*.

Yours sincerely

Jane Smith

cc. Anyshire Council Chairperson
Social Services Committee[4]

Letter 4: Expressing concern about the failure of the NHS to provide adequate speech or language therapy assistance

Ms Jane Smith
Flat 11, Any Street,
Anytown,
AnyShire AE15 7LB
Tel: 01234 56789

The Manager
Shiretown Community NHS Trust[5]
Shire Street
Anytown AE1 0BU

1 February 2001

Dear NHS Community Trust Manager

Formal Complaint: Speech/Language Therapy
Richard Smith born 30 October 1997

I write concerning the failure by your trust to provide adequate speech and language therapy assistance to meet the needs of my son, Richard. As you know:

1. Richard has multiple and profound physical and mental impairments *[describe briefly his impairments and in particular how his communication difficulties manifest themselves]*.

2. On the 5 November 1999 the Shiretown social services department requested that your trust contribute towards the assessment of his need for care and health services.

3. The subsequent assessment of his needs concluded that it was essential that he receive speech and language therapy in order to enable him to engage in general social activity and in particular to express preferences concerning his health and social care needs.

4. I believe that the importance of appropriate communication assistance for disabled children such as Richard has been stressed in much official guidance, as well as the need for health and social services to work together to ensure that they co-ordinate their responses to meet the assessed needs (i.e. the Department of Health's Social Care Group, para. 9.2 Disabled Children: Directions for Their Future Care 1998).

5. The importance of Richard being able properly to express his wishes and opinions is, I also understand, a 'convention right' (as Art.10) protected by the Human Rights Act 1998.

The reason why I am dissatisfied with your authority's response to his needs for language and speech therapy are: *[here explain in as much detail as possible what the trust has failed to do and what it needs to do in order to provide a satisfactory service to Richard]*

I am very concerned that there has been such delay in providing appropriate speech and language therapy and accordingly ask that you treat this letter as a formal complaint about this failure. I want rapid steps to be taken to ensure that he does receive the help he needs.

I am copying this letter to the health and social services authorities and to the community health council.

Please acknowledge receipt.

Yours sincerely

Jane Smith

cc. Director of Patient Care Health authority[6]
Director of social services,[7]
community health council[8]

Letter 5: Requesting the initial involvement of LEA for child under 5

Ms Jane Smith
Flat 11, Any Street,
Anytown,
Anyshire AE15 7LB
Tel: 01234 56789

Chief Education Officer[9]
Education Department
Anyshire Council
Council Offices
Shire Street
Anytown AE1 0BU

1 October 2000

Dear Chief Education Officer

Special Educational Needs Assessment:
Richard Smith born 30 October 1999

I formally request that your department carry out an assessment of my son's special educational needs in accordance with your duties under [section 331 (*if aged under 2*)] / [section 329 (*if aged 2–5 years*)] of the Education Act 1996.

Richard's special educational needs have not previously been assessed and I believe that it is necessary for such an assessment to be made.

Richard was born on 30 October last year and has been diagnosed as having cerebral palsy. *[here explain briefly why it is believed that s/he will probably have:*

significantly greater difficulty in learning than the majority of children of his/her age; and/or

has a disability that prevents or hinders him/her from making use of educational facilities of a kind generally provided for children of his age]

[Here give details, including names and addresses, etc. of any health or social services contacts, etc. with whom you have had contact and with whom it would be sensible for the LEA to liaise.]

I am not presently working and am generally available most mornings (until about midday) on the above telephone number.

I look forward to hearing from you at the earliest opportunity.

Yours sincerely

Jane Smith

Letter 6: Requesting access to files

Director of Social Services/
Health Authority/
NHS Trust/
Housing, etc.
[Address]

Applicant's name
[Address]
[Date]

Access to Personal Information Data Protection Act 1998
Name and date of birth of disabled child

I formally request that you give me access to the personal information held by your authority relating to my *[personal circumstances][son's/daughters personal circumstances and I confirm that s/he lacks sufficient mental capacity to make the request in his / her own name]*

The information I require to be disclosed is all personal information which your authority holds which relates to *[myself][my son/daughter]. [If possible describe as precisely as possible the information that is sought, including for instance where the information is likely to be located, the nature of the information and the dates between which it was collected.]*

I understand that I am entitled to receive this information within 40 days. I also understand that you may wish me to pay a fee for the processing and copying of this information and *[I confirm that I am willing to pay such reasonable sum as you may require (subject to the statutory maximum)]* or *[in order to expedite matters I enclose a cheque in the sum of £10, being the statutory maximum, and would be grateful if you could refund to me, if appropriate, any excess]*[10]

Please confirm receipt of this request.

Signed ...

Notes

1. The address of the social services department can usually be obtained from the Citizen's Advice Bureau or found in the telephone directory under the general heading of your local council. However if you live in an area where there is a county council and a district council, the social services department is located in the county council's offices not the district council.

2. The relevant health authority to whom this letter should be copied will normally be the health authority whose area covers Richard's home address. This will normally be found in the telephone book under 'Health'.

3. The address of the social services department can usually be obtained from the Citizen's Advice Bureau or found in the telephone directory under the general heading of your local council. However if you live in an area where there is a county council and a district council, the social services department is located in the county council's offices not the district council.

4. The name and official address of the chairperson of the social services committee can be obtained from the council offices, or failing that from the central public library.

5. The name and address of the health body which is responsible for speech and language therapy will generally be the local community health NHS trust whose address will be found in the telephone book, although social services or the local community health council (address also in telephone book) should normally be able to provide this information.

6. The relevant health authority to whom this letter should be copied will normally be the health authority whose area covers Richard's home address. This will normally be found in the telephone book under 'Health'.

7. The address of the social services department can usually be obtained from the Citizen's Advice Bureau or found in the telephone directory under the general heading of your local council. However if you live in an area where there is a county council and a district council, the social services department is located in the county council's offices not the district council.

8. The contact details for the local community health council can be obtained from the local library, telephone book or by phoning the Association of Community Health Councils.

9. The address of the education department can usually be obtained from the Citizen's Advice Bureau or found in the telephone directory under the general heading of your local council. However if you live in an area where there is a county council and a district council, the education department is located in the county council's offices not the district council.

10. The 40-day period runs from the date of receipt of the request and any necessary fee. Accordingly provision should be expedited if the fee is actually enclosed.

Useful addresses

AbilityNet
PO Box 94
Warwick CV34 5WS
Tel: 01926 312847
www.abilitynet.co.uk

Action 19 Plus
c/o Campaigns, Scope
6 Market Road
London N7 9PW
Tel: 020 7619 7253

Action for Blind People
14–16 Verney Road
London SE16 3DZ
Tel: 020 7732 8771
www.afbp.org

Advisory Centre for Education (ACE)
1B Aberdeen Studios
22 Highbury Grove
London N5 2DQ
Tel advice line: 020 7354 8321

Anabledd Cymru (Disability Wales)
Llys Ifor
Crescent Road
Caerphilly
Mid Glamorgan CF83 1XL
Tel: 029 2088 7325 (voice and minicom);
email: info@cwac.demon.co.uk

Asian People with Disabilities Alliance (APDA)
Disability Alliance Centre
Old Refectory
Central Middlesex Hospital
Acton Lane
Park Royal
London NW10 7NS
Tel: 020 8961 6773

ASBAH UK (Association for Spina Bifida and Hydrocephalus)
ASBAH House
42 Park Road
Peterborough PE1 2UQ
Tel: 01733 555988
www.asbah.demon.co.uk

Association for Postnatal Illness
Tel: 020 7386 0868

Association for Youth with ME (AYME)
PO Box 605
Milton Keynes MK6 3EX
Tel: 01908 691635
www.ayme.org.uk

Benefit Enquiry Line
Tel: 0800 882200; text tel: 0800 243355
www.dss.gov.uk

Birth Defects Foundation
Tel: 01543 468 888

British Council of Disabled People (BCODP)
Litchurch Plaza
Litchurch Street
Derby DE24 8AA
Tel: 01332 295551; minicom tel: 01332 295581
www.bcodp.org.uk

British Diabetic Association
Youth and Family Services
10 Queen Anne Street
London W1M 0BD
Tel: 020 7323 1531; careline tel: 020 7636 6112
www.diabetes.org.uk

British Epilepsy Association
New Anstey House
Gateway Drive
Yeadon
Leeds LS19 7XY
Tel: 0113 210 8800; freephone helpline: 0808 800 5050
www.epilepsy.org.uk

British Institute of Learning Disabilities (BILD)
Wolverhampton Road
Kidderminster
Worcs DY10 3PP
Tel: 01562 850251
www.bild.org.uk

CANDO (Careers Advisory Network on Disability Opportunities)
Lancaster University Careers Service
Reception Lodge
Ballirigg LA1 4YW
Tel: 01524 594370
www.cando.ac.uk

Careline
Cardinal Heenan Centre
326 High Road
Ilford
Essex IG1 1QP
Tel: 020 8514 5444; helpline tel: 020 8514 1177

Carers National Association
20 Glasshouse Yard
London EC1A 4JS
Tel: 020 7490 8818

Challenging Behaviour Foundation
32 Twydall Lane
Gillingham
Kent ME8 6HX
Tel: 01634 302207

CHANGE
First floor, 69–85 Old Street
London EC1V 9HY
Tel: 020 7490 2668; minicom tel: 020 7490 3483
email: contact@changeuk.demon.co.uk

Child Poverty Action Group
4th floor, 1–5 Bath Street
London EC1V 9PY
Tel: 020 7253 3406

Circles Network
Pamwell House
160 Pennywell Road
Upper Easton
Bristol BS5 0TX
Tel: 0117 939 3917

Commissioner for Local Administration (England and Wales)
21 Queen Anne's Gate
London SW1H 9BU
Tel: 0207 222 5622

The Oaks
Westwood Way
Westwood Business Park
Coventry CV4 8JB
Tel: 01203 695999

Beverley House
17 Shipton Road
York YO3 6FZ
Tel: 01904 630151

Derwen House
Court Road
Bridgend
Glam CF31 1BN
Tel: 01656 661325
www.open.gov.uk/lgo/index.htm

Contact-a-Family
170 Tottenham Court Road
London, W1P 0HA
Tel: 020 7383 3555
www.cafamily.org.uk

Council for Disabled Children
8 Wakley Street
London EC1V 7QE
Tel: 020 7843 6000

Court of Protection
Stewart House
24 Kingsway
London, WC2B 6JX
Tel: 020 7269 7300

Crossroads Care Attendant Scheme
10 Regent Place
Rugby
Warwicks CV21 2PN
Tel: 01788 573653

Cruse Bereavement Care
Tel: 0345 585 565

Cystic Fibrosis Youth Line
27 Spencer Street
Carlisle CA1 1BE
Helpline tel: 0800 454482, Mon, Wed, Fri 2–5 pm
www.CFTrust.org.uk

Deafblind UK
100 Bridge Street
Peterborough PE1 1DY
Tel: 01733 358100
www.deafblind.org.uk

Department for Education and Employment (DfEE)
Sanctuary Buildings
Great Smith Street
Westminster
London SW1P 3BT
Tel: 020 7925 5000

DfEE Publications Unit
PO Box 5050
Sudbury
Suffolk CO10 6ZQ
Tel: 0845 60 222 60; fax: 0845 60 333 60
www.dfee.gov.uk/sen/publicat.htm

Department of Health
Richmond House
79 Whitehall
London SW1A 2NS
Tel: 020 7972 4300
Department of Health (publications section)
PO Box 777
London SE1 6XH

DIAL UK (Disability Information and Advice Line)
Park Lodge
St Catherine's Hospital
Tickhill Road
Doncaster DN4 8QN
Tel: 01302 310123
www.members.aol.com/dialuk

Disability Alliance ERA
88–94 Wentworth Street
London E1 7SA
Tel (minicom available): 020 7247 8776
rights advice line (minicom available): 020 7247 8763, Mon, Wed 2–4 pm

Disability Information Trust
Mary Marlborough Centre
Nuffield Orthopaedic Centre NHS Trust
Headington
Oxford OX3 7LD
Tel: 01865 227592
www.home.btconnect.com/ditrust/home.htm

Disability Law Service
39–45 Cavell Street
London E1 2BP
Tel: 020 7791 9801

Disabled Living Centres Council
Redbank House
4 St Chad's Street
Manchester M8 8QA
Tel: 0161 834 1044
www.dlcc.demon.co.uk

Disabled Living Foundation
380–384 Harrow Road
London W9 2HU
Tel: 020 7289 6111; helpline: 0870 603 9177
www.dlf.org.uk

Disablement Income Group (DIG)
PO Box 5743
Finchingfield CM7 4PW
Tel: 01371 811621, Mon – Fri 9.30 am–5 pm

The Disaway Trust
2 Charles Road
London SW19 3BD
Tel: 020 8543 3431

Down's Syndrome Association
155 Mitcham Road
Tooting
London SW17 9PG
Tel: 020 8682 4001
www.downs-syndrome.org.uk

Dyslexia Institute
133 Gresham Road
Staines
TW18 2AJ
Tel: 01784 463935

Dyspraxia Foundation
8 West Alley
Hitchin SG5 1EG
Tel: 01462 454986
www.emmbrook.demon.co.uk/dysprax/

Employment Opportunities for People with Disabilities
123 Minories
London EC39 1NT
Tel: 020 7481 2727
www.opportunities.org.uk

Enable
6th Floor, 7 Buchanan Street
Glasgow G1 3HL
Tel: 0141 226 4541; helpline: 0800 026 4444

Family Fund Trust
PO Box 50
York YO1 9ZX
Tel: 01904 621115; text tel: 01904 658085
www.familyfundtrust.org.uk

Floyd P! – Forum for Living of Young Disabled People, Independent Living Alternatives
Trafalgar House
Grenville Place
London NW7 3SA
Tel: 020 8906 9265
www.ILA.mcmail.com

Friends for the Young Deaf (FYD)
East Court Mansion
College Lane
East Grinstead
West Sussex RH19 3LT
Tel: 01342 323444

Gingerbread Association For One-Parent Families
Tel: 020 7336 8184

Greater London Action on Disability (GLAD)
336 Brixton Road
London SW9 7AA
Tel: 020 7346 5800 (voice and minicom); email: glad@binternet.com
www.glad.org.uk

Greater Manchester Coalition Young Disabled People's Forum
Carisbrooke
Wenlock Way
Gorton
Manchester M12 5LF
Tel: 0161 273 5153 (voice and minicom);
helpline: 0161 273 5155 (voice and minicom) 9.30 am–4.30 pm

Health Service Commissioners
Millbank Tower
Millbank
London SW1P 4QP
Tel: 020 7276 2035

4th Floor
Pearl Assurance House
Greyfriars Road
Cardiff CF1 3AG
Tel: 01222 394621
www.health.ombudsman.org.uk/health.htm

Holiday Care
2nd Floor, Imperial Buildings
Victoria Road
Horley RH6 7PZ
Tel: 01293 774535
www.freespace.virgin.net/hol.care

Housing Options
78a High Street
Witney
Oxon OX8 6HL
Tel: 01993 705012
www.hoptions.demon.co.uk

Independent Living Fund
PO Box 183
Nottingham NG8 3RD
Tel: 0115 942 8191/8192
www.dss.gov.uk/ba/GBI/5a58b94.htm

Independent Panel for Special Education Advice (IPSEA)
22 Warren Hill Road
Woodbridge
Suffolk IP12 4DU
Tel: 01394 382814/0800 0184016

Listening Books
12 Lant Street
London SE1 1QH
Tel: 020 7407 9417
www.listening-books.org.uk

MENCAP
117–123 Golden Lane
London, EC1Y 0RT
Tel: 020 7454 0454

MIND (National Association for Mental Health)
Granta House
15–19 Broadway
London E15 4BQ
Tel: 020 8519 2122; information line: 020 8522 1725
www.mind.org.uk

Mobility Advice and Vehicle Information Service (MAVIS)
Department of DETR, 'O' Wing
Macadam Avenue
Old Wokingham Road
Crowthorne RG45 6XD
Tel: 01344 661000

Muscular Dystrophy Campaign
7–11 Prescott Place
London SW4 6BS
Tel: 020 7720 8055
www.muscular-dystrophy.org

National Asthma Campaign
Providence House
Providence Place
London N1 0NT
Tel: 020 7226 2260; helpline: 0845 701 0203

National Autistic Society
393 City Road
London EC1V 1NE
Tel: 020 7833 2299; helpline: 0870 600 8585
www.oneworld.org/autism_uk

National Centre for Independent Living
250 Kennington Lane
London SE11 5RD
Tel: 020 7587 1663; text tel: 020 7587 1177; email: ncil@ncil.demon.co.uk
www.bcodp.org.uk/ncil

National Council For One-Parent Families
Tel: 0800 0185026

National Deaf Children's Society (NDCS)
15 Dufferin Street
London EC1Y 8PD
Tel: 020 7250 0123
www.ndcs.org.uk

National Health information Service
Tel: 0800 66 55 44

National Society for Epilepsy
Chalfont St Peter
Buckinghamshire SL9 0RJ
Tel: 01494 601300; helpline: 01494 601400
www.epilepsynse.org.uk

Patients Helpline
PO Box 935
Harrow HA1 3YJ
Tel: 020 8423 8999
www.patients-association.com

People First
Instrument House
207–215 Kings Cross Road
London WC1X 9DB
Tel: 020 7713 6400

Queen Elizabeth Foundation for Disabled People

Leatherhead Court
Leatherhead KT22 0BN
Tel: 01372 841100; information service: 01306 875156
www.qefd-org

RADAR (Royal Association for Disability and Rehabilitation)

12 City Forum
250 City Road
London EC1V 8AF
Tel: 020 7250 3222; minicom tel: 020 7250 4119
www.radar.org.uk

Rathbone

4th floor
Church Gate House
56 Oxford Street
Manchester M1 6EU
Tel: 0161 236 5358; special education advice line: 0800 917 6790

Remap

Hazeldene
Ightham
Kent TN15 9AD
Tel: 01732 883818
www.remap.org.uk

Rett Syndrome Association

133 Friern Barnet Road
London N11 3EU
Tel: 020 8361 5161
www.rettsyndrome.org.uk

RNIB (Royal National Institute for the Blind)

224 Great Portland Street
London W1N 6AA
Tel: 020 7388 1266

Royal National Institute for the Deaf (RNID)

19–23 Featherstone Street
London EC1Y 8SL
Tel: 020 7296 8000; minicom tel: 020 7296 8001; helpline: 0870 605 0123

Scope

6 Market Road
London N7 9PW
Tel: 020 7619 7100; helpline: 0808 800 3333, Mon–Fri, 9 am–9 pm;
email: cphelpline@scope.org.uk
www.scope.org.uk

Sense: The National Deafblind and Rubella Association
11–13 Clifton Terrace
Finsbury Park
London N4 3SR
Tel: 020 7272 7774; textphone: 020 7272 9648
www.sense.org.uk

Shaftesbury Society
16 Kingston Road
South Wimbledon
London SW19 1JZ
Tel: 020 8239 5555
www.shaftesburysoc.org.uk

Shaw Trust
Shaw House
Epsom Square
White Horse Business Park
Trowbridge
Wilts BA14 0XJ
Tel: 01225 716300
www.shaw-trust.org.uk

Sickle Cell Society
Tel: 020 8961 7795

Skill (National Bureau for Students with Disabilities)
4th Floor, Chapter House
18–20 Crucifix Lane
London SE1 3JW
Tel: 020 7450 0620; information service: 0800 328 5050
www.skill.org.uk

Special Educational Needs Tribunal Office
Windsor House, 7th floor
50 Victoria Street
London SW1H 0NW
Tel: 020 7925 6925; fax: 020 7925 6926; email: sentribunal@gtnet.gov.uk
www.dfee.gov.uk/sen/trib1.htm

Spinal Injuries Association (SIA)
76 St James Lane
London N10 3DF
Tel: 020 8444 2121; counselling tel: 020 8883 4296
www.spinal.co.uk

SPOD
(Association to Aid the Sexual and Personal Relationships of People with a Disability)
286 Camden Road
London N7 0BJ
Tel: 020 7607 8851

Stillbirth & Neonatal Death Society (SANDS)
Tel: 020 7436 5881

Tripscope
Alexandra House
Albay Road
Brentford TW8 0NE
Tel: 020 8580 7021
www.justmobility.co.uk/tripscope

Values into Action (VIA)
Oxford House
Derbyshire Street
London E2 6HG
Tel: 020 7729 5436
www.demon.co.uk/uk/via

Winged Fellowship Trust (WFT)
Angel House
20–32 Pentonville Road
London N1 9XD
Tel: 020 7833 2594

Young Arthritis Care
18 Stephenson Way
London NW1 2HD
Tel: 020 7916 1500

Subject Index

AbilityNet 275
access
  to education 93–4
  to files, letter requesting 273
  to information 75–6
  to services 89–90
Access to Work scheme 159
accommodated children 190
accommodation
  discretionary grants 264
  housing and supported living schemes
    153–4
  overnight for parents 99–100
  residential 64
  secure accommodation orders 189
  specific arrangements 200–2
    Care Standards Act 2000 200
    fostering 201–2
    residential care 202
    short-term breaks (respite care) 200–1
Action 19 Plus 275
Action for Blind People 275
adult, becoming an 138–74
  disabled young people and transition to
    adulthood 140–6
    barriers to opportunity 143–6
    quality of life 140–3
  legal commentary
    Disability Discrimination Act 1995 and
      employment 159
    further and higher education provision
      159–64
    housing responsibilities 169–71
    Independent Living Fund 168–9
    local education authority responsibilities
      155–9
    mental capacity and parental wills/trusts
      171–3
    NHS responsibilities 167–8
    social services 164–7
  representation, support and information
    147–8
  service provision and planning for transition
    to adult life 148–54
    careers and employment 151–2
    community care services 152–3
    future plans in education 150–1

health care 152
  housing, accommodation and supported
    living schemes 153–4
  what it means to become an adult 139–40
advice on self-help user groups 105–6
Advisory Centre for Education (ACE) 118,
  125, 275
advocacy and key working 46–8
advocates 61
After Age 16 Whats New? Services and Benefits for
  Young Disabled People (Family Fund) 147
A-level courses 150
Anabledd Cymru (Disability Wales) 276
annual reviews of statements 133
ASBAH UK (Association for Spina Bifida and
  Hydrocephalus) 276
Asian People with Disabilities Alliance (APDA)
  276
assessment(s) 62–4
  and integrated family service provision,
    needs-led approach to 41
  social services assessment 106
    and care planning obligations 230–3
    and service provision obligations 62
  special educational needs assessments 127–8
    and statutory time scales 128–9
  of users circumstances 232
assistance with financial and practical problems
  of daily living 49
Association for Postnatal Illness 276
Association for Youth with ME (AYME) 276
Association of Metropolitan and County
  Councils 227
autonomy and choice for disabled child,
  increasing 113–16
avoidance of disproportionate expenditure 162

barriers to opportunity 143–6
basic care 42
behaviour, services to aid childs development
  and 90–1
Benefit Enquiry Line 276
benefits, social security 105
Bliss 114
boundaries 42
Birth Defects Association 276
Bradford, Mr and Mrs 170
Bradford, Simon 170
British Council of Disabled People (BCODP)
  277
British Diabetic Association 277

British Epilepsy Association 277
British Institute of Learning Disabilities (BILD) 277
British Sign Language 114

CANDO (Careers Advisory Network on Disability Opportunities) 277
careers and employment 151–2
Careers Service 150, 151
  responsibilities 157–9
  special employment assistance for disabled people 158
    Access to Work scheme 159
    supported employment 158
    work preparation 158
Careline 278
care orders 189
carers
  health risks for 134–5
  hospital social workers duties to 100
  and primary care staff 102–3
  social services duties/responsibilities towards 64–5, 238–41
    The Carers (Recognition and Services) Act 1995 238–41
    The Carers and Disabled Children Act 2000 240–1
    young carers 239–40
Carers National Association 278
caring in the home: mothers, fathers and siblings 29–31
Challenging Behaviour Foundation 278
CHANGE 278
changing population of disabled children 28
charging for services
  under Children Act 241–2
  under Chronically Sick and Disabled Persons Act 1970
Child Poverty Action Group 278
children who live away from home 175–205
  implications for policy and practice 182–8
  legal commentary 189–205
    children accommodated by NHS or an education authority 203
      notification duties 203
    duties to children and young people leaving care 198–200
      The Children (Leaving Care) Act 2000 198–200
    local authority duties to looked after children 190–1

specific accommodation arrangements 200–2
terminology 189–90
  accommodated children 190
  care orders and secure accommodation orders 189
  looked after children 190
  parental responsibility 190
limitations of available information 177–88
choice and autonomy for disabled child, increasing 113–16
Circles Network 278
Citizens Advice Bureau 105, 125
codes of practice 56
Code of Practice on the Identification and Assessment of Special Educational Needs 244–50
  fundamental principles of Code 244–5
  guidance on preliminary stages 130, 245–50
  practices and procedures essential in pursuit of principles 245
Commissioners for Local Administration (England and Wales) 77, 278
common needs and problems for disabled children and their families 29–40
  caring in the home: mothers, fathers and siblings 29–31
  critical transitional periods 36–7
  families experience of services 35–6
  material, financial and practical problems 33–5
  need for information 39–40
  needs to be met at home 31–3
  personal consequences for parents, disabled children and their siblings 37–9
communication skills and independent living courses 164
community care
  legislation 231–2
  planning 232–3
    assessment of users circumstances 232
    implementation and monitoring 232–3
    preparation of care package 232
  services 152–3, 235–8
    under s.2 Chronically Sick and Disabled Persons Act 1970 235–8
    laundry assistance under Schedule 8 NHS Act 1977 238
community health services in 100–3
community resources 42
complaint(s)

local authority complaints not covered by specific social services rules 227–8
  education complaints 227
  other local authority complaints 227–8
local authority materials/procedures 223–8
  structure of complaints system 223–7
    formal stage 224–5
    informal or problem-solving stage 224
    review stage 2267
5panel hearings 226–7
  who can complain? 223
NHS complaints materials 255–7
  stage 1 255–56
  stage 2: independent review panel 256–7
procedures for making representations and 76–8
to social services (letter) 269
confidentiality 74–5
Connexions Service 150, 158
Connexions: the best start in life for every young person (DfEE 2000) 151
Contact-a-Family 279
contact visits 197
co-operation with social services and NHS over SEN 130
co-ordination
role of social services 107
of services 45–6
Council for Disabled Children 279
Council of Europe 54
Court of Protection 172–3, 279
critical transitional periods 36–7
Crossroads Care Attendant Scheme 279
Cruse Bereavement Care 280
cultural background, similar (in family placements) 192
Cystic Fibrosis Youth Line 280

Data Protection Commissioner 76
daycare 91–3
Deafblind UK 280
Department for Education and Employment 57, 132, 280
Department of Education 227
DfEE Publications Unit 280
Department of Health 57, 74, 75, 96, 133, 135, 179, 280
developmental needs 41

DIAL UK (Disability Information and Advice Line) 281
Disability Alliance ERA 281
Disability Discrimination Act 1995 materials 258–62
  discrimination 262
  employment 258–60
    justification 260
    reasonable adjustments 259–60
  exclusions 262
  goods, facilities and services 260–2
Disability Information Trust 281
Disability :Law Service 281
Disabled Children: Directions for their Future Care (Ball 1998) 180
disabled facilities grants 171
Disabled Living Centres Council 281
Disabled Living Foundation 281
Disabled Students Allowances 166, 167
Disablement Income Group (DIG) 282
Disaway Trust, The 282
discharge from hospital, planning 97–8
discovering disability 82–5
discretionary grants 264
  accommodation 264
  employment 264
  welfare 264
discrimination 259–62
Downs Syndrome Association 282
duty
  to inform, of social services 65
  to plan and keep registers 62
Dyslexia Institute 282
Dyspraxia Foundation 282

early years 81–111
  accessing education 93–4
  accessing services 89–90
  daycare, playgroups, nursery education and short-term breaks 91–3
  discovering disability 82–5
  establishing a way of living with disability 86–7
  isolation and lack of support 87–8
  legal commentary 94–111
    education departments role in the early years 107–10
    NHS and hospital services 95–103
    social services in the early years 103–10
  need for information 88–9

services to aid childs development and
    behaviour 90–1
ECHR (European Court of Human Rights)
    54–5
education
  accessing 93–4
  complaints 227
  disabled childs perspective of 71
  getting a decent 116–19
  for looked after children 192
  materials 244–54
      Code of Practice on the Identification
          and Assessment of Special
          Educational Needs 244–50
      Special Educational Needs: Transition
          Plan 253–4
      Statement of Special Educational Needs
          250–3
  planning 110
  during school years 124–33
      speech and language therapy and other
          aid/assistance to communication
          126
      special educational needs procedures
          127–33
  future plans in 150–1
education authorities, specific obligations of 66
education departments role in the early years
    107–10
  health and social services educational
      responsibilities for children under five
      109
  planning ahead 110
educational needs, phased response to 128
educational support services 166–7
eligibility for grants 265
emotional and behavioural development 41
employment 42
  assistance for disabled people 158
  and careers 151–2
  and Disability Discrimination Act 1995 159,
      258–60
  discretionary grants 264
  and discrimination 259
  supported 158
Employment Opportunities for People with
    Disabilities 282
Enable 282
ensuring safety 42
environmental factors 42
ethics see human rights, ethics and values

exclusion and lack of opportunity,
    understanding 25–7

facilities
  grants for 171
      discretionary 264
      eligibility for 265
      mandatory 264
      materials 263–5
      timescales 265
  providers of, and Disability Discrimination
      Act 1995 260–2
failure
  of hospital discharge planning, letter
      expressing concern about 267–8
  of NHS to provide adequate speech or
      language therapy assistance, letter
      expressing concern about 270–1
families of disabled children
  common needs and problems for 29–40
  experience of services 35
family
  history and functioning 42
  social integration of 42
  and social relationships 41
Family Fund Trust 44, 105, 283
fathers as carers 29–31
financial problems 33–5
  assistance with 49
Floyd P! – Forum for Living of Young
    Disabled People, Independent Living
    Alternatives 283
fostering 201–2
Friends for the Young Deaf (FYD) 283
further and higher education provision
    159–64
  avoidance of disproportionate expenditure
      162
  further education 160–4
  Further Education Funding Council support
      161–2
  independent living and communication skills
      courses 164
  Learning Skills Council 160–1
  out-of-sector placements 162–4
Further Education Funding Council 150, 160,
    161–2, 163, 164

GCSE courses 150

general obligations and powers of statutory agencies 58–9

Getting Your Rights: A Guide for Young Disabled People (Barnardos) 147

Gingerbread Association For One-Parent Families 283

good practice *see* research and good practice

goods, providers of, and Disability Discrimination Act 1995 260–2

Greater London Action on Disability (GLAD) 283

Greater Manchester Coalition Young Disabled Peoples Forum 283

Growing Up: A Guide to Some Information Sources Available to Young Disabled People and Their Families (Beecher, 1998) 147

guidance 56, 57–8
  and boundaries 42

hardship and poverty 28–9

health
  care 152, 191
  risks for carers 134–5
  services *see* health services

Health Service Commissioners 77, 284

Health Service Ombudsman 77

health services
  in the community 100–3
      primary care staff and carers 102–3
      respite and short breaks 102
      speech and language therapy 101–2
  in school years 135–6
      wheelchairs 136

hierarchy of the law: statutes, regulations and guidance 57–8

Holiday Care 284

home
  care, short-term breaks and support workers 49–51
  caring in: mothers, fathers and siblings 29–31
  needs to be met at 31–3

homelessness 169–70

Hospital Discharge Workbook 97

hospital services and NHS 95–103
  health services in the community 100–3
  hospital discharge planning 97–8
  in-patient treatment 95–7
  role of hospital social worker 98–100
      duties to carers 100
      overnight accommodation for parents 99–100
      transport to and from hospital 99

housing 42
  accommodation and supported living schemes 153–4
  authorities, specific obligations of 66
  responsibilities of authorities 169–71
      Children Act housing duties 170–1
      disabled facilities grants 171
      homelessness 169–70

Housing Options 284

human rights, ethics and values 14–22
  law and its application 21–2
  quality of life and human rights 14–16
  relationships between service users and providers 19–21
  significance of social groupings and divisions 18–19
  understanding disability 17
  whose perspectives? 17–18

identity 41

income 42

independent living and communication skills courses 164

Independent Living Fund 153, 168–9, 284

Independent Panel for Special Education Advice (IPSEA) 118, 125, 284

independent visitors 197–8

inform, social services duty to 65

information
  access to 75–6
  need for 39–40
      in early years 88–9
  on transition to adulthood 147–8

initial involvement
  of LEA for child under 5, letter requesting 272
  of social services, letter requesting 266–7

in-patient treatment 95–7

integrated family service provision needs-led approach to assessment and 41

International Classification of Impairments, Disabilities and Handicaps (Abberly 1992) 178

interventions to enhance childrens development 48–51
  assistance with financial and practical problems of daily living 49

short-term breaks, homecare and support
workers 49–51
isolation and lack of support 87–8

key debates and social trends 25–9
changing population of disabled children 28
disabled childrens perspectives 27
poverty and material hardship 28–9
understanding disability, exclusion and lack
of opportunity 25–7
key working and advocacy 46–8

language and speech therapy 101–2
letter expressing concern about failure of
NHS to provide adequate assistance
270–1
and other aid/assistance to communication
126
laundry assistance under Schedule 8 NHS Act
1977 238
law
and frequently encountered legal obstacles
53–80
confidentiality and access to
information 74–6
disabled childs perspective 69–72
duties of statutory agencies to
co-operate with each other 67–9
general obligations and powers of
statutory agencies 58–9
perspective of parents and siblings 72–4
procedures for making representations
and complaints 76–8
specific obligations of local authorities
60–6
transitional periods in a disabled childs
development 69
what is meant by the law 54–8
hierarchy of the law: statutes,
regulations and guidance 57–8
rights based law 54–6
and its application 21–2
Learning and Skills Council for England 160,
161
Learning Skills Council 160–1
Learning to Succeed (DfEE 1999) 151
leaving care, duties to children and young
people 198–200
leisure, play and social life 120–1

linguistic background, similar (in family
placements) 192
Listening Books 285
living with disability, establishing a way of
86–7
local authorities, specific obligations of 60–6
duties to looked after children 190–8
contact 197
duties during placement 194–6
record keeping 194
reviews 195–6
duties prior to placement 191–2
education 192
health care 191
race, culture, religion and linguistic
background 192
independent visitors 197–8
placement plan 192–3
placements outside England and Wales
193
NHS obligations to disabled children 66
specific obligations of education authorities
66
specific obligations of housing authorities 66
specific obligations of social services
departments 60–6
material, financial and practical problems
33–5
local authority complaint materials 223–8
local education authority responsibilities
155–9
careers service responsibilities 157–9
letter requesting initial involvement of LEA
for child under 5 272
review meeting 156
transitional plan 156–7
local government ombudsman procedures 77
looked after children 190

mainstream schooling, special educational
needs within 127–8
Makaton 114
Making Connections. A Guide for Agencies Helping
Young People with Disabilities Make the
Transition from School to Adulthood (DoH)
147
mandatory grants 264
material hardship and poverty 28–9
MENCAP 285
mental capacity and parental wills/trusts
171–3

Court of Protection 172–3
mental capacity 172
parental wills/trusts 173
*Me, Survive, Out There? – New Arrangements for
    Young People Living in and Leaving Care*
    (consultation document) 198
MIND (National Association for Mental
    Health) 285
Mobility Advice and Vehicle Information
    Service (MAVIS) 285
monitoring care plan 232–3
mothers as carers 29–31
*Move on Up: Supporting Young Disabled People in
    their Transition to Adulthood* (Morris, 1999)
    147
*Moving on Towards Independence: Second Report on
    Transition Services for Disabled Young People*
    (Social Services Inspectorate, 1997) 147
Muscular Dystrophy Campaign 285

naming a school 131–2
National Association of Young People in Care
    188
National Asthma Campaign 285
National Autistic Society 285
National Centre for Independent Living 285
National Council for Education and Training
    for Wales 160
National Council for One-Parent Families 285
National Curriculum 244, 252
National Deaf Childrens Society (NDCS) 285
National Development Team 151
National Health Information Service 285
National Health Service (NHS) 12, 58
    complaints materials 255–7
    Executive 96
    and hospital services 95–103
    obligations to disabled children 66
    responsibilities for disabled young people
        167–8
        NHS funded residential and respite care
            167–8
    services, disabled childs perspective of 71–2
National Society for Epilepsy 286
need(s)
    of individuals and families, personal, material
        and practical support 122–3
    for information 39–40
    -led approach to assessment and integrated
        family service provision 41
    to be met at home 31–3

non-residential services 64
notification duties 203
    educational/social services placements 203
Nottingham County Council 228
nursery education 91–3

Ombudsman, Health Service 77
OPCS (Office of Population, Censuses and
    Surveys) 28, 30, 177, 178, 179, 180,
    181
out-of-sector placements 162–4
opportunity
    barriers to 143–6
    lack of 25–7
overnight accommodation for parents 99–100

panel hearings of complaints 226–72
parental responsibility 190
parental wills/trusts 173
parenting capacity 42
parents
    overnight accommodation for 99–100
    perspective of 72–4
Pathway Plans 199
Patients Helpline 286
People First 287
personal consequences for parents, disabled
    children and their siblings 37–9
personal, material and practical support needs
    of individuals and families 122–3
perspective, disabled childs 69–72
    education 71
    NHS services 71–2
    social services 70–1
phased response to educational needs 128
placement(s)
    educational/social services 203
    outside England and Wales 193
    plan 192–3
playgroups 91–3
play, leisure and social life 120–1
policy guidance 56
population of disabled children, changing 28
*Positive Choices: Services for Disabled Children
    Living Away from Home* (Russell 1995) 177
poverty and material hardship 28–9
practical problems of daily living, assistance
    with 49
practice guidance 56
precedent letters 266–74

complaint to social services 269
expressing concern about failure of hospital
    discharge planning 267–8
expressing concern about failure of NHS to
    provide adequate speech or language
    therapy assistance 270–1
requesting access to files 273
requesting initial involvement of LEA for
    child under 5 272
requesting initial involvement of social
    services 266–7
preparation, work 158
primary care staff and carers 102–3
procedures for making representations and
    complaints 76–8
providers and service users, relationships
    between 19–21
provision of services 106–7

quality of life 140–3
and human rights 14–16
Quality Protects programme 40, 49, 198
Queen Elizabeth Foundation for Disabled
    People 287

racial background, similar (in family
    placements) 192
RADAR (Royal Association for Disability and
    Rehabilitation) 287
Rathbone 287
reasonable adjustments 259–60
record keeping 194
register(s)
of children with disabilities 104–5
duty to plan and keep 62
regulations and orders 56, 57–8
relationships between service users and
    providers 19–21
religious background, similar (in family
    placements) 192
Remap 287
representation, support and information 147–8
representations and complaints, procedures for
    making 76–80
complaints procedures 76–7
Health Service Ombudsman 77
judicial review 78
local government ombudsman procedures 77
research and good practice 23–52

disabled children and their families: common
    needs and problems 29–40
interventions to enhance childrens
    development 48–51
key debates and social trends 25–9
valued service provision 40–8
residential accommodation 64
residential care, NHS funded 167–8, 202
respite
care, NHS funded 167–8, 200–1
and short breaks 102
social services funded 235
Rett Syndrome Association 287
review meeting 156
rights based law 54–6
RNIB (Royal National Institute for the Blind)
    288
RNID (Royal National Institute for the Deaf)
    288

safety, ensuring 42
school, naming a 131–2
school years 112–37
getting a decent education 116–19
increasing autonomy and choice for disabled
    child 113–16
legal commentary 123–37
    education 124–33
    health services 135–6
    social services 133–5
leisure, play and social life 120–1
personal, material and practical support
    needs of individuals and families 122–3
Scope 288
secure accommodation orders 189
self-care skills 41
self-determination 20
self-help user groups, advice on 105–6
Sense: The National Deafblind and Rubella
    Association 288
service users and providers, relationships
    between 19–21
services
to aid childs development and behaviour
    90–1
co-ordination of 45–6
families experience of 35–6
non-residential 64
providers of, and Disability Discrimination
    Act 1995 260–2
provision 40–8

key working and advocacy 46–8
needs-led approach to assessment and
    integrated family service provision
    41
obligations 62
and planning for transition to adult life
    148–54
Shaftesbury Society 288
Shaw Trust 288
short-term breaks 91–3, 102, 200–1
  homecare and support workers 49–51
  social services funded 235
siblings
  as carers 29–31
  perspective of 72–4
Sickle Cell Society 289
Skill (National Bureau for Students with
    Disabilities) 289
Social Fund 99
social groupings and divisions, significance of
    18–19
social life, play and leisure 120–1
social presentation 41
social security benefits 105
social services
  disabled childs perspective of 70–1
  in the early years 103–10
      general advice and information 105–6
        advice on self-help user groups
          105–6
        social security benefits 105
      provision of services 106–7
      register of children with disabilities
        104–5
      social services assessments 106
      social services co-ordination role 107
  letter or complaint to 269
  materials 230–43
      power of social services departments to
        charge for services 241–2
      charging for accommodation
        services under Children Act
        241–2
      charging for non-accommodation
        services under Children Act
        241
      charging for services under
        Chronically Sick and Disabled
        Persons Act 1970 242
    responsibilities towards carers 238–41
    services for disabled children 233–8
        under Children Act 1989 233–5

respite/short break care 235
    under community care legislation
      235
    social services assessment and care
      planning obligations 230–3
      assessments under Children Act
        1989 230–1
      assessment under community care
        legislation 231–2
      care planning 232–3
    in school years 133–5
      health risks for carers 134–5
    and transition to adulthood 164–7
      educational support services 166–7
social services departments, specific obligations
    of 60–6
  advocates 61
  assessments 62–4
  duty to plan and keep registers 62
  power of social services departments to
    charge for services 65–6
  non-residential services 64
  residential accommodation 64
  social services assessment and service
    provision obligations 62
  social services duties towards carers 64–5
  social services duty to inform 65
  social work service 60–1
Social Services Inspectorate 57
social trends and key debates 25–9
social worker, hospital 98–100
social work service 60–1
special educational needs procedures 127–33
  annual reviews of statements 133
  assessments 127–8
      and statutory time scales 128–9
  Code of Practice (1964): guidance on
    preliminary stages 130
  and co-operation with social services and
    NHS 130
  within mainstream schooling 129–30
  naming a school 131–2
  statement 130–1
  transition plan 253–4
  Tribunal 129, 132–3
Special Educational Needs Tribunal Office 289
speech and language therapy 101–2
  letter expressing concern about failure of
    NHS to provide adequate assistance
    270–1
  and other aid/assistance to communication
    126

Spinal Injuries Association (SIA) 289
SPOD 289
stability 42
statement 130–1
Statement of Special Educational Needs 250–3
statutes 56, 57–8
statutory agencies
   duties of, to co-operate with each other
      67–9
   powers of, and general obligations 58–9
Stillbirth & Neonatal Death Society (SANDS)
   289
stimulation 42
support
   isolation and lack of 87–8
   representation and information 147–8
supported employment 158
supported living schemes 153–4
support workers, short-term breaks and
      homecare 49–51

transitional periods in a disabled childs
      development 36–7, 69
   transition to adulthood 140–6
transitional plan 156–7
transport to and from hospital 99
Tripscope 289
trusts 173

understanding disability 17
   exclusion and lack of opportunity 25–7
United Nations 54

values see human rights, ethics and values
Values into Action (VIA) 290
Voice for the Child in Care 188

Wales 92, 160, 162, 164, 193
welfare, discretionary grants 264
Welsh Assembly 96, 161
Welsh Office 92
wheelchairs 136
Who Cares movement 188
Wigan 171
wills 173
Winged Fellowship Trust (WFT) 290
work preparation 158

Young Arthritis Care 290
young carers 239–40

Index of legislation and guidance

Note: This index includes legal cases, statutes (acts), regulations, policy guidance, codes of practice and practice guidance. Figure 4.1 (p. 56) illustrates the relative importance of each of these.

A v UK [1998] 78
Arrangements for Placement of Children (General) Regulations 1991 204
Assessing Children in Need and Their Families, practice guidance (2000) 56, 57, 61, 72, 79, 80, 111
Assevov v Bulgaria [1999] 78

Bradford MC v A [1997] 126

Care Management and Assessment – Practitioners Guide 79, 80, 243
Carers and Disabled Children Act 2000 64, 65, 72, 100, 201, 234, 240–1
Carers (Recognitions and Services) Act 1995 57, 59, 64, 65, 72, 73, 79, 100, 102–3, 238–9
Carers (Recognitions and Services) Act 1995, practice guidance (1996) 56, 57, 2437
Care Standards Act 2000 200, 202
Children Act 1989 21, 22, 55, 56, 57, 58, 60, 61, 62, 63, 64, 65, 66, 67, 70, 72, 74, 79, 92, 99, 104, 106, 107, 121, 165, 166, 170, 172, 174, 179, 181, 184, 189, 190, 192, 193, 195, 196, 197, 198, 199, 202, 204, 205, 223, 224, 225, 230, 231, 232, 233–4, 235, 236, 238, 239, 240, 241, 242
Children Act 1989 Guidance and Regulations, Vol. 2, Family Support (1991) 230–1, 234, 239
Children Act 1989 Guidance and Regulations, Vol. 3, Family Placements (1991) 223, 228
Children Act 1989 Guidance and Regulations, Vol. 4, Residential Care (1991) 204, 205
Children Act 1989 Guidance and Regulations, Vol. 6, Children with Disabilities (1991) 56, 58, 65, 73, 79, 80, 98, 104, 110, 111, 134, 165, 174, 195, 204, 205, 228, 231, 242
Children (Leaving Care) Act 2000 198–200
Children Short Term Placement (Miscellaneous Provisions) Regulations 1995 204
Childrens Homes Regulations 1991 205
Chronically Sick and Disabled Persons Act 1970 62, 63, 64, 65, 121, 134, 152, 164, 165, 166, 167, 230, 231, 235, 236, 238, 241, 242, 243
Citizen Advocacy with Older People: a Code of Good Practice 79
Code of Practice for the elimination of discrimination in the field of employment against disabled persons or persons who have a disability (1996) 262
Code of Practice on the Identification and Assessment of Special Educational Needs 1994 56, 58, 71, 73, 108, 109, 111, 119, 126, 127, 129, 130, 132, 136, 156, 157, 160, 244–50, 253
CI(95)12 (guidance concerning young carers) 239
Community Care (Direct Payments) Act 1996 166
Community Care guidance 61
Community Care in the Next Decade and Beyond Policy Guidance (HMSO, 1990) 80
Contact with Children Regulations 1991 204

Data Protection Act 1998 74, 75–6, 273
see also LASSL (99)16
Disability Discrimination Act 1995 22, 56, 110, 120, 124, 144, 159, 258–62
Disability Discrimination (Employment) Regulations 1996 262
Disability Discrimination (Services and Premises) Regulations 1996 262
Disability Rights Handbook (Disability Alliance 2000) 49, 111, 168
Disabled Children: Directions for Their Future Care (DoH guidance, 1998) 135
Disabled Facilities Grants and Home Repair Assistance (Maximum Amounts) Order 1996 265
Disabled Persons (Services, Consultation and Representation) Act 1986 68, 155, 165, 230

Education Acts 22
  1944 167, 174
  1981 124
  1996 56, 57, 107–8, 109, 125, 127, 128,
    129, 130, 131, 136, 155, 159, 161,
    174, 230, 250
Education (Special Educational Needs)
  Regulations 1994 56, 129, 155, 161,
  250
Employment Relations Act 1996 111
Employment Training Act 1973 261
European Convention on Human Rights
  (ECHR) 54, 55, 96, 102

Foster Placement (Children) Regulations 1991
  201–2
Framework for Assessing Children in Need
  (2000) 41–2, 44
*Framework for the Assessment of Children and their
  Families,* policy guidance (2000) 56, 70,
  74, 80
Further and Higher Education Act 1992 160,
  161–2, 164, 174
Further Education Funding Council Circular
  96/01 164
Further Education Funding Council Circular
  99/02 162–3

Gaskin v UK [1989] 79
*Gillick v West Norfolk & Wisbech Area Health
  Authority* [1985] 80
Guidance on the need for complaints
  procedures (Circular 1/89, DoEd) 227
Guide to Transition Planning for Secondary
  and Special Schools (Dfee, 1999) 254

Health Act 1999 68
Health and Safety Executive Guidance
  HS(G)104 137
Higher Education Act 1992 167
Housing Act 1996 68, 169–70
Housing Grants, Construction and
  Regeneration Act 1996 263
Housing Renewal Grants Regulations 1996
  265
Human Rights Act 1998 21, 54, 55, 56, 96,
  102, 270

Inheritance (Provisions for Family and
  Dependants) Act 1975 173

LAC (96)7 (policy guidance on Carers
  (Recognitions and Services) Act 1995)
  100, 103, 240, 243
LASSL (99)16 (social services guidance on the
  Data Protection Act 1998) 75
Learning and Skills Act 2000 160–1, 174
Local Authority Social Services Act 1970 58,
  79
Local Authority Social Services (Complaints
  Procedure) Order 1990 228

Manual Handling Operations Regulations
  1992 136
Mental Health Act 1983 22, 72, 79, 172, 242

National Assistance Act 1948 60, 79, 166,
  242
National Health Service Act 1977 57, 68, 95,
  101, 235, 238, 242, 243, 257
National Health Service (Functions of Health
  Authorities) (Complaints) Regulations
  1996 257
National Health Service (General Medical
  Service) Regulations 1992 110
National Health Service and Community Care
  Act 1990 62, 63, 68, 71, 79, 230, 231
Norris v Ireland [1985] 79

Osman v UK [1999] 79

Patel v UK (the East Africans case) [1973] 78
Patients Charter 97
Private Sector Renewal: A Strategic Approach
  17/96 56, 58

R v Bexley LBC ex p B [1995] 242
*R v Bradford MBC and the Further Education
  Council for England ex P Parkinson* [1997]
  174
R v Cambridge Health Authority ex p B 96
*R v Further Education Funding Council &
  Bradford MBC ex p Parkinson* [1996] 167
R v Gloucestershire County Council ex p RADAR
  [1995] 80

R v Hampshire Education Authority ex p J [1985]
    136
R v Hampshire Education Authority ex p W [1994]
    136
R v Harrow LBC ex p M [1997] 126
R v Isle of Wight Council [1997] 136
R v Islington LBC ex p Rixon [1996] 58, 227,
    243
R v Lancashire CC ex p M [1989] 136
R v Mid Glamorgan FHSA ex p Martin [1994] 80
*R v North and East Devon Health Authority ex p
    Coughlan* [1999] 95
R v Northavon DC ex p Smith [1994] 79
R v North Derbyshire Health Authority ex p Fisher
    96
R v North Yorkshire CC ex p Hargreaves [1994]
    80, 243
R v Powys County Council ex p Hambidge [1998]
    242
*R v Secretary of State for the Home Department, ex p
    Brind* [1991] 78
R v Tower Hamlets LG ex p Bradford [1997] 170
R v Wigan MBC ex p Tammadge [1998] 170
Race Relations Act 1976 56
Race Relations (Amendment) Act 2000 79
Representations Procedure (Children)
    Regulations 1991 56, 228, 269
Review of Childrens Cases Regulations 1991
    56, 57, 194, 204
Right to Complain, The (1991) 223, 224, 225,
    228

Special Educational Needs and Disability in
    Education Bill (proposed) 136

UN Convention on the Rights of the Child
    1989 54
UN General Assembly Declaration on the
    Rights of Disabled Persons 22
UN International Covenant on Economic,
    Social and Cultural Rights 1966 78
Universal Declaration of Human Rights 22

X & Y v Netherlands [1985] 79

Author Index

Abberly, P. 178
Abbott, D. 178, 181, 182, 183
Abbott, P. 29
Ahmad, W. 18, 26
Aldgate, J. 50
Anderson, H. 144
Appleton, P. 35, 41, 42, 43, 44, 46, 88, 89, 90, 91, 94
Argent, H. 186, 187
Aries, P. 139
Association of Metropolitan Authorities 39, 46, 89, 118, 120, 121
Atkin, K. 26, 29, 31
Atkinson,N. 31, 32, 38
Audit Commission 35, 44, 46, 82, 83, 87, 88, 90, 92, 93, 118

Baldwin, S. 15, 25, 26, 28, 30, 31, 33, 34, 36, 37, 38, 41, 86, 88, 140, 141, 142, 143
Ball, M. 19, 25, 27, 28, 33, 35, 36, 39, 41, 44, 46, 47, 49, 50, 90, 113, 177, 179, 180, 183
Ballard, K. 43
Bamford, C. 40, 51
Barn, R. 176
Barnardos Policy Development Unit 140, 143, 144, 147
Barnes, C. 25, 144
Barnes, H. 144
Barton, L. 116, 140
Bax, M. 91
Baxter, C. 26, 35, 36, 39, 41, 46, 83, 87, 88, 89, 119, 140
Bebbington, A. 175, 176
Becker, S. 31, 38, 48, 114
Beecher, W. 43, 49, 114, 115, 147, 188
Begum, N. 26
Beresford, B. 16, 25, 27, 29, 30, 31, 32, 34, 35, 36, 37, 39, 40, 41, 42, 43, 44, 49, 50, 83, 84, 86, 87, 89, 91, 92, 113, 114, 118, 120, 121, 122, 123, 140, 141, 153, 182
Berridge, D. 176, 186
Bertoud, R. 145
Biehal, N. 176

Blackburn, C. 38
Bone,
Booth, T. 26, 116, 117
Bradley, M. 50
Broad, B. 176
Brodie, I. 176, 186
Bullock, R. 176
Burke, B. 26
Burkhart, L. 49
Butt, J. 26, 35, 36

Cameron, C. 48, 90, 92
Carlisle, J. 25, 28, 31, 34, 36, 37, 38, 41, 88
Cavet, J. 120, 121
Chailey Young Peoples Group 114, 188
Chamba, R. 26, 36, 39, 46, 88, 90
Clark, G. 176, 188
Clements, L. 12, 79, 137, 174
Corbett, J. 140
Court, Report 140
Coventry Who Cares 176, 188
Crawforth, M. 31, 32, 38
Cross, M. 177, 185, 186
Crow, L. 25
Cunningham, C. 42, 83, 84

Dalrymple, J. 26
Dearden, C. 31, 38, 48
DfEE 25, 41, 44, 92, 93, 116, 119, 151
Disability Alliance 49
Dobson, B. 33, 34, 38, 52, 87, 118
DoH 19, 25, 26, 40, 41, 44, 80, 135, 147, 175, 176, 186
Doyle, B. 262
Duckworth, D. 41, 122
Dunning, A. 79
Dyson, S. 26, 36, 84

Family Focus 116
Family Fund 147
Ferguson, T. 140
Flynn, M. 140, 152
French, S. 184

Gandhi, M.K. 21
Glendinning, C. 30, 31, 32, 35, 38, 46, 86, 90
Goodey, C. 27, 36, 82, 89
Gooding, C. 144

Gordon, D. 24, 34, 177, 178, 180, 181, 182, 183, 184, 186
Gordon, P. 184
Gough, D. 36
Graham, H. 30, 38
Green, J.M. 83
Gregory, S. 48, 91

Hall, D. 35, 41, 44, 48, 83, 90, 91
Harker, M. 153
Harrison, C. 175
Hasler, F. 153
Hawley, D. 50
Haylock, C. 32, 35, 40, 41, 46, 48, 87, 88, 89, 90
Heaton, P. 87
Henwood, M. 137
Hevey, D. 27
Hill, M. 26
Hirst, M. 15, 26, 30, 38, 140, 141, 142, 143
Home Office 25, 41, 44
Hubert, J. 36
Humphries, S. 184

Jackson, P. 50
Jackson, S. 176
Jigsaw Partnerships 121
Jones, M. 188
Julyan, A. 188

Kagan, C. 87
Kelly, D. 176
Kennedy, M. 27, 49, 185
Kerr, A. 140
Kerrane, A. 186, 187
King, N. 153
Kestenbaum, A. 145
Knight, A. 183, 184
Kozens, A. 140

Lakey, J. 145
Lambert, L. 176
Lawton, D. 33
Legal Action Group 79, 80
Leighton Project 114
Lenton, S. 43, 46, 87, 88, 89, 90
Lewis, A. 27
Lewis, S. 87
Li, L. 36

Little, M. 176
Lonsdale, S. 144
Loughran, F. 177, 178

McConachie, H. 25, 28, 35, 36, 42, 48, 91
McGucken, R. 83
MacHeath, C. 82
McKay, S. 145
Marchant, R. 27, 49, 114, 177, 185, 186, 188
Marsh, P. 175
Martyn, M. 188
Mason, M. 26, 117
Masson, J. 175, 184
Mercer, G. 25
Middleton, S. 33, 34, 38, 48, 52, 87, 91, 118
Miles, J. 175, 176
Milham, S. 175, 176
Minchom, P. 42, 91
Minkes, J. 27, 114, 121, 188
Mirza, K. 26, 35, 36
Mittler, P. 42
Morgan, D. 30
Morgan, P. 83
Morris, J. 15, 17, 25, 26, 51, 113, 114, 140, 144, 145, 146, 147, 151, 152, 153, 177, 178, 180, 181, 185, 188
Moss, P. 92
Mukherjee, S. 43, 46, 47, 90
Murray, P. 82
Murton, F.E. 83

National Association of Citizens Advice Bureaux (NACAB) 144
Newton, D. 91

OBrien. J. 79
Oldman, C. 34, 153
Oliver, M. 17, 25
OPCS (Office of Population, Censuses and Surveys) 30
Owen, M. 175

Page, M. 27, 49, 114
Page, R. 176, 177, 185, 188
Pahl, J. 83
Parker, G. 140
Parker, R. 28, 176, 177, 180, 181, 187
Pavlovic, A. 175

Penman, J. 82
Penn, H. 92
Phillips, R. 187
Philp, M. 41, 122
Potts, P. 116
Priestley, M. 27
Pugh, G. 92
Pumpian, I. 20, 21

Quine, L. 83, 91
Quinton, D. 175

Read, J. 12, 15, 16, 25, 27, 29, 30, 31, 32,
    38, 41, 48, 82, 83, 86, 90, 92, 116, 118,
    122
Reisser, R. 26, 116, 117
Residential Forum 176
Riddell, S. 139
Robinson, C. 27, 28, 36, 50, 51, 88, 121,
    178, 181, 187
Rowe, J. 176
Russell, P. 23, 27, 32, 37, 41, 43, 47, 49, 50,
    92, 113, 114, 115, 122, 177, 179, 182,
    183, 186, 187

Sachdev, D. 91, 117
Sainsbury, R. 144
Sang, B. 79
Sapsford, R. 29
Scope 81, 82, 83
SCOVO 82, 83, 84
Sebba, J. 91, 117
Sellick, C. 176, 187
Shah, R. 26, 36, 39, 46, 83
Shaw, L. 117
Shaw, M. 18
Sheik, S. 83
Simons, K. 145
Sloper, P. 26, 30, 31, 32, 34, 35, 36, 39, 43,
    44, 83, 87, 88, 89, 92, 120
Smith, A. 184
Smith, P.A. 137
Smyth, D. 91
Social Services Inspectorate 25, 26, 28, 35,
    36, 39, 41, 44, 46, 113, 140, 147, 152
Spastics Society 93, 118
Stalker, K. 36, 50, 88, 187
Stallard, B. 43, 46, 87, 88, 89, 90
Statham, J. 41, 83, 92

Stein, M. 176
Stevens, A. 26
Strong, P. 30
Swann, W. 116, 119

Thoburn, J. 176, 187
Thomas, C. 116
Thomas, N. 176
Thompson, G. 140
Thompson, N. 19, 26
Thornton, P. 144
Townsley, R. 28
Tozer, R. 33
Traustadottir, R. 82
Treseliotis, J. 175
Turner, S. 26, 30, 31, 32, 34, 35, 36, 39, 43,
    44, 83, 87, 88, 89
Twigg, J. 26

Utting, W. 176, 186, 187

Voice for the Child in Care 176

Walker, A. 116, 140
Ward, K. 140
Ward, L. 27, 114, 179
Warner, N. 176
Warnock Committee 140
Warr, B. 176
Westcott, H. 177, 185
Weston, C. 27
Who Cares! Trust 176
Williams, F. 120
Williams, G. 25
Wishard, J. 140
Wroblewska, A. 36
Wynne Oakley, M. 184

Yerbury, M. 35, 44
Younghusband, E. 140